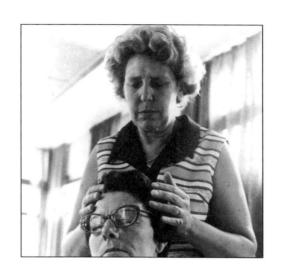

MYSTERIES
OF THE
UNEXPLAINED

MYSTERIES OF THE UNEXPLAINED

BLITZ EDITIONS

Published by Blitz Editions
an imprint of Bookmart Ltd
Registered Number 2372865
Trading as Bookmart Ltd, Desford Road, Enderby
Leicester LE9 5AD

Cover design: Peter Dolton
Text design: Jim Reader
Production Manager: Sue Gray
Editorial Manager: Roz Williams

Printed in the Slovak Republic
50979

ISBN 1 85605 134 X

Every effort has been made to contact the copyright holders for the pictures. In some cases they have been
untraceable, for which we offer our apologies. Thanks to the Fortean Picture Library and the Hulton Deutsch
Collection Ltd, who supplied most of them. Pictures have been provided as follows:
SECTION 1
Hulton Deutsch Collection Ltd (pp 2, 3, 9 bottom, 10, 18, 26, 27, 28 bottom, 29, 30, 33, 40 top left, 41 bottom,
42, 51, 52 bottom, 53 bottom, 54 top, 60–4, 75 top, 76 top, 79). The remainder have been supplied by the
Fortean Picture Library.
SECTION 2
Island Publishing Co (pp 75, 76 top), Popperfoto (p 72), *Psychic News* (pp 68 bottom, 78). The remainder have
been supplied by the Hulton Deutsch Collection Ltd.
SECTION 3
M. De Cet (p 7), Hulton Deutsch Collection Ltd (pp 2–4, 5 middle, 6, 10, 11, 14, 15, 17–21, 22–3 bottom, 24,
28–33, 34 top, 35–8, 42, 43 top left and right, 45 top, 63 bottom, 67–70, 74), McDonnell Douglas Photos (p 5
top), The Mansell Collection (p 22), Mary Evans Picture Library (pp 77, 80), *Psychic News* (p 60). The
remainder have been supplied by the Fortean Picture Library.

Jacket: Fortean Picture Library.

The Authors
Reuben Stone, who has written sections 1 and 3, has long been fascinated by the paranormal
and the mysteries of the unexplained. He is the author of many books and articles on military history,
popular science and technology, and various aspects of anomalous phenomena.

Allan Hall has written section 2. He is a professional journalist currently working in New York as a foreign
correspondent and is the author of several books on mysteries, scandals, and murders.

Contents

MYSTERIES OF THE UNEXPLAINED

THE FRONTIERS of knowledge are being bulldozed back on a daily basis, yet as we lose touch with our deepest instincts and the powers of natural forces, the questions that remain unanswered seem to some to pose a threat to our very existence. The more that science is able to account for, the more we are frightened by the unexplained.

Myths and superstitions, strange places and people, are all investigated, calmly, rationally and objectively in the chapters of this book. The search for truth leads us into the depths of dark oceans and lakes, and high up into the snowclad mountains. It takes us back into the tangled confusion of the past and sweeps us forward into the dangers of the future. And it immerses us in the deepest recesses of the human mind, the tremendous powers of which we are only just beginning to appreciate.

The very latest evidence is presented for us to judge for ourselves the precise significance of the seemingly inexplicable. We must try to understand, for if we fail we may pay the price in terms of our lives, our children's lives, and the life of the Earth itself.

Mysteries of the Unexplained gives us the opportunity to analyse the facts and to penetrate the mysteries...and, ultimately, to help us to accept that, even today, certain events are destined to remain beyond our comprehension.

MONSTERS & MYSTERIOUS PLACES

WHAT LURKS IN THE LAKE?

For over 1000 years there have been authenticated sightings of a monstrous creature living in one of the Earth's deepest lakes. Now scientists have finally begun to take the stories seriously, and are using state-of-the-art technology to get to the bottom of the icy black waters of Loch Ness and the secrets they hide...

There can hardly be a person in the civilized world who has not heard of Loch Ness in Scotland and its famous monster. Possibly rather less commonly known is the fact that Nessie is but one of an army of such unexplained lake monsters. There are about 250 lakes, world-wide, which reputedly harbour creatures that, according to conventional science, should not be there – or anywhere – at all.

The first intimation that something strange might be living in Loch Ness came in St Adamnan's 7th-century biography of St Columba. In about 565 AD the latter apparently confronted a water monster living in the River Ness with the sign of the cross and so, according to Adamnan, caused it to depart the neighbourhood at speed. Over the centuries other sightings were made, although some have the curious feature that the creature was seen on land, not swimming in the Loch itself.

In 1771, for instance, one Patrick Rose saw what he described as a cross between a horse and a camel in the Loch. In 1907 (or 1919, according to some accounts) a group of local children at Invermoriston, which is about five miles from the southern end of the Loch on its western side, saw a 'light brown, camel-like quadruped' slip into the murky depths of this strange stretch of water.

A GAPING RED MOUTH

A curious event occurred in 1857 at Loch Arkaig, which is some 20 miles south-west of Loch Ness but linked to it by the same river system, so there may well be a connection of another kind with the creature reportedly living in Loch Ness.

Lord Malmesbury, a solid, bewhiskered gentleman rolled from the stoutest Victorian makings, went shooting deer near Loch Arkaig that autumn. His memoir of 3 October 1857 reads:

'This morning my stalker and his boy gave me an account of a mysterious creature, which they say exists in Loch Arkaig, and which they call the Lake Horse. It is the same animal of which one has occasionally read accounts in newspapers as having been seen in the

While St Columba was in the Highlands, preaching to the Picts in the late 6th century (above), he chanced on a monster in the River Ness. The record of his encounter is the first written account of a sighting of the mysterious creature that inhabits the deep, peat-stained waters of brooding Loch Ness (opposite).

Above: *The first photograph, taken in 1933, that was alleged to show the Loch Ness monster. Sceptics have remarked that it could show a labrador swimming with a stick in its mouth. Despite often unsatisfactory photographic evidence, there seems little doubt that something unusual lives in Loch Ness.*

Highland lochs, and on the existence of which the late Lord Ellesmere wrote an interesting article...

'My stalker, John Stewart, at Achnacarry, has seen it twice, and both times at sunrise in summer on a bright sunny day, when there was not a ripple on the water. The creature was basking on the surface; he only saw the head and the hindquarters, proving that its back was hollow, which is not the shape of any fish or of a seal. Its head resembled that of a horse.'

Local folk, then, were not unfamiliar with the presence of odd animals in the inland waters of the Highlands. Most witnesses described something with two humps, a tail, and a snake-like head. They often noted a V-shaped wash behind the creature, and commonly reported such details as a gaping red mouth and horns or antennae on the top of its head.

Children of the villages around Loch Ness were told not to go swimming in its waters lest the creatures that lived there attack them, but word of what might be in Loch Ness did not travel far. The bombshell, as far as the world outside was concerned, came in 1933. Up to a point,

this has a simple, material explanation. In that year a road was dynamited into existence along the Loch's north shore, and the view across the water 'improved' by sawing away the vegetation. Tourism into the area immediately increased. So did sightings of the thing in the lake, but now they were not being made simply by local people.

'PREHISTORIC ANIMAL'

On 14 April 1933, a Mr and Mrs Mackay catapulted the Loch Ness monster into the headlines. The Inverness *Courier* reported their account of seeing an unknown creature in the Loch that 'disported itself for fully a minute, its body resembling that of a whale'. More sightings, and photographs to prove them, followed rapidly.

At 4 pm on 22 July 1933, Londoners Mr and Mrs George Spicer were driving along beside Loch Ness on the new road, on their way back from a holiday in northern Scotland, when their car nearly struck a huge, black creature with a long neck. The 'prehistoric animal', as Mr Spicer described it, shambled across the road, slithered through the undergrowth, and splashed into the Loch.

On 12 November 1933, an employee of the British Aluminium Company, Hugh Gray, watched an unusually large 'object' rise out of the Loch. When it had raised itself two or three feet out of the water, Gray photographed it. He estimated the length of the thing to be about 40 ft, and described it as having greyish-coloured, smooth and shiny skin.

His photograph is, to say the least, ambiguous: it's not difficult to see in it the image of a labrador-like dog with a largish piece of wood in its mouth. But in late 1933, a little frivolity from the Highlands was good news to a world wearied by the Depression and worried by Hitler's recent rise to power. The picture was published in papers all over the globe, and the Loch Ness monster became a permanent fixture in the popular imagination. In the year after the release of the Gray photograph, there were over 50 reported sightings of 'Nessie'.

In 1934 two more photographs were taken of the creature. One was by Colonel Robert Wilson, a London doctor. Labelled the 'surgeon's picture' by the British press, Wilson's photo was clear and distinct in comparison with Gray's. It seemed to show the head and neck of a plesiosaur-like creature rising out of the water. In the summer of that year, Sir Edward Mountain organized an expedition to the Loch to investigate the stories and the sightings. A member of the group snapped a picture of something strange breaking the surface of the Loch on 13 July, but hardly any details are visible.

POMPOUS JOKE?

Since then, there have been many pictures taken of things that may or may not be mysterious animals in Loch Ness. Several have been definite hoaxes. One – taken by a notorious self-publicizing 'investigator' – was nothing more than a part-submerged fence post with a sock, or possibly a collapsed Wellington boot, stuck on top to look like the head of a monster. This kind of joke hardly forwards the cause of disinterested research.

Others, even some of those taken by reputable and impartial scientists, have been ambiguous at best, although not necessarily because of what they seem to show. The classic examples are the underwater pictures taken by Dr Robert H. Rines of the Academy of Applied Sciences at the renowned Massachusetts Institute of Technology during thorough surveys of the Loch in 1972 and 1975. One of the computer-enhanced photographs, taken in 1975, seems to show an animal that fits the standard description of Nessie – something rather like an aquatic dinosaur. The other, taken in 1972, apparently shows the creature's flipper.

The doubt arises not just because there is, inevitably, no background or other detail by which to judge the size of the image – Loch Ness's waters are extremely murky thanks to the amount of peat suspended in them – but because of the pompous scientific name dreamed up for the purported animal by the naturalist Sir Peter Scott. Impressed by the rhomboid shape of the flipper, Scott coined the Latin name *Nessiteras rhombopteryx* for the animal, a 'christening' that was taken at the time to be a sign that Nessie had been accepted into the hallowed groves of establishment science.

Then someone – who must have been either a genius with dyslexia or a fanatical crossword buff – realized that the letters of

Above: *The 'surgeon's picture' of Nessie, taken on 19 April 1934 by London doctor Colonel Robert Wilson, showing the classic plesiosaur-like profile of the mystery animal.*

THEY WATCHED, PETRIFIED WITH FEAR, AS THE PREHISTORIC CREATURE SHAMBLED ACROSS THE ROAD, SLITHERED THROUGH THE UNDERGROWTH, AND SPLASHED INTO THE LOCH.

Below: *Nessie as pictured by Cornish magician and monster-hunter Anthony 'Doc' Shiels on 21 May 1977. Like many other photographs of the creature, its lack of background makes it inconclusive as evidence.*

the Latin name could swiftly be rearranged to read 'Monster hoax by Sir Peter S'. Was it a joke? A revelation? A bizarre coincidence? Scott never said, while sceptics have pointed out that the image in the Rines photographs could have been of nothing more mysterious than a lump of wood.

STRIKING CONSISTENCY

If the photographic evidence is largely dubious, the circumstantial evidence that some very odd animal is alive and well and living in Loch Ness is very good. In the 60 years since 1933, there have been more than 3000 sightings of the creature. There is, to begin with, a striking consistency in reports of what people see. Most describe a long-necked, humpbacked animal that can move very fast when it wants to, whether its head is up or down, and that, at other times, will simply rise quietly to the surface for a few minutes and then sink silently below.

It is also a curious fact that apart from Loch Ness itself the world-wide sightings of lake monsters that resemble Nessie (which no living animal known to science does) have all occurred around the isothermic line of 50°F in both northern and southern hemispheres. The animal, or animals, whatever they are, thus conform to a rule of zoology in having a distinct distribution within a specific environmental pattern. They don't pop up just anywhere, and if they did there would be grounds for suspecting that they were more a figment of the imagination (or folklore) than an elusive fact of nature.

Veteran cryptozoologist Bernard Heuvelmans commented crisply: 'One could hardly wish for better circumstantial evidence for their existence.' The unanswered question remains: what might these animals actually be?

INEXHAUSTIBLE APPETITE

There are numerous theories as to the animal's identity. Candidates have included the zeuglodon, a prehistoric, snake-like primitive whale, an unknown type of long-necked seal, giant eels, and more prosaically walruses, floating mats of plants, otters, diving birds and even – someone had to say it – mirages.

A favourite contender has always been the plesiosaur, a marine reptile that has officially been extinct for the last 70 million years. The 'extinct' label affixed by science is not necessarily proof that a species has in fact died out, however; it simply represents the current state of accepted knowledge. Until 1938 the coelacanth, a singularly ugly but otherwise inoffensive prehistoric fish, was reckoned extinct because there were no fossils of it less than 70 million years old and no living specimens had been seen; but then coelacanths were found thriving, and no doubt thoroughly indifferent to the opinions of scientists, in the Indian Ocean. So it is possible that a community of plesiosaurs has survived in the same way.

The mystery of the Loch Ness monster is riddled with paradoxes. When Canadian holidaymaker Jennifer Bruce took the picture opposite of the view across Urquhart Bay from near Temple Pier in 1982, she did not notice the monster in the Loch. But thorough research by scientist Dr Robert Rines in the 1970s (above and left), produced photographic evidence that was no less ambiguous.

Above: *A model of Issie, the monster said to inhabit Lake Ikeda in Japan.*

Right: *Pictish carvings show a strange elephant-like creature, which some believe represents a lake monster.*

Below: *A fossil relic of Tullimonstrum gregarium, which has been claimed to be an ancestor of Nessie.*

They would have had to survive in the sea for the major part of that time, but they could have found their way into Loch Ness with little or no difficulty in the last 10,000 years. Then, after the last great Ice Age ended, the glaciers retreated, and the Great Glen fault – which divides the Scottish Highlands, and of which Loch Ness is a part – opened up to the sea. On the other hand, they would have had to have adapted from being geared to a saline marine environment to survival in the fresh water of the Loch in a very short time (in evolutionary terms). But that again is not impossible.

Loch Ness is a fairly sterile place, partly because of its depth (up to an estimated 1000 ft), its darkness, and the lack of nutrients flowing into it. But a plesiosaur could survive there on a healthy diet of fish without disturbing the Loch's basic ecosystem. At least, it could as long as it had an inexhaustible appetite for fresh salmon. This is because the mature salmon that enter the Loch from the sea, by way of the River Ness, simply don't eat, and so don't affect the rest of the food chain in the Loch. Still more convenient, salmon come into the Loch all year round, so there is a reasonably consistent and plentiful supply of food for any predator that might depend on them for survival.

THE LAST DINOSAUR?

What militates against Nessie being a leftover plesiosaur is the rarity with which it seems to appear on the surface, for the creature would have to live in the top 125 ft or so of the Loch's waters, not only because that is where the food (of any kind) is, but also because below that level the temperature drops dramatically – too low for a cold-blooded reptile (even of the 'monster's' reported size) to survive. Even the warmer level of the Loch is at the extreme end of such an animal's range. On top of that, reptiles have lungs, not gills: they need to breathe fresh air. So why aren't the 'reptiles' of Loch Ness seen on the surface more often?

Most reptiles, too, would have to come – and stay – ashore for a brief period at least once every year to lay their eggs. No one has seen that happen yet at Loch Ness. It is, of course, again possible that the creatures move from the Loch out to the ocean for some of the year, perhaps especially in the breeding season. Nevertheless, it's surprising that this hasn't been seen happening on some rocky Scottish shore by someone at some time.

Even the possibility that the creature's elusiveness – not to say virtual invisibility

– is the result of there being only a very small family of monsters in the Loch, is hardly a conclusive argument. To be viable, there would need to be a community of an average of at least three monsters alive at any one time. The Loch's surface area is no more than 45 square miles, that is 15 square miles of surface water for every monster. The surface area of the Mediterranean is some 900,000 square miles, or 20,000 times bigger. The estimated population of the rare and endangered monk seal in the Mediterranean is between 300 and 600 or, at best, one every 1500 square miles – 100 times the area for each Loch Ness monster. Seals are mammals and have to breathe air; they surface to do so. And they are seen every year, at all seasons, and recognized with delight for what they are, by all kinds of people all over that huge inland sea. There is no mystery about the monk seal, although they are far more sparsely distributed over a much vaster area than the extremely mysterious Loch Ness monster would seem to be.

A SWIMMING ELEPHANT?

None of that, however, is a conclusive argument against there being something – or some things – living in the Loch. It may not be a reptile at all. It may be a fish of a

Above: *In 1984 'Doc' Shiels proposed that Nessie was a gigantic elephant squid.*

Left: *A coelacanth, a fish believed to have been extinct for 70 million years until one was caught in 1938. Could lake monsters too be living examples of reptiles officially deemed to be extinct?*

THE HIDEOUS COELACANTH HAD BEEN OFFICIALLY EXTINCT FOR **70** MILLION YEARS UNTIL IT WAS DISCOVERED TO BE ALIVE – AND STILL SWIMMING – IN **1938.**

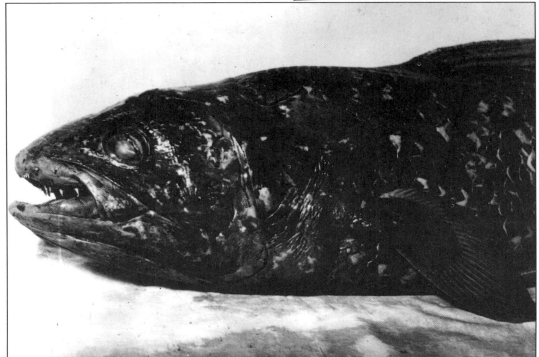

Above: *The plesiosaur, which of all known animals most resembles 'typical' lake monsters as seen in Europe and North America.*

THE INTREPID COLONEL TRACKED THE ANIMAL AS IT RETURNED TO ITS LAIR.

rather unusual variety. It may be something utterly unexpected. In August (not April!) 1979, two highly qualified academics, Dr Dennis Power and Dr Donald Johnson, suggested in the columns of the august journal *New Scientist* that the creature of Loch Ness might be a swimming elephant. While this may have started as a lighthearted article, a correspondent to *Fortean Times* gleefully pointed out a fine, ironic coincidence with this proposal. Ancient Pictish rock carvings showed (among many recognizable creatures) an animal that scholars had been unable to identify and had called either just 'the Pictish beast' or – here it comes – 'the swimming elephant'.

Certainly one of the odder aspects of the Loch Ness monster is its apparent ability to travel over land. In June 1990, retired Colonel L. McP. Fordyce published an account in *Scots Magazine* of his experience in April 1932 – some 12 months before the event usually credited as the first 'modern' sighting of the denizen of the Loch. He too mentioned the resemblance to an elephant.

Colonel Fordyce and his wife were driving south in their six-cylinder Morris Isis, along the minor road on the south side of the Loch from Foyers to Fort Augustus. At one point the road leaves the shoreline and winds through woodland. Colonel Fordyce wrote:

'Travelling at about 25 mph in this wooded section, we were startled to see an enormous animal coming out of the woods on our left and making its way over the road about 150 yards ahead of us, towards the loch.

'It had the gait of an elephant, but looked like a cross between a very large horse and a camel, with a hump on its back and a small head on a long neck.'

Colonel Fordyce was not a soldier for nothing. He got out of his car and followed the animal on foot 'for a short distance. From the rear it looked grey and shaggy. Its long, thin neck gave it the appearance of an elephant with its trunk raised.'

THE MONSTER BITES BACK

So, the mystery deepens and, in its way, becomes almost as murky as the peat-ridden waters of the Loch itself. But one of the most persuasive arguments that a large, strange animal of some kind is living in (or near) Loch Ness is the variety of different traditions and sightings from other, similar lakes around the world that share certain geographic and topographical features with Loch Ness. For the mystery animals are all reported from lake and river systems that either are connected to the sea or have been in the past, and they all either harbour or once harboured migratory fish. Many of the lakes that fit this pattern are also deep and cold.

One such is Lake Storsjön in central Sweden, which is connected by river systems with the Gulf of Bothnia, a spur of the Baltic Sea. For 350 years or more there have been reports of a monster in the lake, and since 1987 alone the local Society for Investigating the Great Lake has collected over 400 reports of sightings. Few, unfortunately, are consistent, so there is no clear idea of what the creature might really look like. Some witnesses have seen an animal with a large neck that undulates back and forth and looks like a horse's mane. Others described a large worm-like creature with distinct 'ears' on its head. According to reports, the beast's size may vary from 10 to 42 ft in length.

By a brilliant irony, one famous sighting was made by a local fisheries conservation officer, Ragnar Björks. The 73-year-old official was out checking fishing permits among anglers on the lake in the 1970s

Left: *An attempt in 1969 to trap the strange animal that several witnesses have reported seeing in Lough Auna, in Ireland's wild Connemara region.*

THERE ARE STARTLING SIMILARITIES BETWEEN THE LAKES AROUND THE WORLD WHICH ARE REPORTEDLY INHABITED BY MONSTERS.

when he had the fright of his life. A huge tail suddenly broke the calm surface near Björks's 12 ft rowing boat. The creature that owned the tail seemed to be 18 ft long, and was grey-brown on top with a yellow underbelly. Björks struck at it with his oar and hit it on the back. The creature reacted by slapping the water mightily with its tail: Björks and his boat were ignominiously hurled about 10 ft in the air. During his brief flight Björks became a convinced believer in lake monsters.

WREAKING VENGEANCE

Inconsistent reports also come from Ireland, where in Connemara a wilderness of rocks and peat-bog is broken up by a patchwork of loughs of all sizes. Here, as in the Highlands of Scotland, it's possible that the unidentified denizens of the loughs move from one to another. Such migration would help explain why so many very small stretches of water in Connemara seem to house so many animals and such large ones to boot. But there seem to be several kinds of the creatures, if the witnesses' reports are accurate.

In the evening of 22 February 1968, farmer Stephen Coyne and his son were gathering peat beside Lough Nahooin, a tiny peat tarn, only some 100 by 80 yds in extent, near Gladdaghduff. Alerted to something weird in the water by the behaviour of their dog, Coyne sent the boy to fetch the rest of his family to watch it. The seven-strong family were joined by four other local children.

They agreed that the creature was probably about 12 ft long, hairless, with 'eel-like' black skin. It had a 'pole-like' neck, in diameter about 12 in, and apparently horns on its head that may have been protuberances housing its eyes, and a pale mouth. When it put its head underwater two humps showed above the surface. The group caught only glimpses of a tail.

This is entirely different from the animal spotted in Lough Dubh, another small lake in County Galway, near Glinsk. Three men saw a monster there in 1956, and in 1960 three of them were seen in the lough. One day in March 1962, schoolteacher Alphonsus Mullaney and his son Alphonsus Jr went fishing there for pike, and took rod and line stout enough to

Below: *Joseph W. Zarzynski, director of the research group Lake Champlain Phenomena Investigation, prepares sonar equipment in the hope of tracking 'Champ', the lake's famous but mysteriously elusive inhabitant.*

Above: *A model of Ogopogo, the monster of Lake Okanagan in British Columbia, Canada. Local Indian lore acknowledged the creature centuries before it was first sighted by European settlers.*

handle these hefty fish. Mullaney caught more than a fish:

'Suddenly there was a tugging on the line. I thought it might be on a root, so I took it gently. It did not give. I hauled it slowly ashore, and the line snapped. I was examining the line when the lad screamed.

'Then I saw the animal. It was not a seal or anything I had ever seen. It had for instance short thick legs, and a hippo face. It was as big as a cow or an ass, square faced, with small ears and a white pointed horn on its snout. It was dark grey in colour, and covered with bristles or short hair, like a pig.'

The thing, hurt and furious, was trying to get out of the water and wreak vengeance on its hapless fishers. Mullaney and his son fled. A posse of local men later returned with guns to search for the creature, but they found nothing. Nothing like it has been reported since from Lough Dubh.

Different again was the monster seen in Lough Auna, 3 miles or so north-east of Clifden, the 'capital' of Connemara. Air Commodore Kort, who had moved to Ireland after retiring from the Royal Netherlands Air Force, was about to go indoors at the end of a barbecue party in the summer of 1980 when he and one of his guests saw what seemed to be the sawtooth,

reptilian dorsal fin of an animal moving slowly across the lough. The fin was about 5 ft long and stood 12 in out of the water. 'The uncanny thing about it,' said Kort, 'was the gliding movement without any disturbance of the water on the surface.'

WATER SERPENT

In North America, monsters such as the frequently seen but so far unidentified inhabitant of New Brunswick's Lake Utopia and 'Manipogo' of Lake Manitoba in Canada, and those of Lake Erie (where there were many sightings in 1991) and Flathead Lake in Montana, were all locally renowned long before 'Nessie' grabbed the world's headlines.

One such lives in the 109 mile long Lake Champlain, which adjoins New York State, Vermont and Quebec. Lake Champlain's monster, nicknamed 'Champ', has been sighted over 240 times, nearly half of them since 1982. The first really detailed report came in July 1883. The Sheriff of Clinton County, New York, Captain Nathan H. Mooney, was on the north-west arm of the lakeshore when he saw a huge water serpent about 50 yds from him. The creature rose about 5 ft out of the water, which was rough. He reckoned the animal was 25 or 30 ft long. Its neck was about 7 in in diameter, with visibly contracting muscles, and was curved like that 'of a goose when about to take flight'. Mooney noted that there were round white spots inside the creature's mouth.

Candidates for the identity of 'Champ' are identical to those offered for the Loch Ness monster, with the plesiosaur leading.

There are a number of photographs of the creature. Perhaps the most significant was taken on 5 July 1977 by Sandra Mansi of Connecticut, who described the thing as a 'dinosaur' with its neck and head some 6 ft out of the water. The Mansi photograph has been examined by scientists and declared to be a genuine original of something in the water. But what?

THE 'REMORSEFUL ONE'

The best-known Canadian lake monster, 'Ogopogo' of British Columbia's Lake Okanagan, also made its debut long before Nessie. Reports go back to 1850, although

the local Indians were familiar with the beast long before that, and indeed named it the 'remorseful one'. Indian legend says the creature was once human – a murderer turned into a serpent as punishment for his crimes. In 1926, the editor of the Vancouver *Sun* wrote of the creature: 'Too many reputable people have seen it to ignore the seriousness of actual facts.'

A recent sighting shows how witnesses are convinced that there is indeed something odd in Lake Okanagan. In the summer of 1989, hunting guide Ernie Giroux and his wife were standing on the banks of the lake when an animal about 15 ft long surfaced from the calm waters and swam 'real gracefully and fast', as Giroux later told reporters. The creature had a round head 'like a football'. Several feet of the creature's neck and body came up out of the water. The Girouxs saw the monster at the same spot where, a few

weeks before, British Columbian car salesman Ken Chaplin had taken a video of what he described as a dark green, snake-like creature about 15 ft long.

Wildlife experts who saw the video said the animal was more likely a beaver or a large river otter than a 'monster'. Ernie Giroux was unimpressed.

'I've seen a lot of animals swimming in the wild and what we saw that night was definitely not a beaver,' he said bluntly.

At the other end of the Americas is 'Nahuelito', the denizen of Nahuel Huapi Lake at the foot of the Patagonian mountains in southern Argentina. The lake, which covers 318 square miles, is in a popular resort area. Dozens of tourists and local people have seen the creature.

Accounts of the animal vary. Some describe a giant water snake with humps and fish-like fins; others speak of a swan with a snake's head, while yet others liken

Above: *An early effort to trap the creature of Loch Ness – a huge steel cage, built in 1933.*

THE BEAST HAD ONCE BEEN HUMAN.

it to the overturned hull of a boat or a tree stump. Estimates of the creature's length range from 15 to 150 ft. 'Nahuelito' seems to surface only in the summer, when the wind is still. A sudden swell of water and a shooting spray usually precede a sighting.

Patagonia, mountainous and desolate at best, has long been the source of tales of monstrous animals, and even human giants. Patagonian Indians told the first colonists of a huge lake-dwelling creature without head, legs or tail. The rumoured existence of a Patagonian plesiosaur was given additional fuel in the early 1920s, when a gold prospector named Sheffield followed an unusual spoor and found a bizarre water beast at the end of the trail:

'I saw in the middle of the lake,' he reported, 'an animal with a huge neck like that of a swan, and the movement in the water made me suppose the beast to have a body like that of a crocodile.' An expedition, led by Dr C. Onelli, director of the Buenos Aires Zoo, set out to catch or photograph the animal, but sadly failed.

THE LATEST TECHNOLOGIES

What would solve the mystery of the world's lake monsters?

Naturalists are agreed that only the capture of a live specimen or the discovery of a carcass (scientists tend to disapprove of investigators 'acquiring' dead specimens by ballistic means) would admit the monsters into the charmed circle of conventional science. But hunting lake monsters is not the world's easiest task. No live monsters have been caught, yet.

No carcasses have been found either that might be anything other than recognizable animals. Dead specimens may be elusive because the typical monster haunt is a very deep lake. A dead monster would sink to the bottom, where the water pressure would slow down the rate of decomposition – leaving time for eels and other creatures to consume the remains.

Giant nets, submarines, underwater cameras, sonar, lake and loch-side crews of observers have all failed to come up with unambiguous and unimpeachable evidence that would prove to the world that there is an actual monster in any of their reputed haunts. If the animals as reported do exist, they are quite possibly frightened away by the sounds made by the very devices that are being used to track them – as well as by engine noise from the boats.

But until that solid evidence turns up, these strange animals will remain classic mysteries. And credible witnesses will continue to report them, take fuzzy photographs, and keep the lake monster legends alive and swimming.

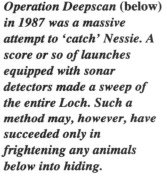

Operation Deepscan (below) in 1987 was a massive attempt to 'catch' Nessie. A score or so of launches equipped with sonar detectors made a sweep of the entire Loch. Such a method may, however, have succeeded only in frightening any animals below into hiding.

NOT QUITE HUMAN

Modern reports of strange, over-sized, ape-like wild men have mainly come from the Himalayan mountains, China, Australia, and the American Pacific Northwest, but they are also part of European folklore. In England the creatures were called woodwoses (previous page, carved into the font in Sibton church, Suffolk, and far right).

As he began his descent down the mountain through the heavy mist, the professor thought he was hearing the echo of his footsteps. Terror seized him when he realized that the footsteps belonged to something different – to something malignant...

Abominable snowmen and other horrid hairy man-beasts are strictly contained in the Himalayas, the wilderness of the USA, and the remoter parts of China. Or so you thought.

At 4296 ft Ben MacDhui is the highest peak in Scotland's Cairngorm mountains, and the second highest in the country. Many who have scaled Ben MacDhui are convinced that a malignant entity – which locals call *Am Fear Liath Mor*, the Big Grey Man – lives on the mountain.

The first report from anyone outside the area that something sinister haunted Ben MacDhui came in December 1925 at the Annual General Meeting of the Cairngorm Club. Professor Norman Collie told his suitably astonished audience that in 1891 he had been climbing through heavy mist down from the summit of Ben MacDhui, when, he said, 'I began to think I heard

Right: The Blue Mountains of New South Wales, Australia, which are said to be the haunt of the yowie, the antipodean version of the mysterious man-beast.

something else than merely the noise of my own footsteps. For every few steps I took I heard a crunch, and then another crunch as if someone was walking after me but taking steps three or four times the length of my own.'

At first he thought his imagination was working overtime, but the sound persisted, although whatever was making it remained hidden in the mist. Then, as the eerie crunching continued, Collie said, 'I was seized with terror and took to my heels, staggering blindly among the boulders for four or five miles.'

Collie vowed never to return to the mountain alone, and remained convinced that there was 'something very queer about the top of Ben MacDhui'.

His chilling account was soon picked up by the newspapers, with the result that other mountaineers came forward to record that they too had had similar experiences of uncontrollable and inexplicable fear and panic while on Ben MacDhui. Some had barely managed to avoid lethal falls in their compulsion to get away as quickly as possible from the terrifying presence.

This sounds like a paranormal presence, but some witnesses have actually seen the thing, reporting a huge, man-like figure, and many accounts mention the same heavy footsteps with the unusually long stride that Collie heard.

Plenty of explanations have been put forward for these experiences. They range from the presence of yeti-like man-beasts and optical illusions to the (inevitable) 'base for extraterrestrial aliens' and (more plausibly) hallucinations brought on by lack of oxygen. This latter most probably accounts for some of the more exotic reports of the Big Grey Man, which mention strains of ghostly music and sepulchral laughter wafting across the mountain during its appearance.

But leaving the wonkier propositions aside does not mean dumping the 'man-beast' explanation entirely. There is a long tradition that hairy man-beasts inhabited the British mainland in the past. Known as 'woodwoses', or more mundanely as 'wild men of the woods', their images can be seen carved into the decorations in many old East Anglian churches. There is not much forest on Ben MacDhui, and it is a long way from East Anglia, but the

possibility that a colony of these legendary creatures has survived in Scotland remains to tantalize the imagination.

FOUL ODOURS

Although conventional zoology says that one wouldn't expect to find apes of any kind, let alone 'ape men', living in South America or Australia, any more than in the British Isles, both continents can boast plenty of eyewitnesses who would swear that the contrary is true and that the scientists are wrong.

Australia's man-beast is known as the 'yowie'. Most reports have come from

Below: *The enigmatic female beast shot by members of a geological survey team led by François de Loys on the Venezuela–Colombia border in 1920. Controversy still rages over the true nature of the creature.*

HERE WAS CONCLUSIVE PHYSICAL PROOF AT LAST — THE CARCASS OF THE FEMALE BEAST.

New South Wales and Queensland, and the creatures have been seen by settlers since the mid-19th century at least. The Aborigines have known about them since long before then. Like North America's 'bigfoot' and 'sasquatch', the yowie can remain remarkably unperturbed when surprised. When George Summerell, who was riding a horse, came upon one bending down to drink from a creek near Bemboka, New South Wales, on 12 October 1912, it simply 'rose to its full height, of about 7 feet, and looked quietly at the horseman', according to an item in the Sydney *Morning Herald*. 'Then stooping down again, it finished its drink, and then, picking up a stick that lay by it, walked steadily away...and disappeared among the rocks and timber 150 yards away.'

Footprints around the shore of the creek showed that the creature had been there at least a fortnight before, as well, and that the animal had only four toes – a feature of other man-beast prints taken around the world. But the yowie has two other features commonly reported by witnesses of the North American man-beasts: no neck, and the ability to emit revolting smells at will.

In early 1978, an Australian National Parks worker was cutting timber near Springbrook in Queensland when he saw 'this big black hairy man-thing' about 12 ft away from him.

'It had huge hands,' he said, 'and...a flat, black shiny face, with two big yellow eyes and a hole for a mouth. It just stared at me and I stared back. I was so numb I couldn't even raise the axe I had in my hand. We [were] staring at each other for about 10 minutes before it suddenly gave off a foul smell that made me vomit – then it just made off sideways and disappeared.'

THE BEASTS ATTACK

The most intriguing and controversial encounter with a South American man-beast took place along the Tarra River on the Venezuela–Colombia border in 1920. A 20-strong team of geological surveyors, led by Swiss geologist Dr François de Loys, had set out in 1917 but at the end of three years had been reduced to a handful by disease, venomous animals, and the poisoned arrows of hostile Indians. One day in 1920, this ragged band saw coming through the foliage ahead of them two 5 ft tall, ape-like but tail-less creatures, walking upright on their hind legs.

When the beasts – one male and the other female – saw the geologists, they became plainly agitated, tearing angrily at the vegetation around them. They got so excited that both defecated into their hands and flung their excrement at the scientists. Then they moved forward – as if to attack, it seemed to the geologists, who responded with a hail of small-arms fire. The female died instantly. The male fled.

The geologists examined the carcass, noted its details, and photographed it. Most of the pictures were lost when the party's boat capsized later in the expedition, but one survived. On returning to Europe, De Loys showed it to the French anthropologist Professor George Montandon. He was convinced that it showed a species comparable to the Old World's apes – chimpanzees, gorillas, orang-utans and gibbons. He formally named it *Ameranthropoides loysi* – 'Loys's American ape'. Other scientists were less impressed.

The creature did look somewhat like an over-sized and tail-less spider monkey, and

Below: *It was in tropical jungle like this that De Loys and his party came upon and shot at a pair of aggressive man-beasts in 1920.*

most zoologists maintained that it was some form of spider monkey. Some even hinted, none too subtly, at a hoax. Montandon answered all the criticisms in painstaking detail, but his critics were unmoved: as far as establishment science was concerned, De Loys's find was not an ape, and the issue was soon simply ignored.

But there is plenty of circumstantial evidence in favour of creatures like the one De Loys shot and photographed. Indian tribes in the jungles all over South America have long believed in the existence of ape-like beasts that walk upright and lack tails. And among the ruins of various South American and Mexican ancient cities are sculptures of gorilla-like creatures quite unlike any known New World primate – but they do resemble the South American ape woman shot by De Loys's party. Further, there is no ecological reason why such an ape should not be able to survive in the South American environment – but conventional science always prefers to ignore awkward little questions and hair-splitting logic like that.

OUT OF AFRICA

In contrast to the areas we've looked at so far, it would make sense if hairy man-beasts were to be found living in Africa. Apart from its vast areas of wilderness in which such creatures could roam free, with little risk of being detected by people, the continent is now known to be the 'cradle of mankind' – the place where humans, *homo sapiens*, evolved.

The oldest African fossils of hominids are the australopithecines, which first appeared over three million years ago. Some types were notably slender, others more robust – and so it is just possible that these or other ancient evolutionary forms, somewhere between apes and men, have survived out of sight in Africa to this day. And if one goes by the huge dossier of eyewitness reports, Africa is indeed home to an enormous variety of unidentified man-beasts.

Living specimens of slender aus-tralopithecine would look like several unidentified man-beasts as witnesses have described them. Among these are Zaïre's 'kakundakari', the 'fating'ho' of Senegal, and Tanzania's 'agogwe'. According to

witnesses, the agogwe is small, russet-furred, and man-like, and sometimes mixes with other primates such as baboons. Elders of the Mandinka tribe of Senegal speak of the fating'ho as if it were just as real as any of the known animals inhabiting their lands, though it is rarely seen nowadays (perhaps simply because it has become rarer).

Other man-beasts seem to resemble the robust species of australopithecines. Among these are the 'kikomba' of Zaïre, and Sudan's 'wa'ab'. These may even be surviving examples of humanity's direct evolutionary ancestor, *Homo erectus*.

The French anthropologist Jacqueline Roumeguere-Eberhardt has concluded that there are no less than five different species of man-beast living in Kenya. She has cautiously dubbed them 'X One' through to 'X Five'.

X One is a typical bigfoot-like being, hairy, huge, and possibly social, since it's been seen carrying buffalo meat rather than gorging it on the spot. It also defends itself with a kind of sardonic gentleness. A young hunter who was cornered by the beast said it simply removed his arrows from their quiver, broke them up and put them back.

Above: *Cryptozoologist Loren Coleman, who was the first to note the extraordinary similarity of the environments in China and the USA where man-beasts have been sighted.*

Right: *One of over 1000 footprints apparently made by a company of bigfoot near Bossburg, Washington State, in 1969. The creature's deformed foot was over 16 in long.*

Below: *Two prospectors made these sketches of their sighting of a sasquatch near Pitt Lake, British Columbia, on 28 June 1965.*

X Two is a cave-dwelling creature with a hairless, beige-coloured body with curly black hair on its head. A noticeably human-oid beast, it is tall and thin, and seems to live in nuclear families.

X Three is tall, and uses tools for hunting. Males have been seen to fell buffalo 'with an uprooted tree with its roots carved into spikes'. The beast then wields 'a spear-like knife' to cut out its prey's internal organs, 'which are then eaten on the spot'.

X Four is a hairy-chested, fat-bodied pygmy-like hominoid that, witnesses say, is often to be seen carrying a digging stick, which it uses to uproot tubers.

X Five is exclusively vegetarian, a man-beast that carries bows and arrows and is apparently capable of making leatherwork bags.

Despite the wealth of sightings of African man-beasts, no one has yet caught

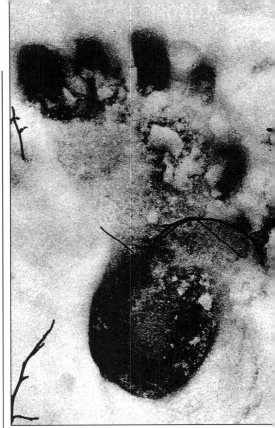

or killed one, or found a skeleton that would provide conclusive proof of their existence. But Africa has given zoologists plenty of surprises in the 20th century alone. As the saying goes, 'There is always something new out of Africa.' So, perhaps, as the English cryptozoologist Dr Karl Shuker has put it, the most secretive of continents may be saving its most sensational surprise for the future.

THE INCREDIBLE HULK?

As far as the West is concerned, the grand-daddy of all hairy man-beasts is, of course, the so-called 'abominable snowman' or 'yeti' of the Himalayas. The existence of what, correctly translated, the local people call 'a man-like living thing that is not a human being' first came to the West's attention in 1921, when Lt-Col C.K. Howard-Bury was surveying Mt Everest for a forthcoming attempt to reach the summit. On 22 September that year he came across huge footprints on a snowfield where, earlier, he had seen dark, man-like forms moving around. News of these two events sped round the world, and have been reinforced by sightings from virtually every mountaineering expedition into the area since.

The term 'abominable snowman' is not only a mistranslation of the Nepalese term

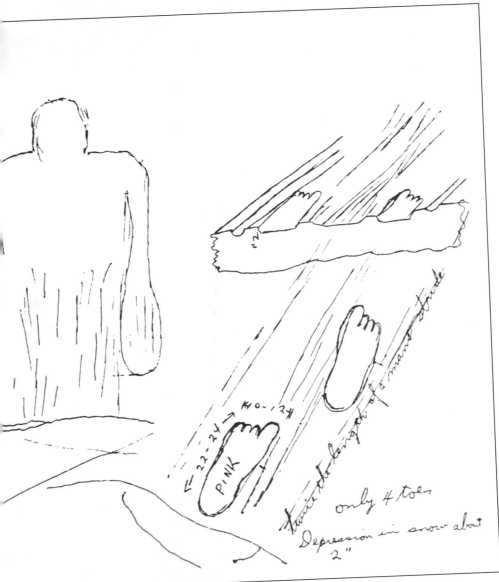

for these creatures – it's irritatingly misleading. There seems to be nothing particularly abominable about the yeti, and they appear on the high Himalayan snowfields only when making their way from one hot and humid valley, where they seem to spend most of their time, to another. And the term also implies that there is only one of these creatures. Not only are there many individuals, if reports are to be trusted, but there are at least three different kinds of yeti.

The word yeti itself is a Sherpa term that means, roughly, 'That-thing-there'. Investigator (and oil millionaire) Tom Slick was the first to conclude, from his expeditions to the Himalayas in 1957 and 1958, that there were at least two types of creature that local people had seen.

The 'original' yeti is the *meh-teh*, a man-sized creature that sports a conical head set on a stout neck, with a jutting jaw and a wide, lipless mouth. The body is covered in thick, reddish-brown fur. Prints show short, broad feet. Meh-teh eat plants and small animals, including birds, which they hunt in the upper forests of the mountains.

There is also a pygmy man-beast of the Himalayas, *teh-lma*, which means 'man-like being'. Standing about 3–4 ft tall, these creatures live deeper in the valleys than meh-teh, surviving on a diet largely of frogs and insects. Their thick fur is dark red, with a slight mane on the back.

The third species of yeti is known in the Himalayas, but only by repute. Called *dzu-teh* – 'hulking living thing' – these beasts are huge, far taller and bulkier than a human, with a dark shaggy coat, a flat head with beetling brows, long powerful arms and hands, and large feet that leave prints with two pads under the first toe, which points out and away from the others on the foot. They live not in the Himalayas but in eastern Tibet and northern China, on a mainly vegetarian diet.

This matter of the two pads (and other features) showing in the dzu-teh's footprint is important, and so is the animal's habitat. American cryptozoologist Loren Coleman first pointed out that both plant and animal species in the areas of China where dzu-teh (called 'yeren' in China) are consistently reported bear an uncanny resemblance – they are often related to, or the same as –

Tracks made by a bigfoot on Blue Creek Mountain, California, in the late summer of 1967 (above left) were measured by investigator René Dahinden at 15 in (above).

So, are bigfoot (alias sasquatch) and yeren (alias dzu-teh) related – or even separate communities of the same animal? And if so, what animal?

The favourite candidate is a species of giant ape, named *Gigantopithecus*, which lived in southern China until it – apparently – became extinct 500,000 years ago. Its anatomy is somewhere between ape and human. Gigantopithecus, as its name implies, was huge. Males probably weighed around 800 lb and females around 500 lb. This is easily the largest primate that ever lived. Gigantopithecus also, almost certainly, stood and walked in a human manner.

Humans and all apes share a unique set of anatomical traits in the arms, shoulders, and thorax, since all evolved to swing through trees. Humans gave up this form of personal transport long ago, preferring walking, horse-riding and eventually the Ford Model T. As a result they lost their tails. Gigantopithecus also belonged to this

Above and below: *Frames from the famous movie of a bigfoot filmed by Roger Patterson on 20 October 1967 at Bluff Creek in northern California. Expert opinion says the film was not faked.*

those found in the Pacific Northwest of North America. And this is where bigfoot and sasquatch are most often seen. And the footprints of yeren and bigfoot are strikingly similar in the configuration of their pads, ridges and disposition of the toes.

group of higher primates, but it was too large to swing through trees, and probably, therefore, also lost its tail. Its wide chest, broad shoulders, and lack of tail would make it conspicuous among apes – and remarkably like a human in appearance.

Gigantopitheces had ape-like faces and were covered with body hair. Their faces would have had the ape's retreating forehead and blunt nose, but with a more human set to the mouth and jaw. They did not make tools and had less-than-human intelligence. They probably did not live in close social groups. All these features are remarkably consistent with the reported appearance and behaviour of bigfoot/sasquatch.

Most authorities presume that Gigantopithecus is extinct because the most recent fossil teeth (from northern Vietnam) are 300,000 years old. Other finds date back a million years. But one early Gigantopithecus jaw from India is at least five million years old. Thus, the animals survived for four million years although we have no direct physical evidence that they did. So they could have survived during the 300,000 years since the owner of the most recent fossil remains died off and still leave no sign of being here.

'I RAN OUT OF FILM'

Although many American Indian tribes of the Pacific Northwest tell tales of bigfoot, and in them treat the creature just as they do less elusive animals, it was not until 1958 that the American public at large became aware of the bigfoot phenomenon. In the summer of 1958 strange, giant footprints cropped up around some road-making equipment at Bluff Creek in northern California. The tracks appeared several nights in a row, alarming the workers who found them. Once the major San Francisco papers picked up the story, it soon got national attention. Bigfoot had become the ultimate reclusive media star.

The next major sighting, which also netted a major piece of evidence, came in 1967. On 20 October that year Roger Patterson and Bob Gimlin of Yakima, Washington, went to Bluff Creek in the hope of catching sight of a bigfoot after hearing that tracks had been seen again in the area. They went on horseback, and

were 40 or 50 miles from the nearest road when they rounded a bend on the trail and came to a creek. In Gimlin's words: 'Here this thing stood by the creek, just stood. We were on one side of the creek, the creature on the other and our horses went crazy. Roger's little horse just went bananas.'

Patterson managed to haul out the 16-mm movie camera, loaded with colour film, that he was carrying in his saddlebag.

'This creature turned,' said Gimlin, 'and started to walk away from us, just slow like a man would if he were just walking down the street, but as it did this, Roger ran across the creek behind it, but then he stumbled on a sandbar…He was shooting the camera while he was running. He hollered back for me when he stumbled and fell. He said, "Cover me!" and, naturally, I knew what he meant.

'So I rode across the creek on my horse and took my .30-06 rifle out of the saddle scabbard and just stood there (pointing but not aiming the rifle at the beast). When I did this, this creature was…about 90 feet [away] – and it turned and looked at me; just turned as it was walking away. It never stopped walking. And then…I heard Roger say, "Oh, my God, I ran out of film."'

Above: *Bob Gimlin, who was with Patterson at Bluff Creek, holds two casts that the pair made of tracks left by the bigfoot. The prints measured over 14 in long.*

'ROGER'S LITTLE HORSE JUST WENT BANANAS.'

Above: *Detailed drawing of the Bluff Creek bigfoot's head, made by Russian researcher Dmitri Baynov after studying the movie.*

FORTY POLICE SPECIALISTS WERE FORCED TO CONCLUDE THAT THE FOOTPRINTS WERE MADE BY A GENUINE BIGFOOT.

Below: *Leading US bigfoot researcher Grover Krantz, with a cast of a bigfoot print.*

Gimlin remains adamant that he and Patterson saw a genuine bigfoot that day. Two things support his contention. First, Patterson is now dead, and Gimlin has more to gain financially from a confession to a hoax than stoutly maintaining the opposite – after all, he owns no rights in the film.

Second, the oft-mentioned possibility that a third party hoaxed the two bigfoot-hunters seems highly unlikely. To begin with, such a prankster would have had to have anticipated the pair's moves over many miles of rough country, seeing them but not being seen. Even if the hypothetical hoaxer had managed that feat of fieldcraft, only an idiot would risk getting in the way of a shot from Gimlin's powerful hunting rifle; the .30-06 round will down a bear.

And some expert scientific opinion backs the men's claim. One expert who studied the film, Dmitri Donskoy, Professor of Biomechanics at the Soviet Central Institute of Physical Culture in Moscow, noted that the creature's gait was that of an animal with enormous weight and strength, and that the movement of the whole body was fluid and confident. 'These factors…allow us to evaluate the gait of the creature as a natural movement without any sign of the artfulness that one would see in an imitation,' he concluded. 'At the same time, with all the diversity of locomotion illustrated by the creature of the footage, its gait as seen is absolutely non-typical of man.'

Another expert, Donald Grieve, Reader in Biomechanics at the Royal Free Hospital in London, was similarly impressed, but had a reservation. He felt that if the camera speed – which Patterson did not know for sure – had been set at 24 frames per second, the film could be showing a large, walking man. But if the film had been shot at 18 frames per second, no human being would be able to match the movements shown. He concluded with rare honesty: 'My subjective impressions have oscillated between total acceptance of the Bigfoot on the grounds that the film would be difficult to fake, to one of irrational rejection based on an emotional response to the possibility that the Bigfoot actually exists.'

The leading US authority on bigfoot, Professor Grover Krantz of Washington State University, made a detailed analysis of the movie in 1991, and concluded that it was indeed shot at 18 frames per second. The animal's movements, he believes, were impossible for a human to imitate, and convincingly show the creature's massiveness and strength. And he noted that its huge size, and muscles to match, were well outside the normal range of human variation. In other words, if Patterson's bigfoot had been a man in a fur suit, he would have been a giant who had pumped an awful lot of iron.

DEAD OR ALIVE

More impressive evidence for the reality of bigfoot comes from a set of footprints that were discovered and cast by US Forest Service workers in 1982, in the Blue Mountains along the Washington–Oregon border. The prints were made in very fine soil that was slightly damp. All the casts show ridges on the skin under the toes and on the soles. These are just like finger-prints, and only the palms and soles of higher primates have them. Forty police fingerprinters have studied these casts over the years, and have all concluded that the footprints must have been made by one or more genuine bigfeet.

Opinion among anthropologists and primatologists who have seen the casts is mixed. Many suggested that the casts had

been made from human footprints that had somehow been enlarged – a latex mould of a footprint will expand by 50 per cent when soaked in kerosene. This trick also expands the spacing between the ridges by 50 per cent. All the fingerprint experts noted that the ridges on these footprints were spaced just like those on the skin of other primates.

Despite all this circumstantial evidence, the only thing that will convince mainstream science of the reality of bigfoot will be part or all of a specimen itself, dead or alive. Professor Krantz remarks that 'a single lower jaw would be enough to establish not only its existence, but whether Gigantopithecus is still with us'.

INFESTED WATERS

Bigfoot is by no means the only mystery man-beast in North America, nor the strangest. The prize for the most bizarre has to go to a nightmarish creature nicknamed Lizard Man.

Witnesses describe it as 7 ft tall, walking upright like a man – but with green scaly skin, glowing red eyes, three toes on each foot and three fingers – each sprouting a 4 in long claw – on each hand. This grotesque animal, or apparition, first introduced itself to humanity around 2 am on 29 June 1988, near Scape Ore Swamp, outside the one-horse town of Bishopville in Lee County, South Carolina.

Seventeen-year-old Christopher Davis had just finished changing a flat tyre on his car when he saw 'something large' running toward him across a nearby field. As the creature came nearer, Davis leaped into the vehicle and tried to slam the door – only to see the thing seize it and try to wrench it open. Davis had plenty of time – more than he would have liked – to note the fine details of its unlovely appearance. Davis eventually got the car going and made his getaway. When he got home, shaking with fright, he found long scratches on the car roof, and the wing mirror in serious disarray.

Others encountered Lizard Man that summer, but none helped solve the mystery of what the creature was. However, records show that scaly and apparently aquatic man-beasts have been reported before, in many parts of North America.

Such creatures sound like a fantasy, or a hoax, or merely the effect on surprised witnesses of a person in a diving suit. But there is an odd twist to the Lizard Man tale, especially if one bears in mind the possibility that bigfoot and its international relations may be a surviving form of the officially extinct Gigantopithecus. In 1982, paleontologists Drs Dale A. Russell and R. Séguin of the Canadian National Museum of Natural Sciences published a paper in which they set out what a dinosaurian equivalent of a human being may have looked like, had the dinosaurs survived to the present. They suggest it would have been a two-legged creature with three-fingered hands, and in general would have looked startlingly like Lizard Man.

THE 'HUMAN DINOSAUR' ATTACKED WITH A VICIOUS FEROCITY.

Below: *As shown by this artist's impression, bigfoot towers over an average-sized man.*

MONSTERS FROM THE DEEP

Since pre-Biblical times, sailors have returned home from long voyages with tales of huge monsters and cunning sea serpents. Many stories can be attributed to the lonely nights at sea, and alcoholic solace, but should these include the testimony of senior naval officers, and the unidentifiable carcasses washed up upon remote shores?

'He had a large body and a small alligator-like head. The neck seemed to be medium size, matching the size of the head. The body was very large, shaped somewhat like a seal. There was a mane of bristly hair or fur which ran down the middle of his head.

'He would surface the upper part of his body and glide out of the water with the lower part of his body remaining submerged. The portion of his body which was visible measured about 40 feet in length. We estimate his weight to be between 35 and 40 tons over all.

'At no time did the whole body show. He stayed on the surface no longer than 40 seconds at a time. You could hear the heavy weight of his upper body when he dove below, creating a large splash and a subsequent wake. He surfaced four times in 20 minutes during which we were trying to stay clear of him. The Captain changed course to steer away from him and the queer fellow surfaced on our starboard beam…

'Another peculiar thing about him was that when he'd surface he would turn his head looking towards us and it seemed to us he was playful and curious. Another point was that on the upper part of his body there were two flippers, similar to those of a seal.'

So runs part of a report of a sea-monster sighting on 3 September 1959 by the cook, Joseph H. Bourassa, of the scalloper *Noreen*. The ship was 120 miles out from Bermuda, east of Pollock. Bourassa had been at sea for 20 years, and had never before seen anything like what he saw that day.

'IT SEEMED TO US HE WAS PLAYFUL AND CURIOUS.'

Opposite: *A 16th-century artist's rendering of a sea serpent. Of the thousands of such creatures that have been sighted over the centuries, surprisingly few conform to this stereotype. Sea serpents are as bewildering in their variety as in every other aspect of their existence.*

Below: *A German U-boat of World War 1 vintage. When one such craft torpedoed a British freighter, a 60 ft long sea serpent was blown out of the water at the same time.*

Morgawr, the Cornish sea serpent, as photographed by witness 'Mary F.' in early February 1976. Although much smaller, the animal bears a distinct resemblance to many descriptions and photographs of the Loch Ness monster.

Right: *Strong drink and sailors have always been boon companions. Some of the wilder reports of monsters seen at sea may fairly be put down to the effects of the demon booze.*

NAVAL REPORTS

What are sea monsters? How many kinds of them are there? Compare Bourassa's account with this, from an officer of the Imperial German Navy who was aboard the U-boat U28 when, during World War 1, the submarine blew the British *Iberian* out of the water in the North Atlantic:

'A little later pieces of wreckage, and among them a gigantic sea-animal, writhing and struggling wildly, were shot out of the water to a height of 60 to 100 feet…the animal sank out of sight after 10 or 15 seconds… It was about 60 feet long, was like a crocodile in shape and had four limbs with powerful webbed feet and a long tail tapering to a point.'

If this creature bears little enough resemblance to the animal in the first account quoted, try this one:

'Then I saw this great eel-like monster rear its head like a Scotch terrier struck by curiosity. Its eyes were red and green, like the port and starboard lights of a ship. It was about ninety feet long. As we approached within 200 feet, it rose out of the water, with its seven humps like a camel and its face like a cow, and didn't make any noise, but I thought it should have mooed. Then it uttered an eerie bellow, like a bull whale in its last agony and reared up, perhaps thirty feet, perhaps fifty, and flopped over on its back. Along its flanks was a phosphorescent glow. By this time we had five searchlights on it, and it turned to the side and dived.'

The report came from First Officer A.E. Richards, who witnessed the episode from the bridge of the liner *Santa Lucia* in the long thin dawn light of 21 October 1933. The ship was off Sheringham Point near Victoria, in Cadboro Bay, Vancouver Island, British Columbia. The bay is famous for its resident sea monster 'Caddy' or, more pretentiously, *Cadborosaurus*.

One more example will drive home the point to which we are making so laborious a pilgrimage:

'It looked like an elephant waving its trunk, but the trunk was a long neck with a small head on the end, like a snake's head. It had humps on the back which moved in a funny way. The colour was black or very dark brown, and the skin seemed to be like a sealion's...the animal frightened me... I do not like the way it moved when it was swimming.'

'The animal' is called *morgawr*, the Cornish Celtic word for 'sea giant'. It made many appearances off the Cornish coast in the 1970s, and this particular witness, known only as Mary F., actually managed to photograph it, in February 1976, as it played in the sea off Rosemullion Head near Falmouth. The creature bears a striking resemblance to the popular image of the Loch Ness monster, and for all anyone knows may be of the same family, although Mary F. estimated its length to be no more than 15–18 ft – a veritable infant beside Nessie, and a positive midget compared to the monstrous 'eel-like' animal that First Officer Richards saw disporting itself off Vancouver Island.

PANDORA'S BOX

And there lies the rub. On the face of it, no one sea monster seems to bear much likeness to another. So what are we dealing with? The usual catalogue of possibilities and explanations presents itself unbidden – hallucinations, misidentifications, bored sailors livening up a ship's log to bemuse posterity, tired and emotional witnesses (considerably less of a rarity at sea than monster sightings: many long-haul freighters are navigated through a sea-fog of alcohol).

Or are we back in the world of officially extinct or simply officially overlooked animals? There is some reason to believe that some apparently extinct creatures have survived in the sea. The ostensibly fresh-water Loch Ness monster, for instance, may be a marine animal, a surviving plesiosaur, that merely visits the Loch on occasion. On the evidence, there is no compelling reason to suppose for an instant that scientists have catalogued all the animals that live in the world's oceans. The waters, after all, cover roughly two-thirds of the surface of the Earth, and they keep on presenting little surprises to our friends in the laboratory coats. Just to cite three examples: in 1958, a previously unknown species of porpoise, now called the 'cochito', was found in the Gulf of California; eight years later 'megamouth' was discovered, hauled up on the anchor of an Hawaiian survey ship – a shark so different from other sharks that zoologists had to create an entire new family to accommodate it, and it duly entered the record books, too, as the third largest known species of its kind; and in 1983 a new species of killer whale, the Prudes Bay, peculiar to the Antarctic, was added to zoology's roll of honour.

Honest scientists know that they have not plumbed the depths of the riches of life hidden in the oceans. The same honesty makes their hair, quite rightly, stand on end at the thought that untold biological riches are being destroyed in the Amazon rainforests every day. Biologists do not know what we may be losing as the fires of greed consume trees, herbs, insects, mammals and birds by the square mile every minute. They only know such a vast and fecund area must be a living treasure house. So it is with the seas of the world.

Above: *This shot of Earth from space shows just how much of the surface of the planet is covered by water. With millions of square miles of ocean unfrequented by humanity, it would be astonishing if there were no rare and unusual animals still unknown to science.*

There have to be creatures there waiting, willingly or not, to be discovered, but the seas of the world are harder, vaster, more expensive and more treacherous to explore than any rainforest, and that is the scientists' problem.

MONSTERS OF THE BIBLICAL SEAS

Our problem, for the time being – perhaps in the forlorn hope of persuading scientists to recognize that there is a potentially fruitful field of research waiting to be taken up – is to make sense of such material as we have. There is plenty of circumstantial evidence that sea monsters exist: but how good is it? Leaving aside the mistakes, hallucinations, hoaxes and misperceptions of drunken sailors, we are left with two basic possibilities as to the origin or reality of sea monsters.

First is the possibility that some, at least, of the reported sightings are of animals that have survived their official 'extinction'. Second is the possibility that these are creatures – some rare, some perhaps less so – that have simply eluded the eyes of science. They are not 'unknown' or 'unexplained' animals, but simply unidentified ones.

Whatever we are dealing with, there is nothing new about them. Large and terrifying animals have been known to exist since Old Testament times, and from the days before those ancient texts were written as well. Jonah was swallowed by a 'whale'. The other monster of the Biblical seas, Leviathan, is also mentioned in greater or lesser detail in various places in the Psalms of David, and the Books of Isaiah and Job. One senses that these passages reveal what only the Lord can know of creatures that swim beneath the face of the deep.

'HUGEST OF LIVING CREATURES'

The most extensive description of Leviathan comes in Chapter 41 of that dark, bejewelled hymn to an ancient existentialism, the Book of Job. In this, the Lord continues to upbraid Job for his presumptions, and paints a picture of such power that one cannot help feeling not only that the passage seems to be celebrating the tremendous vitality of this creature, but that it is revered even by the one that created it:

'Canst thou draw out leviathan with an hook? or his tongue with a cord which thou lettest down?

Wilt thou play with him as with a bird? or wilt thou bind him for thy maidens?

Shall the companions make a banquet of him? shall they part him among the merchants?

Lay thine hand upon him, remember the battle, do no more.

Behold, the hope of him is in vain; shall not one be cast down even at the sight of him?

None is so fierce that dare stir him up…

Who can open the doors of his face? his teeth are terrible round about.

His scales are his pride, shut up together as with a close seal.

The flakes of his flesh are joined together: they are firm in themselves; they cannot be moved.

When he raiseth himself up, the mighty are afraid: by reason of breakings they purify themselves.

He esteemeth iron as straw, and brass as rotten wood.

Below: *Jonah is regurgitated from the belly of the 'whale' – clearly not a conventional whale since, despite their size, these huge sea-going mammals are not capable of swallowing anything as large as a man.*

The arrow cannot make him flee: sling-stones are turned with him into stubble.

He maketh the deep to boil like a pot: he maketh the sea like a pot of ointment.

He maketh a path to shine after him; one would think the deep to be hoary.

Upon earth there is not his like, who is made without fear.

He beholdeth all high things: he is a king over all the children of pride.'

All the elements of a sea-monster sighting seem to be here: the terrific size, the sense of its enormous strength and invulnerability, the confident – even casual – indifference of the creature to its puny human observers, and its sheer, awe-inspiring strangeness.

A 17th-century English poet, John Milton, a mere bricklayer in comparison to the Hebrew architect of language, was also entranced by this creature, but he could only grope blindly to recapture the drift of his predecessor's magnificent vision:

'There Leviathan
Hugest of living creatures, on the deep
Stretch'd like a promontory sleeps or swims,
And seems a moving land…'

But what was Leviathan? Can we tell, at this distance in time?

A TWISTED SERPENT

The translators of the Anglican Church's Authorized Version of the Bible appointed by King James did not actually translate the original Hebrew word, which was *livyathan*, probably because they could not connect its meaning to anything they knew in their own world. Literally, it means 'twisted serpent'.

The 5th- or 6th-century BC Jewish poet who recorded the trials of Job seems himself to have had only a sketchy idea of what Leviathan was. The ancient Hebrews, curiously, were not a seafaring nation, although they were always within reach of the Mediterranean sea. Possibly all sea beasts were somewhat mysterious to them, although they would have been aware that some were of unnaturally large size.

The vision of a monstrous sea animal that possessed the poet who wrote the Book of Job was possibly, and in part, derived from sightings of whales or sharks. The most likely source was probably foreign sailors' accounts of sperm whales, the animals on which the neighbouring Phoenicians – known in the Bible as Canaanites, and living in what is now Lebanon – based their whaling industry.

The Biblical story of Job is based on a Middle Eastern (not Hebrew) legend much older than the poet who re-created it, and his notion of Leviathan was almost certainly influenced by regional tales of dragons. Images of monsters mentioned in the myths of Egypt or Assyria, such as Tiamat and Apophis, would also have influenced the poet's vision. 'Leviathan', then, means any great sea or land monster.

The Belgian zoologist Dr Bernard Heuvelmans, who has made the most detailed study of sea-monster reports in modern times, suggests that Chapter 41 of Job, quoted in part above, suggests not the whale but a melodramatic account of a long-necked sea serpent.

The phrases describing a creature that

the noise of his Tabernacle

of the Clouds

Also by watering he wearieth the thick cloud He scattereth the bright cloud also it is turned about by his counsels

Of Behemoth he saith. He is the chief of the ways of God Of Leviathan he saith, He is King over all the Children of Pride

Behold now Behemoth which I made with thee

W Blake invenit & sculpt

Above: *The Lord shows Job the might of Behemoth and Leviathan in William Blake's engraving. Later scientific researchers have come to the same conclusion as the visionary Blake: that Leviathan is a scaly serpent of the sea.*

Right: *Sketches by zoologist Dr Karl Shuker, based on eyewitness Owen Burnham's descriptions, of the weird creature washed up on a Gambian seashore in June 1983. The dead animal was about 15 ft long.*

K.P.N. Shuker.

THEY WERE TRYING TO
SEVER ITS HEAD.

'raiseth himself' up out of the water and 'beholdeth all high things' certainly suggest an animal with a long neck. And 'the flakes of his flesh [translated elsewhere as 'the members of his body'] are joined together' may be a half-explanatory reference to the sinuous humped appearance of these creatures that (now as then) so many modern reports of sea monsters also mention.

This aspect of Leviathan rather qualifies the possibility that the true source of its reputation is the sperm whale or sharks. This is also the moment to remark on the sceptics' claim that the 'humps' of sea monsters are really a misperception of dolphins leaping in line. This is the kind of dozy (and pretty desperate) rationalization that could only come from people who have never seen dolphins in the sea. They are unmistakable for anything but dolphins.

Was Leviathan no more than a compound of mythical beasts, hearsay, and ignorance? Or was it all that, but with the hearsay relating directly to actual sea monsters? This seems at least possible. Leviathan, then, is at least partly a genuine unidentified creature.

BEEF-RED FLESH

In June 1983, amateur naturalist Owen Burnham was on holiday with his family on the coast of the Gambia, west Africa, taking a break from their home in neighbouring Senegal. During the night of 11/12 June, a large unidentified animal was washed ashore on the beach near where they were staying. They heard about this the following morning. At 8.30 am Burnham, together with his brother and sister and father, went down to the shore to look for the creature. They found it easily enough, along with two Africans who were trying to sever its head so that they could sell the skull to tourists.

The animal was battered, distended with internal gas, and smelled foul, but it was essentially complete and had not begun to decompose. It had not been dead long. Burnham was familiar with all of the major land and sea creatures native to the region, but he was unable to identify this one. The group persuaded the two native entre-preneurs to stop for long enough to let them measure the animal. Burnham, lacking a camera, also made sketches of it and counted the teeth.

The animal was smooth-skinned, with four flippers. One hind flipper had been torn off, and the other damaged. Its overall length was about 15 ft, of which 5 ft were taken up by a long, pointed tail whose cross-section was like a rounded-off triangle.

The animal had a slightly domed forehead, and at the end of its 18 in long snout were what looked like a pair of nostrils. Thinking it might be some form of marine mammal (a whale or dolphin), Burnham looked for a blowhole, but found none. Nor could he see any mammary glands. If there were any male organs they were too damaged to recognize. The creature's long, thin jaws were very tightly closed; Burnham said he had 'a job' to prise them apart. He counted 80 teeth, which he noted were evenly distributed, very sharp, and similar in shape to a barracuda's but whiter and thicker.

The flippers were round and solid. There were no toes, claws or nails. When the Africans returned and completed their work of removing the head, the witnesses could see that the animal's vertebrae were very thick. It took the men 20 minutes' dedicated hacking with a machete to sever it. The animal's flesh was dark red, 'like beef'.

Burnham speaks Mandinka, the local language, fluently and asked the men the name of the animal. They told him *kunthum belein*, Mandinka for 'cutting jaws'; this is what the coastal fishermen call dolphins. Burnham later described the unknown animal to many native fishermen in the area in the hope that they might be able to identify it, but none had ever seen anything like it. He concluded that the butchers on the beach had called it a 'dolphin' because it looked vaguely like one.

Burnham then wrote to various authorities on wildlife to try to get further leads, but got no real help. Most suggested animals that he had already been able to rule out thanks to his familiarity with the denizens of the region.

Burnham also said that he 'looked

Below: *A massive sea serpent was spotted from HMS Daedalus in 1848, and this engraving was based on an eyewitness's drawing sent to the Lords of the Admiralty by Captain M'Quhoe, the ship's commander.*

Right: *A Victorian representation of 'the legendary sea serpent'. The animal seen here would probably now be classified by cryptozoologists as a 'super-eel'.*

Below right: *A giant squid, some 24 ft long, is caught off the Canary Islands by crew of the French gunboat* **Alecton** *on 30 November 1861. Giant squids may well be responsible for many 'monster' sightings at sea.*

'TO SEE SUCH A THING WAS AWESOME.'

---

through encyclopedias and every book I could lay hands on' in trying to identify the mystery animal. Eventually, he found a photograph of the skull of the extinct Australian *Kronosaurus queenslandicus*, which he felt was the nearest thing he had seen so far. However, he noted that that skull was 10 ft long: clearly it was not the same as the creature he had seen.

AWESOME

Burnham's detailed reports of his find, and the sketches and measurements he made, were analysed at length by zoologist Dr Karl Shuker in the mid-1980s. Shuker rapidly ruled out a number of near-contenders, and realized that the only creatures that at all resembled Burnham's find had long since died out – and, what was more, had been extinct for more than 60 million years. One was the pliosaur, a family of short-necked plesiosaurs that included the *Kronosaurus* whose skull Burnham had recognized but rejected. The other was a group of non-scaly sea crocodiles, called thalattosuchians, who had slender bodies and four paddle-like limbs. Their tails had a dorsal fin, but a thalattosuchian whose fin had been torn off or scuffed away would look amazingly like the beast of Burnham's sketches. And if thalattosuchians had survived into the present, it is possible that they would no longer have such a fin.

Without any physical remains for direct examination, however, the Gambian creature cannot be positively identified one way or the other. But the Gambian find suggests, at least, that not all of the reptiles of prehistory died out with the dinosaurs.

Burnham himself says: 'When I think of the coelacanth I don't like to think what could be at the bottom of the sea. I'm not looking for a prehistoric animal, only trying to identify what was the strangest thing I'll ever see. I couldn't believe this creature was lying in front of me. Even now I can remember every minute detail of it. To see such a thing was awesome.'

ESCAPING DETECTION

The *magnum opus* of sea-monster studies is Belgian cryptozoologist Dr Bernard Heuvelmans's *In the Wake of the Sea Serpents*. In this, Heuvelmans analysed 587 sea-monster sightings made between 1639 and 1964. After disposing of hoaxes, misidentifications and reports too vague to be useful, he was still left with 358 sightings, and was able to sort these into nine basic types.

These are the 'long necked' sea serpent – the most often-reported of all sea monsters, with four flippers, a cigar-shaped body and a capacity for swimming very fast indeed – which grows to between 15 and 65 ft long; marine saurians, seen only in tropical waters in mid-ocean, which may reach 60 ft in length; merhorses; many-humped monsters; super-otters (not reported since 1848 and possibly now extinct); many-finned monsters; super-eels; fathers-of-all-the-turtles; and yellow-bellies. The last Heuvelmans believes may be an as yet unidentified fish, possibly a shark.

There is no logical reason why the seas should not be hiding any number of unidentified species of animal (especially if they are both shy and few in number) from the official catalogues of marine science. They will doubtless continue to roam the oceans, bemuse and astonish those few who are lucky enough to spot them, and be overlooked by the guardians of orthodoxy. Probably the creatures themselves would prefer it to stay that way.

Above: *The alleged sea monster photographed by Robert Le Serrec at Stonehaven Bay, Hook Island, Australia, on 12 December 1964.*

PAGAN PLACES, PAGAN POWERS

The ancient remains of powerful pagan civilizations cast long shadows into the present. The bright light of scientific investigation only deepens the mysteries surrounding the strange occurrences and unnerving experiences, and makes the shadows darker still...

While the Earth is full of strange, unexpected and inexplicable creatures, it is no less replete with mysterious and enigmatic works of mankind itself.

The ancient remains of lost civilizations – the great monuments of Stonehenge in England, Carnac in France, the Serpent Mound in Ohio, USA, the stone circles of West Africa – are only the most renowned of a myriad of such sites whose purpose is still obscure and whose meaning has been all but lost with the passing of those who built them.

Yet the world's mysterious places exercise a perennial fascination. They do so not simply because we still do not really understand them, or because they are awesome in themselves; but partly, at least, because we sense that they were enigmatic even to the people who created them.

Very strange things are traditionally said to happen at ancient sites. Very strange things still happen in such places today.

THE PETRIFIED MAIDENS

According to the pioneeering 'Earth mysteries' researcher Paul Devereux, a number of people have had bizarre

The Pipers, in Cornwall (right), are reputedly the petrified remains of the musicians who incited the Merry Maidens (below) into such a frenzy that they danced till they collapsed – and themselves turned to stone.

experiences while passing along a particular 300 yd long stretch of a country lane that runs past the ancient stone circle called Rollright in Oxfordshire, England. One, a member of the Dragon Project research group, was watching a car containing two people approach the stone circle along the road – when the vehicle vanished. On another occasion, a scientist saw a huge, dog-like creature with coarse grey hair momentarily appear and then vanish. Another witness, a woman, saw an old-fashioned gypsy caravan briefly appear and then disappear in much the same way.

Odd occurrences have been associated with such megalithic sites since time immemorial, and the stones, then as now, have been held to possess mysterious powers. There is nothing new about stone circles attracting, or generating, spectres, visions of fairies and other odd creatures from folklore such as black dogs (an instance of which was, presumably, what was seen by the scientist noted above). At the Bryn-yr-Ellyllon mound near Mold in Wales, for example, a huge golden figure has been seen on many occasions – and the name of the barrow itself means 'hill of the goblins'.

It is commonly believed that the number of individual stones in certain circles cannot be counted, although many sites are associated with specific numbers, most often the key mystical figures of three, seven and nine. Possibly one reason they

cannot be counted is that, so the legends say, they can move of their own accord. Many stones are reputed to resist any attempt to move them but, if they are shifted out of place by some means, will put themselves back where they came from. Others are still more independent. One such is the Enstone near Oxford – it is particularly regular in its habits: it reputedly takes a drink every midnight at a neighbouring stream.

There may be a connection between this kind of belief and the tradition that many standing stones, especially groups of them,

were once people, now petrified. The Merry Maidens in Cornwall are so called because that is what they once were – a mite too merry, perhaps, as they danced themselves to exhaustion and turned to stone where they collapsed. Nearby are the musicians presumably responsible for whipping them into their frenzy: the Two Pipers, and the Blind Fiddler, now pillars of granite. The Rollright Stones are reputedly a king and his knights, petrified by a witch.

Not all the powers associated with the ancient stones are so spooky: many have the reputation of being able to heal or impart healing properties. Water that has been splashed on the stones at Stonehenge will cure ailments. Sick children were traditionally passed through the hole in the famous Men-an-Tol in Cornwall. Other sites have the same capacity, especially those associated with water such as holy wells and ancient spas. There is evidence that the baths at Bath, for instance, have been regarded as curative for some 7000 years.

All these unexpected properties have one thing in common: they suggest that there is something strangely alive about these places. They are, in other words, places where a peculiar kind of energy concentrates. This half-hidden idea is reflected in another tradition about ancient places – that many of them are associated with dragons. Stories, myths and legends occur in virtually all cultures, all over the world, of a serpent, worm or dragon whose qualities are, to say the least, peculiarly ambiguous. So it is worth taking a brief

Serpents have always been seen as both threatening and promising, from the Garden of Eden (above) to St George's encounter on behalf of an endangered virgin (below). Dragons might be defeated by the most irreverent means (above right), but gaining the treasure or knowledge in their keeping would always bring fresh challenges.

survey of dragon-lore before pondering how it fits into the puzzle of the ancient sites.

THE DRAGON GUARDS

In the oldest Indian and Babylonian myths, which are roughly 4000 years old, the destruction of an enraged dragon brings the release of life-giving waters. These myths are not moral fables, but creation myths – poetic accounts of how the world was made. The importance of the dragon in these stories is that it releases an indispens-

able source of life and energy into the world – but at the price of having to confront the creature.

Everyone familiar with Genesis is aware of the double nature of the serpent in the Garden of Eden. It is an actual, physical presence, and also it represents a singular moral dilemma. To follow the path of the serpent, as Adam and Eve do, is to lose paradise and innocence but to gain knowledge and moral responsibility – free will.

This theme runs through all serpent myths, all over the world. In Anglo-Saxon Britain, the epic – and essentially pagan – poem *Beowulf* revolves in part around a fire-breathing 'worm' – in other words, a dragon – who is enraged because one of the aging Beowulf's subjects has stolen a cup from the hoard of treasure it has guarded for three centuries. (The poet makes a point of saying that dragons seek out and hoard treasure.) In killing the dragon, Beowulf is mortally wounded. Once again, the serpent is associated with something desirable and yet destructive. His power is also, finally, irresistible, and is potent in the cause of both good and ill.

Anglo-Saxon culture, like any other, had many roots. What we see in *Beowulf* is the fruit of tendrils that reach back to Norse and Celtic mythology, and beyond that to legends that have their known beginnings thousands of years ago, in the mythology of the Indo-European peoples of Central Asia. From the point of view of an investigation of prehistoric sites, what is also significant in this European dragon tradition is its connection with another piece of lore about the sites themselves: that is that many of them are reputed to be built on hoards of buried treasure.

The golden spectre seen at Bryn-yr-Ellyllon may be a reflection of this folk-memory. Like the stones themselves, some hoards have minds of their own. At the neolithic mound of Willy Howe in north-eastern England, there is a tale that local people once attempted to dig out the chest of gold concealed at its centre. They tried to drag it from the earth with horses, but the chest simply burrowed deeper into the ground. As might be expected, many such prehistoric hoards are said to be guarded by dragons.

TREACHEROUS ELEMENTS

It's clear that in Western and Middle Eastern dragon-lore, the creature has both a material and a spiritual energy, but it is one that is neither simple nor entirely trustworthy.

Take the paradox that these fiery creatures have an affinity for water, for example. Water is the most treacherous element as well as the most vital. The same may be said of fire, the other 'element' that is inseparable from any concept of dragons. One hidden lesson here seems to be that both the most basic materials of survival and the great abstractions like moral freedom have a potential for both good and evil. Another hidden message is that struggle is inherent in all our dealings with the contradictory forces of life, despite the fact that we depend on them – or perhaps *because* we depend on them.

The most fundamental lesson that underlies these perceptions is that these are eternal verities; they are the very basic stuff of life. And so the spirit of the dragon never entirely dies. Indeed, in the Babylonian myth, the dragon was also the mother of all living things and, despite being slain, continues her immortal

Above: *The Neolithic mound called Willy Howe, in Humberside, rumoured to hide a hoard of gold that physically resists any attempt to remove it.*

Below left: *The raw power of water – an element for which the fiery-breathed dragon, paradoxically, has a special affinity. In Babylonian myth, the dragon who is mother of all living things reveals herself in ferocious storms at sea.*

> **AS THEY ATTEMPTED TO DRAG THE TREASURE CHEST FROM THE GROUND, IT BURROWED DEEPER INTO THE EARTH.**

Above: *Chinese dragons control the weather – a realm as changeable and unpredictable as dragons themselves.*

WE ARE CONFRONTED WITH SOMETHING ABSOLUTELY FUNDAMENTAL IN THE HUMAN PSYCHE.

existence as a monstrous serpent who makes herself visible in wild storms at sea.

Dragons are everywhere associated with the most fundamental aspects of life. In the Mayan culture of central America, which flourished between about AD 150 and AD 900, the serpent was 'lord of fire and time', and was also responsible for causing floods, earthquakes and storms. It is strange, given the distance between the Americas and Asia, that Chinese dragons are so similar in this respect.

In China, a vast and intricate dragon-lore grew up that detailed not only how long a dragon might live (5000 years) and how many scales it had (81 or 117, depending on the school of thought) but the medicinal virtues of its teeth, liver or saliva and the significance of its behaviour as an augury of the weather.

Chinese dragons are, by Western standards, quite benevolent, but they too have an ambiguous nature. They are capable of shape-shifting, appearing in the guise of familiar animals at will, and, most importantly, they control the weather – which, as everyone knows, is neither predictable nor always benign. And to this day the Chinese believe that their dragons must be appeased and placated. The art of *feng shui*, which means 'wind and water', is entirely devoted to avoiding any disturbance to the 'paths of the dragon' (*lung mei*) when siting buildings in the landscape. Expert geomancers – 'earth diviners' – make elaborate calculations to ensure that this balance of nature is maintained. A famous modern example of their work is the alignment of the Hong Kong and Shanghai Bank in Hong Kong.

One of the most baffling and yet fascinating of all the enigmas associated with prehistoric sites and 'Earth mysteries' studies is the universal nature of dragon-lore. That the same image should reflect so many similar intuitions in so many different cultures, separated by huge gulfs of time and geography, suggests that we are confronted by something absolutely fundamental in the human psyche. And more: that this in turn suggests that the human mind has grasped something crucial about the nature of the Earth itself.

We have, in the dragon, an extraordinary concentration of ideas: a mythical beast that guards material or spiritual riches; the

energies of the elements; and a connection with sites of 'Earth energy'. Researchers have also established that there is a connection between the ancient sites, the so-called ley lines that often connect them, and UFO sightings. Is it possible that dragons and UFOs are different forms of the same 'Earth energy'? And if so, are they shaped by the mind into the form most suited to a particular epoch – or do they cause the mind to perceive them in the most acceptable way?

That there are energies in the Earth, that they are most powerful around prehistoric sites, and that they have real effects on human consciousness, is attested not only by the *feng shui* geomancers and the long traditions of folklore – but by modern reports too.

WEIRD SENSATIONS

Paul Devereux collected one such account from local government official Peter Thornborrow. He was walking through the stone circle called Long Meg and Her Daughters in Cumbria, when he was suddenly assailed by a bizarre sensation of dizziness. He felt, he said later, as if he was 'not really there…not really in the same time'. He leaned against one of the stones to recover his normal senses. It responded by giving him what he could only describe as 'an electric shock'.

Devereux has also recorded that in 1986, as a young couple were driving on a country lane beside Carn Ingli, a peak and sacred site in the Preseli Hills in Pembrokeshire, west Wales, the girl felt a weird sensation of physical discomfort. She was sure the feeling was caused by the peak. The pair decided to test the idea. They drove on until the girl felt normal again, and then turned the car around and drove back over the same route. Once again, as they neared Carn Ingli, the strange and uncomfortable sensation returned.

Modern experience and traditional lore thus combine to confirm the strangeness of prehistoric sites. There is a long-standing belief that experiences like the two recounted above and the legacy of folklore clinging to these ancient places indicate that some form of paranormal or psychic energy is at work in them. Since the turn of the century, psychics have attempted to

Left: *The ancient stone circle known as Long Meg and Her Daughters in Cumbria. Virtually all such sites were created with stones in places that show anomalies of magnetism, gravity, or radioactivity. This may account for the bizarre psychic experiences that some have reported having at Long Meg and other similar locations.*

Below: *Local co-ordinator for the long-standing Dragon Project research group Roy Cooper tests the Rollright Stones for radioactivity.*

pick up the local 'vibrations' at standing stones, circles, barrows and mounds, and since the 1930s dowsers too have tried to unravel the secrets of these places. Unfortunately, the claimed results and 'discoveries' at any one site have been as many and various as the number of psychics or dowsers who have tried their skills there.

The aptly named Dragon Project was launched in England in 1977 to bring a comprehensive set of research methods to bear on the question of what kinds of energies might be present at prehistoric sites. The project decided to pursue two parallel lines of investigation: there would be room for dowsers and psychics to follow their own form of detective work, while a variety of scientific detection instruments would be used to search out and record the more conventional physical attributes of the sites.

This has involved recording levels of magnetism, radioactivity, infra-red radiation, among known physical forces, as well as recording and studying unexplained but theoretically conventional effects such as the strange light phenomena that have long been reported at or near many ancient sites. The psychic side of the research has been as inconclusive as any of the other attempts to use mind power to probe the secrets of the ancients, but the second, scientific line of enquiry has thrown up some intriguing results. Although this kind of monitoring deals in the standard scientific measures of physics, the actual

levels discovered at the sites have been by no means conventional or consistent with normal, average ('background') levels for the areas concerned.

Science has begun to confirm folklore.

Right: *A kiva – an underground chamber used for ritual purposes – once used by the Anasazi people of Mesa Verde, Colorado.*

Below: *Possibly one of the world's holiest places – the Chalice Well at Glastonbury, whose waters are mildly radioactive.*

SECRET KNOWLEDGE – SECRET PURPOSES

At Long Meg, where Peter Thornborrow had the bizarre experience described earlier, Dragon Project researchers found that several of the standing stones there had small patches on them that were emitting a constant stream of gamma rays – in short, they were radioactive. The stones concerned were granite, which is naturally radioactive, but not to the degree of these particular stones. And it is distinctly unusual for granite to emit radiation of any kind from concentrated energy points such as these stones possessed.

This may or may not have been responsible for Thornborrow's experience, but researchers have noted that in places where natural radiation – from granite or other radioactive minerals, or from radon gas seeping from the ground – is higher than normal, some people have experienced apparently altered states of consciousness. Monitoring the radiation levels around the Rollright Stones revealed a fascinating fact about the 300 yd stretch of country lane where at least three people – whose accounts we gave above – had reported seeing spectral visions. Geiger counters showed far higher than normal background readings of radiation here.

Its source, the researchers concluded, was probably in energetic rocks in the hardcore used to lay the road's foundations. This, like the stones at the ancient site, had come from local quarries – which suggests that whoever put the Rollright Stones in place was aware that the local rock had very special qualities. Those qualities were

interesting to them because they served their purposes. The key question after that is: what were their purposes?

Some other odd qualities of ancient sites may help to get us nearer the answer to this crucial question.

RADIOACTIVE BURIAL CHAMBERS

People have experienced different strange effects at other sites with greater than the usual 'background' natural radiation. At Boleigh Fogou, an Iron-Age underground stone chamber or 'souterrain' built from granite in Cornwall, a psychologist saw mysterious swirls and points of light moving over the inner rock surfaces. Similarly, inside the 5000-year-old Cornish dolmen called Chun Quoit, archeologist John Barnatt and photographer Brian Larkman both saw bands of light flashing along the underside of the capstone.

Most of Europe's ancient underground chambers of this kind are in areas whose basic rock formations are of granite, or where uranium has been found, so it can hardly be insignificant that in North America, Pueblo Indian underground ritual chambers, known as 'kivas', were likewise built in uranium-rich areas of what are now the Southwestern States. Bearing that in mind, it comes as no surprise to learn that the King's Chamber in Egypt's Great Pyramid was specially clad in granite, and that when members of the Dragon Project monitored the King's Chamber they found

ONE OF THE HOLIEST PLACES IN THE WORLD IS SAID TO BE — RADIOACTIVE.

Left: *Stones at the top of the Akapana pyramid at Tiahuanaco, Bolivia, twist a compass needle out of kilter.*

Below: *Castlerigg stone circle near Keswick, Cumbria, where weird lights have been seen, and whose westernmost stone has unusual and powerful magnetic properties.*

Above: *Gors Fawr stone circle in Wales. Rough and desolate today, this was once a major ritual centre, like Stonehenge* (**opposite**), *the most elaborately built of all the ancient megalithic sites.*

enhanced radiation levels there, at levels at least as high as those found inside the granite monuments of Britain.

The great stone sites of the ancient world are not unique among ancient monuments in registering unusually high – although by no means dangerous – levels of nuclear radiation. Holy wells, too, can be mildly radioactive, and there is evidence to suggest that at such 'homeopathic' levels nuclear radiation is actually beneficial, not harmful. As mentioned earlier, the famous hot springs at Bath, England have been known as healing waters for some 70 centuries, and are mildly radioactive. The waters of Chalice Well, Glastonbury – one of the holiest places in the world, if the legends are to be believed – are said to be radioactive. Dragon Project researchers have also recorded higher-than-average readings from geiger counters at a number of holy wells in the Celtic fringes of Britain in Wales, Cornwall and Scotland.

MAGNETIC MAGIC

Ancient sites, stone circles and solitary standing stones have all been known for decades to have strange effects on compasses and lodestones. Go to a standing stone or similar ancient site and the

chances are it is in a place where there are peculiarities in the Earth's local magnetic field, or that it throws the standard measuring equipment – the gaussometer – out of true by a marked margin.

The Dragon Project found that scattered about Carn Ingli were areas where there were powerful anomalies in the local magnetic field. In these places, compass needles point south instead of north, and gaussometers show unexpected readings. As for individual stones creating bizarre magnetic effects – or being carefully placed where those effects are most marked – there is a host of instances. At Castlerigg, Cumbria, only the westernmost stone, alone among 38 stones at the circle, affects a compass needle. At the Gors Fawr stone circle in Wales, the outlying pillar, which indicates the direction of the midsummer sunrise, is also the only magnetic stone at the site. A serpentine outcrop on Mount Tamalpais, San Francisco (a magical place for the local American Indians), similarly causes compasses to spin. There are many other examples, and they can be found all over the world.

Still more strange is another magnetic anomaly that Dragon Project researchers have found at many ancient sites. They discovered that some standing stones show sudden fluctuations in their magnetic fields that last for only a few hours. Similar effects were found, quite independently of the Dragon Project work, at the Rollright Circle by the retired engineer Charles Brooker, who reported his discoveries in the international journal *New Scientist* in 1983.

The nature of these short-lived magnetic pulses is not understood by modern science, so what significance they may have had for the ancients so many thousands of years ago must be today entirely a matter for speculation. But then so is the means whereby the peoples of the ancient world, lacking modern instrumentation, recognized these qualities in the sites and in the stones they chose, in the first place. And *why* they chose them for these qualities is another question altogether.

THE STONES ARE SINGING

Some of the unexplained phenomena at ancient sites would not have needed any

exotic instruments to detect. One is the often-reported appearance of peculiar and apparently intelligent lights in, around or near prehistoric remains. Another is the persistent presence of inexplicable noises at these places.

While alone inside Stonehenge one early morning in 1983, Gabriele Wilson heard a 'ringing' sound from one of the stones. At midsummer in 1987, Michael Woolf and Rachel Garcia heard 'a sudden, muffled thunderclap' that seemed to come 'from beneath the earth' at the 11 ft tall Blind Fiddler stone in Cornwall. Other researchers at the Rollright Stones have reported curious clicking noises issuing from the ground at night.

The ancients themselves witnessed such odd sounds at their sacred sites, as well. The two 60 ft tall statues known as the Colossi of Memnon, in the Valley of the Kings in Egypt, were cracked during an earthquake in 27 BC. After that, the northernmost of the two statues began to emit a strange sound at dawn each day. The noise was variously described as 'soft' and 'bell-like', 'a musical note' and even (by contrast) like 'a cord snapping'. People flocked from far and wide to the massive statue in the belief that it would act as an oracle. The sounds stopped when the cracks were eventually repaired.

Whatever the cause of these particular noises, modern researchers have long known that sounds at extremely high 'ultrasound' frequencies – well beyond the range of normal human hearing – can be detected at dawn coming from standing stones.

In January 1987 Dragon Project workers discovered that a 3 ft band around the middle of the tallest stone at the Rollright Circle was the source of a signal being picked up by their ultrasound receiver. The signal always ebbed away as the day wore on. It is possible that these signals were the by-product of transmissions from nearby military telecommunications stations, resonating in crystals in the stones. There is nothing secret or occult in the fact that crystals are sensitive to radio waves. On the other hand, the effect could be caused by some unknown process occurring in the Earth itself.

CENTRES OF POWER

The folklore interpretation of the weird sounds and lights that have been heard and seen around ancient sites has been quite

THE GREAT STONE STATUES BEGAN TO EMIT A STRANGE SOUND AT DAWN EACH DAY.

The Colossi of Memnon in Egypt, which gave out bizarre singing noises after they were cracked by an earthquake in 27 BC.

logical, but it has also probably been back-to-front.

People who have intuitively recognized something strange about the ancient places have attributed other signs of their uniqueness to the spirits, ghosts or even fairies to whom they feel these places belong. But almost certainly this view is the wrong way round. It is much more likely that the sites for stone circles, burial mounds, kivas and other ceremonial centres were chosen exactly because they were (in the eyes of the builders, those who saw them first) already magical. Throwing out strange noises and weird darting lights,

such sites were advertising themselves as ideal for magical purposes.

As we have seen, these signs were also signals – that still stranger effects would take place in these places on the minds of those brave enough to enter them. How those effects were taken advantage of and controlled is one of the central mysteries of the purpose of the prehistoric sites.

This mystery may not be entirely unsolved, but even to glimpse the solution, we must first look at the stars, the Sun and the Moon, the tree at the centre of the world, and at mysterious patterns on a parched desert floor.

CELESTIAL SIGNS IN SACRED PLACES

Right: Professor Aubrey Burl (at right), an authority on Stonehenge, whose work has helped demolish the myth that the site was an astronomical 'observatory' rather than a temple.

Stonehenge, with its toppled stones and sad grandeur, is but the last in a series of sacred temples which changed drastically in both appearance and purpose over several thousand years. The original Stonehenge was a place of earth and timber – and rotting corpses.

Stonehenge (previous page and below) is perhaps the most impressive of all megalithic monuments – yet its architectural splendour hides the slow spiritual decay of those who built it.

The curious physical qualities of the sites where the ancients built their sacred places must have had specific advantages for those who used them. But what did they use them for?

One tenacious myth that has taken hold in many a mind is that the prehistoric temples and stone circles were used as astronomical observatories. This idea has been going the rounds since the late 19th century, when archeologists first recognized the way that Stonehenge, on Salisbury Plain in England, was built to coincide with a number of seasonal astronomical events. It was full of 'sight-lines' between the stones to significant sunrises, sunsets, phases of the Moon, and movements of the stars.

Many of the conclusions drawn by the early pioneers of astro-archeology have since been found to be – not to put too fine a point on it – wildly wrong. In spite of this, their ideas were revived in the 1960s. It is in fact illogical and outmoded to believe that a place like Stonehenge could have been used to watch and mark the behaviour of the Sun and Moon and stars.

The illogic of such an idea is easily exposed, for to build these sites in the first place, someone must have known *beforehand* all the astronomical phenomena to which their stones are so precisely aligned. The builders of the great prehistoric monuments had already made their observations of the sky and taken their

measurements on the ground long before they laid a single stone. It is an especially piquant notion that such a massive construction as Stonehenge could ever have had the flexibility that is essential to a real observatory. Such places are not evidence of some kind of primitive science, as the first researchers believed, and as many who mourn for the 1960s still do today.

'No astronomer-priests surveyed the skies there,' Professor Aubrey Burl has written plainly of Stonehenge. 'Superstition, not science, dominated the minds of its builders.'

COSMIC DRAMA

Not only did the ancients see the material world in a different way from us, they seem to have found a link between space and time, and between solid reality and the realm of the spirit. Ancient astronomy was a religious quest, and Stonehenge is one of the most dramatic and visible pieces of evidence of that. Its role was not that of being a record or marker of a scientific view of the Universe and the Earth within it. It was built as a stone stage set for a cosmic drama. But by the time it reached its most complex form in stone, it was not even the greatest of such constructions in the ancient world.

Stonehenge seems to be a symbol of enormous stability, and that it is a monument to an apprehension of cosmic reality that has long since been lost only makes the splendour of the place, emptied now of its original meaning, all the more moving. But the toppled stones and magnificent relics of grandeur that we see today are in reality the last and, amazingly, the least complicated of a series of temples that were built on this single site over a period of some 16 centuries.

A TEMPLE OF DEATH

The very first Stonehenge was made not of stone, but of earth. Around 3200 BC the skin-clad peasants of the farming tribes of Salisbury Plain dug out a wide circular earthwork known as a henge. It had an inner bank broken by what seemed to be two entrances. One was 35 ft wide on the north-east arc of the henge. The second was narrower, and was set precisely south

of the centre of the henge. The builders probably found this point by halving the distance between the points on the horizon where the midwinter Sun rose and set.

In 1723 the antiquarian William Stukeley (who also discovered the other great prehistoric site in southern England, Avebury) noticed that the south-west-to-north-east axis of this original construction, and thus the north-eastern 'entrance', was almost in line with the midsummer sunrise. Later researchers realized that Stukeley had made an error. The builders had been interested in another heavenly body: not the Sun, but the Moon.

Outside the north-east gap in the earthwork each year, they had set up a post in line with the most northerly rising-point of the Moon. Unlike the rising-point of the midsummer Sun, this moves gradually

Above: *The Moon, not the Sun, was the most important heavenly body to the builders of the first Stonehenge.*

Above: *The Heel Stone casts its shadow toward the circle at Stonehenge.*

THE FIRST STONEHENGE WAS A TEMPLE TO THE MOON, NOT THE SUN; AS SUCH IT WAS A TEMPLE OF DEATH.

---

across the horizon between two extremes, over a period of 18.61 years. The ancient builders had recorded this slow motion over six cycles and more than a century of observations, until they were certain of the most northerly point where the Moon rose. They aligned one side of the north-east 'entrance' with this point.

The first Stonehenge was a temple to the Moon. It was also a temple of death.

ROTTING CORPSES

For more than a millennium the ancestors of the first builders of Stonehenge had buried their dead in long barrows that pointed to the Moon somewhere between its midwinter rising-point in the north and its midsummer rising in the south. For these people, death and the Moon were inextricably bound up together.

The north-east 'entrance' was in fact a window, one side aligned to the midpoint of the Moon's arc, the other to its northernmost rising. Marking these lines of sight were pairs of tall stones at the edges of the causeway. On its eastern side the middle of the lunar cycle was marked by the now-fallen Slaughter Stone. The famous Heel Stone, beyond it, was never a pointer for the midsummer sunrise. It was always a lunar marker.

At the centre of the first Stonehenge was a 100 ft wide roofed building where corpses were laid until their flesh had rotted, and then the bones would be buried in the long barrows on the plain outside. This rite was long practised in Neolithic Britain and was always associated with the Moon.

The power of this strange holy mortuary was enhanced by more dead, deliberately acquired. In ditches at the ends of both entrances through the earthwork lie the bones of adults and children, sacrificed to the cold-faced, sky-sailing, shape-shifting silvery goddess of death that these people worshipped.

A TEMPLE OF THE SUN

Around 2200 BC, a new people arrived in the region and converted Stonehenge into a temple of the Sun. Whether they were a branch of what archeologists call Beaker Folk or not, their characteristic remains are bright-red, geometrically patterned beaker pots. Teams of men dragged Welsh bluestones into the already ancient earthen enclosure and set them up in two concentric circles. Some of the slabs were shaped as lintels, imitating the earlier timber building.

The stones themselves had come from the Preseli mountains in south-west Wales. Legend said they were brought the 200 miles from those bleak, rainswept hills by none other than Merlin, the mysterious guardian mage of Camelot and King Arthur. Later, theories as elaborate as any concocted to account for the building of the pyramids in Egypt sprang fully formed from the brains of unwary academics to explain the logistics of moving the giant

Example from Suffolk (right) of an intricately patterned artefact of the Beaker Folk.

Left: *Carn Meini in the Preseli Hills in Pembrokeshire. Bluestones from here were used in building Stonehenge, and how they made their way from west Wales to Salisbury Plain long remained a mystery.*

blocks to Salisbury Plain in an age that lacked the wheel. The favourite theory had copper prospectors hauling the things on logs and floating them down rivers.

The real history of Stonehenge is full of surprises. The intrepid-stone-age-trucker theory is even less likely to be true than the rather more pleasing image of Merlin wafting the stones across the Severn with his wand. Archeologists have found a Welsh bluestone in a barrow that was abandoned 10 centuries before Stonehenge was built, yet only seven miles from the site. The prosaic truth is that the bluestones were literally lying about the local landscape, waiting to be used by anyone who was minded to do so. They were dumped there by glacial action, perhaps as long as 8000 years before Stonehenge was even thought of.

The people who brought the stones changed the axis of the henge. They widened the right-hand side of the north-east 'entrance', so that the middle of the break in the earthwork was now in line with the midsummer sunrise. On either side of the Heel Stone, they dug an avenue that led downhill towards the River Avon.

For these people, beakers and Sun-worship went together. Tissue-thin discs of gold have been found with the pots in their distinctive round barrows and are decorated with circles and crosses, and they seem to be symbols of the Sun.

The newcomers placed four stones at the corners of a large rectangle around the unfinished stone circles. Now called the Four Stations, these created three sightlines. The short side of the rectangle they made indicated the midsummer sunrise, while the long side pointed to the northern moonset. Down the line of one diagonal one saw – can still see – the point on the horizon where the Sun sets on May Day, later to be celebrated by the Celts as another Sun festival, Beltane, which means 'the shining one'.

Death was still the essential reason for the existence of the rearranged temple. The burials round about, in the new round barrows, continued apace, dug with sweat and toil from the chalky downland. And on the new axis of the henge, not far from the centre of the stone circles, the newcomers dug the grave of a man, and laid his bones

HUMAN SACRIFICES – ADULTS AND CHILDREN – WERE MADE TO THE SHAPE-SHIFTING SILVERY GODDESS OF DEATH.

Below: *Representation of the death of Arthur. The Arthurian age is linked in legend with the stones that make up Stonehenge.*

At the height of the Early Bronze Age, around 2000 BC, Stonehenge was remade yet again – into the form whose battered and crumbling remains we can see today. By then, great cemeteries of round barrows were crowded into the landscape around the temple. In them lay the bodies of chieftains and their women, clothed in finely woven wool, with their weapons, and household items made of bronze, copper, jet, amber, faience and gold. In a few centuries Stonehenge had changed from being a simple peasant mortuary chapel to a grand cathedral, the exclusive last resting-place of the rich, the powerful, the hard and the mighty.

One might speculate easily on how the new Stonehenge was pressured into being. Possibly the warrior chieftains had grumbled about the poor place the temple was, until their demands forced a monument befitting their status from a servile priesthood and a crushed people. Possibly the priests themselves had become the real powers behind these tiny thrones, and flaunted their power in this last grand architectural gesture. In any case, Stonehenge was rebuilt, but it was no longer a place for the common people. It became weighty and overwhelming, with room only for the priests, their acolytes, and the privileged.

The bluestones were torn out at the

Above: *A Bronze Age warrior. About 4000 years ago, Stonehenge was rebuilt for the last time to create the monument whose remains we know today* (**below right**).

in it with the head to the north-west, looking towards the midsummer Sun. His life gave life and strength – it consecrated – the magical place on the borderline between here and there, the present and the future.

roots. From the Marlborough Downs, 20 miles away, gangs of the faithful or coerced somehow found the energy to drag massive sandstone blocks to the site, where they were shaped and erected in the circle that everyone now knows as Stonehenge. Thirty uprights supported 30 lintels. These stones, bizarrely, were finished by using carpentry techniques – as if no one knew how to dress stone, and as if the builders could not tear themselves away from the memory that this site had once sported a timber building. Inside this forbiddingly atavistic ring of stones, in a monstrous horseshoe pattern, were set five trilithons, five separate, towering archways, each of two pillars topped by a lintel.

The axis of the henge was reversed yet again. The horseshoe of trilithons was open to the north-east but rose in height toward the tallest of them, to the south-west, where the Sun would be seen setting at midwinter – but only by the few for whom there was room in this spectacular but now cramped and darkened place. Astronomically, it was, quite literally, but a gigantic shadow of its former self. The only cosmic matter of interest to its priests was the single alignment to the midwinter sunset.

Whole epic novels might be written about how the mighty slowly but surely toppled after that. The process took 1000 years, and no doubt the last of them were the most tragic, dramatic, bloody and meaningless. The system decayed; the great stones became empty at the heart. By 1000 BC Stonehenge had been deserted. The place was left to the shrieking crows, the wind, and the teeth of the rain – and to the curiosity of those who came nearly 30 centuries later, and wondered what the place had ever been for.

ANCIENT LIGHTS

The builders of the ancient sites did not create them all solely as places from which to peer out and watch the Sun and Moon performing in predictable order. The events and effects they designed them for may have been predictable, but they could be far more spectacular than a mere moonrise or a sunset. One of the ways the ancients celebrated their festival days was to create dramatic lighting effects within the very monuments themselves.

These ancient lightshows, as veteran earth mysteries researcher Paul Devereux has dubbed them, needed a dark stone interior for their full effect to be seen and felt, and, without exception, they were designed to form part of some kind of religious ritual. A good example of this mixture of exploiting astronomical observation and religious significance can still be seen at Burro Flats in the Simi

Below: *The passage-tomb at Newgrange, Ireland, in whose interior astonishing effects of sunlight and shadow are created at midwinter.*

Above: *Karnak temple in Egypt, which is aligned to the midsummer sunset.*

Hills, near Los Angeles, California. Here, a panel of Chumash Indian rock paintings marks the site of a long-dead medicine man's shrine. The paintings are of centipede-like creatures, winged human forms, clawed animals, and handprints. These are traditional and ancient signs of sanctity in American Indian lore.

For most of the year, rock overhangs shelter the paintings at Burro Flats but, on midwinter's day, the rising Sun sends a shaft of light through a natural gap in the rocks that surround the shrine, pointing a pencil of light across the paintings. Thus the inner world of the Earth and of human art, spirit, the emotions, and the mind – and the outer world of the sky and its heavenly bodies were linked.

Nowhere is this link between the inner and the outer universe made more clearly or more spectacularly than at the complex of monuments in the Boyne Valley, Ireland. The best-known of these is the vast Newgrange mound, which is a huge construction penetrated by secret passages and chambers whose ultimate purpose can only be guessed at. Inside the mound, a passage 60 ft long leads to a high stone chamber at the heart of the mound. Here, the rising midwinter Sun sends its light through a roof-box built above the entrance to the passage. Only on midwinter's day can the beam of sunlight reach to the back of this central chamber.

On the Loughcrew Hills of Ireland, US artist Mark Brennan and his research colleagues found that at the equinox – the two days in the year when night and day

are of equal duration – the rising Sun shines into a cairn there, and that it frames a rock carving at the back of the inner chamber. The carving was a Neolithic symbol for the Sun. The eight rays emanating from its centre represented the eight ancient divisions of the year.

The temple builders of Neolithic Europe used this kind of effect in many sacred mounds. The entrance passage of Maes Howe, Orkney, for instance, is aligned with the midwinter sunset. The passage forms part of an intricate web of alignments that cover the whole island.

Inside the 5000-year-old stone chamber of Gavrinis in northern France, a block of quartz stands exactly half-way along the length of the entrance passage. It can hardly be an accident that it was placed at a point where the beams from the sunrise, pouring down the passage at midwinter, would intersect those from the Moon at a key point in the 19-year lunar cycle. Archeologist Aubrey Burl suggests that the builders of Gavrinis used quartz in this place because it would glow dramatically white when the Sun and moonbeams played on it.

THE HEART OF THE EARTH

Similar effects were put to work at the temple of Karnak in Egypt. Much of the surviving temple complex dates from the New Kingdom (1567–1085 BC), but the place was regarded as sacred for centuries before that. Through all its long history, the major astronomical axis of the site remained the same. In the 1890s, the astronomer Sir Norman Lockyer calculated that this axis pointed towards the midsummer sunset. He pictured the dying rays of the Sun reaching in to illuminate the image of the god kept in the darkened sanctuary that lay on the axis deep within the temple.

In the southern hemisphere is the Torreon, in the Inca citadel of Machu Picchu, Peru. The north-eastern window of the inner sanctum of the temple was cut to receive the beams of the midwinter sunrise (which occurs on 21 June in the southern hemisphere). Beneath this inner window is an altar-like rock that has been carved so that a sharp cleft, at right angles to the window, divides it in half. When the Sun

rises at midwinter, its light floods in through the window, falling parallel to the cleft. It is possible that originally a frame hung from the carved knobs that protrude from the otherwise featureless wall in the Torreon, supporting a plumb line that would have thrown its shadow along the cut edge on the altar stone at the same time as the slice of sunlight lit it up.

On a ledge near the top of the 430 ft high Fajada Butte in Chaco Canyon, New Mexico, three fallen slabs of rock allow sharp shafts of sunlight through onto the rock wall behind them. A thousand years ago the Anasazi Indians (who lived here and to whom the place was sacred) carved two spirals into the rock face so that these 'Sun daggers' would cast their shadows on them in distinctive patterns at the equinoxes and at midsummer and mid-winter.

Further west along Chaco Canyon is the ruin of the Anasazi's great kiva, Casa Rinconada. This 12 ft deep, 63 ft wide circular ceremonial structure was built so that it lay north–south, east–west, and like Stonehenge has an opening in its wall to the north-east. The rising midsummer Sun casts a beam of light through this aperture onto the opposite wall of the kiva, illuminating one of six irregularly spaced wall niches.

The ancient builders thus symbolized how the outer universe of Sun and Moon always penetrate to the heart of the Earth. But this truth, which is reminiscent of the black and white dots in the ancient Chinese yin/yang symbol, was a fact of life to these people, whose lives reflected the constant interaction of both. Earth and sky were but aspects of the same thing to them.

THE HITCHING POST OF THE SUN

As the Sun gives light, so it also casts shadows. This fact was not lost on the ancients in their ceremonies and in the way they built their sacred places.

In Mexico, the Indians used shadow in a particularly flamboyant fashion, and with perfect symbolism. The so-called Castillo at Chichen Itza on the Yucatan peninsula is a Toltec-Mayan stepped pyramid originally dedicated to Kukulcan, the Feathered Serpent god. A spectacular light-and-shadow picture forms on the Castillo at the spring and summer equinoxes. In the last hour before sunset, the stepped, north-west corner of the pyramid throws a serrated shadow onto the west-facing balustrade of

Below: *The entrance stone at Newgrange, Ireland. Its enigmatic markings, and those on the kerbstones* **(opposite)**, *may represent the Sun – or may be a record of images seen by entranced priests. The stones all play a part in the 'sacred lightshow' that takes place at Newgrange at the midwinter sunrise.*

its northern staircase. This produces a pattern of sunlight and shadow that looks strikingly like the body markings of the rattlesnake common to the region. At the bottom of the balustrade are serpents' heads, carved in stone. To these the shadow attaches itself, completing the image of the sacred snake, writhing down the holy pyramid.

In the last refuge of the Incas, the mountain-peak citadel at Machu Picchu, Peru, the small but highly significant Intihuatana is carved from a granite outcrop that sits on a naturally pyramid-shaped spur. The Intihuatana is an upright pillar, no more than a foot high, projecting from a complex, asymmetrical platform made up of a variety of odd surfaces and projections.

The name Intihuatana means 'hitching post of the Sun', which is a sure indication that this strangely fashioned (or adapted) feature must have played a vital part in the major Inca festival of Inti Raymi. This took place every winter solstice – the shortest day of the year – to 'tie the Sun'. The ritual prevented the Sun from moving any further north in its daily round and stopped it being lost for ever.

SHADOWS OF THE SUN

At Ireland's Newgrange, the American artist Martin Brennan noted something else besides the entry of the midwinter sunbeam into the great mound. He found that the entrance stone and another 'kerbstone 52' were part of the solar alignment of the site, and that some of the stones in the huge stone circle surrounding the mound also play a part in creating astonishing light-and-shadow effects on that crucial day of the year. And it was crucial: the prehistoric people of the Old World, like the Incas in Peru half a world away, also feared that the Sun might disappear for ever at midwinter.

At midwinter sunrise, as the roof-box at the entrance directs the Sun's rays deep into the mound, the shadow of one of the circle's stones points like a finger to the entrance stone and its vertical marking. At the same time, the shadow from a nearby stone strikes another carved kerbstone. With the complex interplay of shadow and light at the site, it is, as one commentator has said, 'almost as if the builders of Newgrange have left software running in their hardware'.

At nearby Knowth, another mound built like Newgrange with an inner passage and central chamber (and at about the same time, around 3700 BC), Brennan discovered that when the Sun sets at the equinoxes and sends its light down the entrance passage, a standing stone outside likewise throws its shadow onto the vertically grooved entrance stone.

At Castlerigg stone circle in Cumbria, England, photographer John Glover saw an extraordinary phenomenon during the midsummer sunset in 1976. Just as the Sun was sinking to the ridge on the horizon, Glover glanced behind him, and was amazed to see that the tallest stone of the circle was throwing a huge shadow right across the valley.

When the path of the shadow was surveyed later, the researchers found that the slope of the ground beyond the site was such that the shadow fell parallel to it and so extended far beyond the immediate ground. A conifer plantation stands in the way today, but originally it would have stretched for more than two miles across the moor.

THE LIGHT IN THE DARKNESS

Can we deduce anything from these alignments and angles, the subtle interplay of light and shade, or even from the final dark centuries of Stonehenge, with its fixation on midwinter and death, about

the meaning of these astonishing constructions?

The answer is, tentatively at least, yes. As was remarked earlier, the symbolism of these ancient places indicates that for those who fashioned them with such care and attention, Earth and sky were not separate, but parts of a whole. There is more to be quarried here, however. Even the monumental morbidity of Stonehenge speaks of a fixation with wholeness – and by implication with *balance*, as if the ancients had anticipated and written in stone and ritual the words of Cranmer's prayerbook: 'In the midst of life we are in death…'

In the same way, the penetrating light of the Sun at sites all over the world is balanced by shadows; the dark created by light, the light known only in the darkness of a hidden chamber. Earth and cosmos were tied together by threads of light and a network of shadows in a kind of symbiosis. The one could not exist without the other, the ancients saw, and dramatized their intuition in their sacred architecture.

To them, Earth, Sun and Moon coexisted in a cosmic marriage. Part of the drama played out by the stones is conjugal: the long hard light of the Sun penetrating the secret passage of the Earth; the phallic

shadow stretching itself and growing across the surface of the Earth's vast body. This was not a crass cartoon, a huge slide-show of sex and fertility, but an enactment of ultimate cosmic union.

And wherever this celebration of balance, of wholeness, of cosmic passion took place, the people could see that they were at the centre of the Universe, for here all things met as one. The ancient places were at the core of all existence.

> **THIS WAS NO SLIDE-SHOW OF SEX AND FERTILITY, BUT THE ULTIMATE COSMIC UNION.**

THE MYSTIC
LANDSCAPE

For the ancients the Earth was a woman – a mother to be worshipped and cherished, and a lover to be erotically embraced. The secret places of her body were the most sacred sites of the pagan religions, but their true purpose remains mysterious…

A sense of centrality inspired the builders of the world's ancient monuments: they treated their creations as if they truly were at the centre of things, and placed them where the whole surrounding landscape reinforced and reflected that feeling. If need be they would mould whole landscapes to underline the importance of a particular site.

The image of the world's centre took a number of forms in the ancient world. One was the *omphalos*, the navel of the world. Another was the 'world egg'. Another was the 'world tree'. Derived from the Tree of Life were any number of more portable icons and symbols: particular, living, sacred trees, or so-called totem poles, or even a simple rod stuck in the Earth. Wherever these were, there – for the purpose at hand – was the centre of the world.

Marking that central point of the world was the first great magical act in creating sacred geography. Its spiritual importance is nowhere better illustrated than in the creation myth of the Zuni American Indians of New Mexico, who are probably descended from the Anasazi who built Chaco Canyon.

According to their myth, the first Zuni wandered for a long time, looking for a place of peace and stability, where they would settle. Frustrated in their search, they finally summoned *K'yan asdebi*, the water-skate, because his long legs could point in all the directions. A centre of a kind himself, he could surely identify the centre of the world.

This he did. He rose into the sky and stretched out his legs in the six great directions: the four cardinal points of the compass, and above and below. Gradually he came back to Earth, saying, 'Where my heart and navel rest, beneath them mark the spot and there build a town of the midmost, for there shall be the midmost place of the Earth-mother, even the navel…'

A VIEW OF THE GODS

The idea of the sacred centre is really an extension of the individual's perception that he or she already exists at the centre of his or her own world. Each of us looks out upon the world with an intuitive idea of six basic directions: front, back and sides, with the Earth beneath our feet, and the heavens above us. Wherever we are, we are always at the centre of our world.

At its deepest level, the meaning of a sacred site made itself felt through the action of the landscape on the mind, and the *reaction* of the mind to the landscape. Ultimate reality could not be apprehended

Above: *A Quechua boy. These Peruvian Indians still maintain an elaborate mythology of Earth and stars that places their settlement at the very middle of the Universe.*

Opposite: *The Athenian treasury at Delphi. This sacred site is a 'navel' of the world – the centre of the cosmos for those who worshipped there.*

THE SACRED CENTRE WAS THE HOLIEST OF PLACES: IT WAS THE PLACE WHERE THE ACTIONS OF THE GODS – AND SOMETIMES THE GODS THEMSELVES – COULD BE SEEN.

without this exchange between mind and landscape. The place represented a whole that fused together three things: time – made visible as a result of the astronomical alignments of the place, and its play of light and shadow; space, in the form of the landscape that reflected the work of the gods; and man-made imagery, the sign of human consciousness and awareness.

The sacred centre was sacred exactly because it was the place from which the movements of the Sun and Moon were observed and measured against the skyline, and because it was the place from which the actions of the gods – sometimes, even their very shapes – could be witnessed. It was the centre because all things were joined there.

THE ORACLE OF DELPHI

The best-known omphalos in the Old World is the temple complex, sanctuary and ancient home of the oracle at Delphi, Greece. According to Greek myth, Delphi was founded after the chief of the gods, Zeus, sent out two eagles from the far ends of the Earth; where their flights crossed would be the centre of the world. The eagles met over Mount Parnassos, on whose southern slopes Delphi was built.

Reflecting this legend, some classic depictions of omphalos stones (which existed at numerous sacred sites in ancient Greece) show two birds perched on them, facing in opposite directions. Two such stones survive at Delphi today. One is in the complex of temple ruins and is a cone of grey stone shot through with quartz veins. The other is now in Delphi's museum. It is egg-shaped, about 3 ft high, and covered by a delicate interlaced pattern carved in bas-relief.

THE STOREHOUSE OF THE DEAD

The Andean Indians have a very different concept of the stars in the sky than the Western notion of a series of constellations like a picture-book of mythical beings. To the Quechua Indian community of Misminay, who live near the Vilcanota River, about 30 miles north-west of Cuzco, Peru, the Milky Way is the key feature of the night sky.

They call the Milky Way *Mayu*, 'River'. They see it as the heavenly version of their River Vilcanota, which flows from south-east to north-west, and in Quechua myth is said to dump its waters off the edge of the Earth into the encircling void of the heavens. These waters are collected in the

Below: **Sioux Indians in an ecstatic dance, with their medicine man or shaman in a buffalo hide. The centre of the cosmos for the Sioux is Mount Harney, and the shaman's staff is also a symbol of the 'world axis' around which Heaven and Earth revolve.**

north-west by the Milky Way which carries
them through the sky before letting them
fall to Earth and rise again in the east. As
the waters are carried overhead, some of
the moisture drops to Earth again as rain.
The terrestrial and celestial rivers fertilize
land and sky.

From Misminay (as from any fixed point
on the Earth), the Milky Way appears to
swing across the sky, so that every 12 hours
its southern and northern ends respectively
appear to rise from the south-east and north-
east. In a 24-hour period, this apparent
movement draws two lines across the sky
that intersect directly overhead. The Quechua call this zenith point *Cruz Calvario*,
the 'cross of Calvary', borrowing the term
from Christian missionaries, whose work
among them was not entirely successful.

This division of space by the Milky Way
is reflected on the ground in the layout of
the Misminay settlement itself. Two
footpaths and irrigation canals running side
by side form an X-shaped cross on the
ground. Their intersection is called
Crucero, 'the cross'. This corresponds to
the 'crossing point' of the Milky Way in
the sky overhead – Calvario.

Crucero is the place in Misminay from
where the horizons of the 'four quarters' of
the world are marked by the local people.
Each direction is meaningful in Quechua
mythology, and the meaning of each is
reflected in house groupings in the village
and in the significance the people give to
certain sacred peaks beyond. The north-
west–north-east quarter, for example, is
associated with the ancestors, and the holy
mountain on the horizon in that direction is
called *Apu Wanumarka*, the 'Storehouse of
the Dead'. Here again we have a linking of
Earth and sky, life and death, past and
future, the interpenetration of space and
time in which each part gains its meaning
and nourishes the spirit only because it is
part of the whole image of the Universe
that the people entertain.

THE GOLDEN NAVEL OF THE EARTH

Most ancient peoples possessed some
concept of the sacred centre, and it could
take many forms. It could be stone, as at
Delphi or Delos in Greece, a holy city like
the Incas' Cuzco (the name means 'navel'
in the Quechua tongue), or a rock, as it is
for the Semangs of the Malay Peninsula,
where *Batu-Ribn* emerges at the centre of
the world. It is a rock, too, at Jerusalem,
that great centre sacred to Judaism,
Christianity and Islam alike, and it is a rock
too in Mecca.

The world centre could also be a peak, a
'world mountain'. To the Sioux Indians of
the American Great Plains, the centre of
the world was on Mount Harney. Israel
may boast *three* world centres including
Jerusalem – Mount Tabor, whose name
may mean 'navel', according to the
historian Mircea Eliade, and Mount

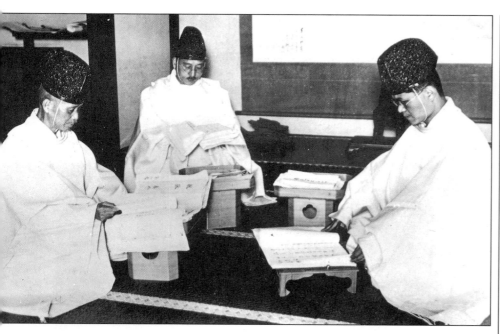

Above: *Priests of the Japanese Shinto religion, which is the world's oldest and is based on a celebration of the mysteries of the Earth.*

THE TREE OF LIFE IS A SYMBOL OF WHOLENESS AND SPIRITUAL STABILITY, BUT AT ITS ROOTS GNAW THE CORRUPTIONS OF MODERN CIVILIZATION.

Gerizim, which, Eliade maintains, was 'undoubtedly invested with the prestige of the centre, for it is called "navel of the earth"'. Buddhists too have their world centre in Mount Kailash in Tibet, the legendary 'Mount Meru', centre of the cosmos to believers. People still make pilgrimages to the remote mountain, to make a ritual tour around it. Some even make the circuit on their knees. In Japan, the volcanic cone of Mount Fujiyama is sacred; the Shinto religion centres on living earth mysteries.

The notion of the holy peak is deeply

embedded in the human psyche. Croagh Padric in the west of Ireland, sacred to the great Christian saint of the island, is likewise a centre of pilgrimages and rituals, which are possibly not Christian at all in origin but an adaptation of a far older tradition.

Besides appearing in stones, rocks and mountains, the centre of the world might be represented by a pole, or even a pit dug in the ground. The 'world tree', in particular, was a universal form of the sacred centre. The world tree connected the heavens and the underworld, but was also the axis from which the middle world, the Earth, oriented itself. It was the 'still point of the turning world', but also a kind of conducting rod between the upper and lower parts of the whole cosmos.

The Yakut tribes of Siberia believe that at the 'golden navel of the Earth' stands a tree with eight branches. In Norse and Old German mythology, the world tree was named Yggdrasil, and trees that symbolize the sacred centre live on in traditions as diverse and distant from one another as those of the Australian aborigines and American Indians.

Like the sacred mountain, the roots of the world tree reach into the human mind, and the sap still rises in this ancient image. It is found in (relatively) modern opera, in Wagner's reworking of the German myths in *The Ring*, and even in English literature.

The German composer Richard Wagner (right) *and the English novelist D.H. Lawrence* (far right) *both used the ancient symbol of the World Tree in their work.*

Left: *The Paps of Anu in County Kerry, Ireland – the bare breasts of the Earth Goddess Anu, who is still regarded with awe today.*

In *Women In Love*, written in the 1920s, D.H. Lawrence was still conjuring with the tree of life as a symbol of growth, wholeness and spiritual stability, at whose roots gnaw the corruptions of modern 'civilization'.

A SLEEPING BEAUTY

Gazing out from their cosmic centre across the landscape, the ancients saw a very different world from the one we think we are looking at. Agriculture, where it existed, was neither a cosy calling pursued by a romanticized minority nor a business, but a battle with nature that involved most of the tribe most of the time. Nor were the deserts dead but photogenic places. The whole of the landscape was alive.

Since Earth and the heavens enacted a cosmic marriage, it is not surprising that many ancient peoples around the world saw in the hills and moors, deserts and mountains around them the shape of a vast goddess, the Earth Mother. She did not *give* life to the land; she *was* its life, and they saw her in it.

The island of Jura off the west coast of Scotland has a range of mountains called the Paps: the central peaks are symmetrical and rounded like breasts. At Ballochroy, on the Kintyre peninsula on the mainland, the central stone of three menhirs has a smoothed side that faces the most northerly of the Paps, Beinn Corra, 19 miles distant across the sound. Behind this peak the Sun sets at midsummer.

On Lewis, the most north-westerly of the major Hebrides islands, the Pairc Hills are known locally as the 'Sleeping Beauty': they resemble the profile of a woman lying on her back. From the cluster of stone circles and settings known as the Stones of Callanish, it seems that when the Moon rises at its most southerly point during its 19-year cycle, it comes forth from the Pairc Hills. At this one time in the cycle it is as if the Sleeping Beauty gives birth to the Moon.

Two symmetrical, rounded hills near Killarney, Ireland, are known as the Paps of Anu. In the Irish myths, Anu is the mother of the last generation of gods to rule the Earth, the legendary Tuatha de Danaan. According to Celtic scholar Dr Anne Ross, these hills are still regarded with awe today. They 'personify the powers of the goddess embedded in the land', and Anu 'is still regarded as the local fairy queen'.

From the Greek island of Poros, off the north-east coast of the Peloponnisos, the mountains on the mainland are seen by local people as outlining the form of a woman lying on her back. 'The resemblance is indeed persuasive,' says the American historian Vincent Scully almost primly in *The Earth, the Temple and the Gods*, although he notes with some relish the shapes of 'the head low on the north, a long neck, high breasts, arched stomach, long legs with the knees drawn up'.

UPLIFTED BREASTS

In *Symbolic Landscapes*, earth mysteries scholar Paul Devereux draws attention to the vast number of Bronze Age Cretan figurines that exist of a goddess with her

---

THE LANDSCAPE RESEMBLED A WOMAN WITH HIGH BREASTS, AN ARCHED STOMACH AND LONG LEGS WITH THE KNEES DRAWN UP.

Below: *Scholar Paul Devereux, whose studies have contributed vastly to understanding the use and meaning of the ancient world's sacred sites.*

Right: *Part of a ley discovered in Gwent, Wales, by Alfred Watkins, a pioneer in the study of enigmatic alignments in the landscape. The track in the foreground leads directly to Llanthony Priory, and continues (unlike any conventional path) in a straight line up the hillside.*

arms raised in a characteristic and apparently curious gesture. The best-known example is the faience Snake Goddess found at Knossos, the heart of the ancient Minoan empire on Crete. Both the figure's upraised arms and its breasts, emphasized by an open bodice, create a cleft shape that is a direct echo of the sacred landscape of the island. The courtyard of the palace at Knossos opens to the distant, cleft-peaked Mount Yiouktas. The palace's *propylaia* or entrance is precisely aligned with the mountain.

The Minoan bull ritual, in which young men and women seized the horns of a charging bull and were propelled over its back, also echoed the horned peak of Mount Yiouktas. We know about the ritual because it is detailed in frescos found at Knossos, and it was performed under the eye of the horned mountain.

'The landscape and temples together form [an] architectural whole,' Vincent Scully wrote of the ancient Greeks' perception of their surroundings. He believed that the Greeks had 'developed an eye' for 'specific combinations of landscape features as expressive of particular holiness'.

This perception of the interchangeability of land and spirit was not confined to Knossos by any means. Other Cretan palaces were built in a deliberate relationship with horned mountains.

Among them are Mallia, which points toward Mount Dikte, and Phaistos, which is aligned to Mount Ida. At Gournia, the palace faces two hills that Scully described as 'so close and rounded that a more proper analogy would seem to be more directly to the female body itself and they do closely resemble the uplifted breasts' of the goddess. He remarked too that the enclosed landscape around Gournia gave the 'inescapable impression' that the palace was being embraced in the arms of the Earth Mother.

Similarly, the characteristic gesture in representations of the goddess is found throughout the Mediterranean. The small terracotta goddess figurines of Mycenae on the Greek mainland have the same raised arms. Tombs in the Castelluccio cemetery in Sicily were carved to show a powerful figure with upraised arms, breasts and head. Pieces of pottery of the same period from Sicily, the Lipari Islands and southern Italy all have horn-like handles to create an image of a goddess with raised arms.

The motif is thousands of years old. Female figurines and pottery decorations from pre-dynastic Egypt, for instance, feature this sacred gesture of upraised arms. The psychologist Erich Neumann has suggested that this universally repeated gesture of the Earth Mother indicates prayer, invocation or a magical conjuring of the deity. What he might have added is

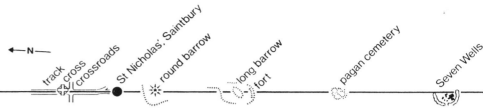

the reflection that it also reinforces the impression that the ancients saw their world as a cosmic union in which spiritual energy is constantly cycling through the whole of creation.

For it can hardly be insignificant that the goddess is always portrayed as herself in an attitude of worship. The Earth Mother was not separate from the rest of the Universe, complacently receiving its supplications, but herself takes part in a mutual – and mutually invigorating – reverence. Time and space, people, gods, spiritual energy, Earth, Sun, Moon and landscape were all aspects of one another. The world was whole, and holy.

HOLY LINES

Of all the conundrums posed by the ancient world's mystical landscapes, the most baffling is the fact that most are built on, or in, straight lines of one kind or another. This puzzling feature takes many different forms around the world. Every one of them brings us back to one of the most familiar, yet most fundamental, of the 'Earth mysteries': the riddle of 'ley lines'.

The usual story is that leys were discovered by Alfred Watkins one sunny June afternoon in 1921. As the 66-year-old businessman was sitting in his car, gazing out over his native Herefordshire from Blackwardine, he glanced down at the map in front of him. It was then, in a sudden epiphany, that he realized that the prehistoric mounds, earthworks and standing stones of the country before him were arrayed in arrow-straight lines across the landscape.

Watkins was not, in fact, the first to notice this. Numerous researchers had recorded their findings prior to Watkins's 'discovery' of 1921. As early as 1846, for instance, the antiquarian Edward Duke had proposed that Stonehenge and Avebury, some 20 miles apart, were part of an invisible straight line across the countryside that passed through another stone circle and two prehistoric earthworks. Other scholars throughout the 19th century noticed similar alignments, and in 1904, Hilaire Belloc published *The Old Road*, in which he described medieval pilgrimage routes linking old churches in England and, drawing on his observations while travelling in the USA, the straight tracks of American Indians.

Watkins, however, provided a comprehensive account for the ancient lines on the land. He believed they were the remaining signs of prehistoric traders' trackways, and they were straight because they had been laid out by line-of-sight. Watkins kept finding distinctive boulders on the lines he explored. He was convinced these were part of the original, prehistoric survey, and consequently called them 'markstones'. He also found old churches and crosses on the alignments which, he argued, were pagan – i.e. prehistoric – sacred places that had been commandeered by Christianity.

Watkins called his alignments 'leys' because he noted the word recurring in placenames on the lines. It comes from the Welsh word *llan*, which originally meant 'sacred enclosure'. The possible significance of this passed Watkins by, possessed as he was, like any good Victorian

Left and above: *The Saintbury ley in Gloucestershire runs for about 3.5 miles through the Cotswold hills. The photograph shows a section near St Nicholas's church, facing south.*

> **A**LONG THE INVISIBLE LEY LINES **C**HRISTIAN CHURCHES AND CROSSES HAD BEEN BUILT IN AN ATTEMPT TO DESTROY THE POWER OF THE SACRED PAGAN PLACES.

Right and below: *The Old Sarum ley in Wiltshire. The photograph shows the ruin of Old Sarum with Salisbury Cathedral in the distance.*

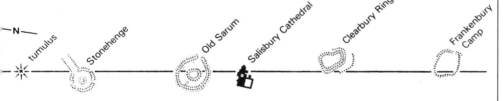

merchant, with the idea that the leys must have been trade routes. But the point was not lost on his contemporaries, the German researchers Josef Heinsch, who noted lines linking hills and old churches, and Wilhelm Teudt, who called the German alignments he discovered *heilige Linien*, 'holy lines'.

MYSTERIOUS ROADS TO NOWHERE

As Hilaire Belloc had realized, mysterious straight lines running through the landscape between ancient sites, and utterly regardless of their practicability as paths as they shot up sheer inclines and blithely disappeared over precipices, were not an exclusively European phenomenon. And as research and surveying and archeological digs continued, it became apparent that nowhere are there such enigmatic lines in the landscape as in the Americas.

The American Indians of antiquity made what are literally old straight tracks – they too ignored practicality for the sake of a ruler-like precision – and equally straight lines of sacred sites, shrines, holy rocks and wells. The remains of this curious practice can be seen all over the Americas, and it obsessed many diverse and distant American Indian cultures. One of the most intriguing of all these prehistoric straight-line systems is in the American Southwest: the 'Chaco roads'.

These are centred on Chaco Canyon, in the high mesa country of north-west New Mexico. They were made by the Anasazi, whose name is actually a Navajo Indian term meaning 'the enemies of our ancestors'. The Anasazi thrived in the Four Quarters area of New Mexico from about AD 800 to about 1300; some of them, in these latter years, clashed with the Navajo as they migrated into the region from AD 1000. The Anasazi developed a distinctive style of flat-roofed buildings

made of mud, rock and wood, called pueblos.

Chaco Canyon was the prime Anasazi ceremonial centre. Here, the culture reached its height. Over the years, the pueblos grew into multi-storeyed terraced complexes now known as 'Great Houses', with walls, courtyards, and 'Great Kivas' – very large ceremonial chambers. There are nine Great Houses within Chaco Canyon itself, all built between AD 900 and 1115. The largest was Pueblo Bonito, covering some three acres.

CARVED THROUGH LIVING ROCK

The Anasazis' mysterious roads radiate in straight lines for many miles around Chaco Canyon. They are fully engineered, a fairly constant 30 ft wide, with spur roads about half as wide. At their borders are earthen ridges, lines of stones or drystone walls. Their surfaces were laid with compacted earth – or cut straight into the bedrock. The true extent of the Chaco roads became apparent only in the 1970s, when aerial photography revealed how vast the network was. With ground surveys and digs, archeologists have now mapped some 400 miles of these enigmatic highways.

Like similar sacred 'routes' elsewhere, the Anasazi roads are no respecters of difficult terrain if it stands in their way. When they reached the canyon walls, the Anasazi engineers carved staircases up to 25 ft wide from the living rock, straight down the canyon sides.

The Chaco roads throw up a host of questions. Why did a people with neither horses nor the wheel need these elaborate highways? Are they roads as such at all? Recent computer-enhanced infra-red aerial pictures taken by NASA only deepen the mystery. These have revealed the existence of rows of sections running parallel to the roads. What were they for?

There is a consensus among archeologists and scholars that the roads were ceremonial or sacred ways that linked the Great Houses, which seem to have been

Above: *An Anasazi Indian settlement huddles under a cliff face at Canyon de Chelly, Arizona. The whole of this bare and seemingly hostile landscape was sacred to this vanished people.*

Right: *The 'Cliff Palace', the largest of the Anasazi settlements perched high within the escarpment at Mesa Verde in southern Colorado.*

THE DESERT WAS LIKE A VAST DRAWING-BOARD COVERED WITH PRECISE AND MYSTERIOUS PICTURES — PICTURES THAT COULD BE SEEN ONLY FROM THE AIR.

ritual centres. Fragments of pottery have been found in limited areas along some of the roads, notably near Great Houses. Breaking pottery vessels has been an act of consecration in numerous societies in widely distant places all over the world. It was often associated with the dead. It is possible that the Anasazi considered the roads themselves to be holy. It remains – officially at least – a mystery as to who used them, and why they were so broad and so finely made.

INVISIBLE HIGHWAYS

Virtually every sacred site in the prehistoric world was linked with others, major or minor, by a radiating network of straight lines. Few were as elaborate or as easily detected in their heyday as the Anasazis' strange highways. Most were invisible, like the leys of Europe – which makes them, in a way, all the more mysterious. In rare cases like the Ohio effigy mounds and the vast drawing-board that covered the desert floor at Nazca, Peru, entire sites were devoted to creating miles of straight lines and, still more bewildering, very precise pictures that could be appreciated only from the air.

In cultures that enjoyed such a comprehensive world-view, and that had such a magical sense of the continuous life rolling through the whole of creation – which today we sterilize and alienate by calling it the 'environment' – the lines, visible or invisible, had to have meaning. Where do they fit in the weft and warp of this most tightly woven of all mythologies?

This has been the greatest enigma of all in the study of the ancient sacred places. It was also, as a handful of researchers have now realized, the biggest clue of all to the meaning and use of the prehistoric sites, and it was staring them in the face all the time.

A MAP FOR THE MIND

Previous page: Parallel lines drawn on the desert floor at Nazca, Peru, disappear mysteriously into the distance. Straight lines like these, some miles long, are found on the Earth at ancient sites all over the world. Why were they so important to those who made them?

AT ANCIENT SITES THE HERE AND NOW HAD LINKS WITH THE SPIRIT WORLD.

Below: Michael Persinger, whose research suggests that ancient sites have qualities that enhance psychic perceptions.

Fault lines, strange lights, magnetic and gravitational abnormalities – how do all of these fit together in the world's mysterious places?

So far, we have gathered up various enigmatic bits of information about the world's mysterious ancient places. They were most often built on fault lines, and these are places where strange lights and magnetic and gravitational anomalies abound. We've seen that these places can have bizarre *psychic* effects on people. Research by Professor Michael Persinger of Laurentian University in Ontario has even suggested that individuals become especially receptive to extra-sensory perception in the presence of the phenomena that cling to the ancient sites.

We know too that these places were seen by the people who built them as *cosmic centres* on which the Sun and Moon were deliberately focused. Most probably, the cosmic light shows were arranged to reinforce the sense of *universal* centrality of the shrine – its place between the Otherworlds. At the sites, too, the here and now was strangely interfused with the spirit world – whether in the form of the Earth Goddess or through the link between Heaven, Earth and Underworld that was symbolized by the 'world tree' or some other equally potent image. Many sites are associated with the dead. Finally, we have seen that these perplexing places are linked, or infested, by straight lines both visible and invisible.

How, or where, do all these aspects fit together? What is the missing link? A brief tour around one of the most problematic of these baffling monuments may let slip a few more clues.

DESIGNS IN THE DESERT

Probably the most famous of American Indian straight lines are the markings on the desert pampas around Nazca, Peru.

The Nazca lines were drawn by removing the desert surface to reveal the lighter soil beneath. The lines can be anything from a few dozen yards to several miles long, and pass straight over ridges. Interspersed among the hundreds of straight lines are a variety of line drawings, made in the same way, of animals, sundry geometric forms and irregular and regular abstract shapes.

It is easier to say what the lines and drawings at Nazca are not than to summarize what they might be. That they are not and never did form a landing-strip for 'ancient astronauts' is a statement scarcely worth making: the idea was never worth ten seconds of anyone's time. Nor are the lines aligned to the heavens in any more conventional archeo-astronomical sense. Work in the 1980s co-ordinated by Anthony F. Aveni of Colgate University, New York State, confirmed the finding by Gerald Hawkins of the Smithsonian Institution in the 1960s that none of the lines had any significant astronomical function.

Aveni and his colleagues did find that there is some pattern to the apparently random layout of the lines on the ground. Nazca's resident researcher Maria Reiche had noted what she called 'star-like centres', from which lines radiated like

rays from a sun. Aveni's team identified over 60 of these centres. They are set on natural hills or mounds, and at least one line from each centre connects it with another.

At these 'star-like' centres are deposits of small stones, shells and broken pottery fragments: signs of some kind of offering to the dead, as were found along the 'roads' in Chaco Canyon. In the 1920s, an elder of the Navajo Indians made the cryptic remark to archeologist Neil Judd that although the Chaco lines looked like roads, they 'were not roads'. The Nazca lines are not tracks, although they look like tracks. They start nowhere and end anywhere.

And the most impenetrable fact of all about Nazca is the line drawings. Why spend energy, which could barely be spared from the hard business of survival, on making pictures that no one could see?

Or *could* someone see them? And if so – how could they?

PATHWAYS FOR THE SPIRITS

Now let us go back to the straight lines. These are traditionally significant in other contexts. Here is another clue to the hidden meaning of the lines on the Earth – and of the ancient places themselves. There is a very ancient tradition that spirits – good and bad – move in straight lines. There is a huge global lore concerning the usefulness of knots in defending oneself against evil spirits, for instance. But straight lines can be used to encourage the intervention of the most beneficial spirits – most interestingly, in many widespread traditions, by using threads to provide a path for them.

Among some Australian Aboriginal tribes, a healer would treat a sick person by running a spider thread from the head of the 'patient' to a nearby bush. This, said the healer, was where the sufferer's spirit had fled from the ailing body. The filament provided a path for the spirit to return, making the patient whole again and banishing the illness.

Similarly, when dealing with sickness, the shaman (colloquially known as the tribal 'witch doctor' or 'medicine man') of the Buryat peoples of Siberia would place an arrow on the ground beside the patient's head and lay a red thread in a straight line, out through the entrance of the sick

Above: *The complexity of the lines and patterns at Nazca becomes clear when they are seen from the air. But why?*

STRAIGHT LINES ARE BY TRADITION THE WAY TAKEN BY THE SPIRITS – AND A THREAD COULD ENCOURAGE THEM.

Above: *Seen at close quarters, the lines at Nazca seem almost insignificant. Yet enormous energy and devotion went into their design and maintenance. But how did their makers get to see the full effect of their work?*

SHAMANISM PERHAPS CAME TO THE AMERICAS ACROSS THE BERING STRAITS MORE THAN 15,000 YEARS AGO. IT REMAINED STRONG AMONG THE INDIAN TRIBES UNTIL RECENT TIMES.

---

person's tent, to a birch pole that he had previously stuck in the ground outside. The pole stood for the world tree, the link between this world and the realms of spirit, while the thread gave the sick person's soul a route along which to return to the body. The principle is almost identical to that of the Australian tradition.

Among the Maoris of New Zealand, the stem of a plant could be taken as a spirit 'line'. The *tohunga* ('healer') put the stem on a sick person's head and called on the evil spirit that was causing the illness to leave by the 'road' offered by the stem of the plant.

In terms of straight lines, the spirit world and ancient places, the most provocative of all these traditions of healing belongs to the Kalahari !Kung people. When they hold a trance dance, which involves hours of rhythmic movement and continuous chanting in the hypnotic presence of a fire, it's not uncommon for people to leave their bodies – to have what we would call an out-of-the-body experience. The !Kung call this state *kia*. Once in it, they can climb 'threads' up to 'where God is'. When they are with God, they can become healers. The !Kung say that then they are able to gaze into people's bodies with X-ray vision to see where any disease has taken root, and can then pull it out.

Here is a very clear indication that straight lines, contact with the spirit world *and* a state of trance are all closely related.

THE THREE WORLDS SYSTEM

The key that unlocks the mystery connecting straight lines and the sacred sites lies in the central fact about the ancient places themselves. That is: they were, exactly and literally, *central* to existence. The sacred centre was not only a place from which to make and take earthly bearings. It linked the 'middle world' of the here and now with the worlds above – Heaven – and below – the Underworld. The realms above and below were kingdoms of the spirit. Anthropologists call this cosmology the 'three worlds system'. It seems to have originated, possibly hundreds of thousands of years ago, with a form of religion known as shamanism.

When and where shamanism began is anyone's guess, but it probably arrived in the Americas with the peoples who migrated across the old land bridge over the Bering Straits somewhere between 15,000 and 25,000 years ago. The shamanic tradition remained strong and healthy among the American Indian tribes until very recent times because the Americas did not suffer the same cultural changes over the centuries as Eurasia did.

What is a shaman? The term itself comes from *saman*, the word the Tungus peoples of Siberia had for the 'elected member' of the tribe who could journey to the spirit worlds seeking healing for tribal members, finding lost or confused souls or seeking help for those in this world by divining the future or peering into the

Above: *Maoris performing invocation. Traditional Maori healing rites embody the concept of spirits using straight lines as pathways.*

Left: *A yarn picture made by the Huichol Indians of central Mexico. In the upper left of the picture are shamans, directing the life force of the Sun's rays as they fall on a cornfield. Note in particular what appear to be wings growing from the shamans' bodies – an indication of their capacity for magical flight in the realm of spirit.*

The Biblical image of Jacob's ladder (above) *as a connection between the spiritual realm and earthly life is echoed in shamanic traditions throughout the world. Like many shamans, too, Jacob had his visionary dream while sleeping on a sacred rock.*

THE SHAMAN'S CHANT, OFTEN OF EERIE BEAUTY, DISTRACTS THE LISTENER AND IS BOTH HAIR-RAISING AND HYPNOTIC.

remote past. The shaman was the intermediary between the tribe and the Otherworld of spirit, and he went to the Otherworld through an out-of-the-body experience. To his conscious self, this experience seemed to be the equivalent of flight above the Earth.

We can infer that this experience of flying was universal from many pieces of evidence. To begin with, shamans all around the world use strikingly similar metaphors to describe their journeys to the Otherworld. They say their spirits rise on smoke, ride along a rainbow, follow a flight of arrows, travel up a sunbeam – and so on. A particularly common image they use is the ladder, stretching from Earth to Heaven – just as Jacob's does in the Bible. He, significantly, also slept on a sacred stone.

ROUTES TO A TRANCE

The shaman used – and still uses – a variety of techniques to achieve the trance state. Among them were prolonged dancing, fasting and chanting. This last, incidentally, was not ordinary chanting. A large choir of Russian Orthodox monks sounds like a tin whistle with the croup in comparison to a shaman in full voice, and

the greatest cantor in Brooklyn might as well be a mosquito.

There are few sounds in the world more *un*earthly than the vocal performance of a Siberian shaman as he prepares to leave the mundane world. Bizarre but distinct whistlings come down from his sinuses and out of his nose and mouth, while he uses an astonishing, fundamental muscular control to produce a grim, low, rhythmic roaring from the diaphragm. On top of these various abnormal noises and mesmeric drones, he manages to produce a conventional human chant, often of eerie beauty, to distract the astounded listener. It comes as something of a surprise to discover that this last, most recognizable, sound is not actually coming out of his ears. The whole effect is both hair-raising and hypnotic, as well as inhuman – as it is surely meant to be, for him as much as for his audience.

Shamans may use other ritual tools at the same time or separately to induce trance. They include exposure to extremes of heat or cold, and a range of more or less horrifying methods of inducing pain and, hence, sensory deprivation. Shamans may also use hallucinogenic plants, foods or smoking mixtures (the 'peace-pipe' had a number of applications, but the ultimate effect was usually very peaceful, not to say positively dreamy).

The hallucinogens that the shamans used are interesting because many of these drugs gave their user a strong impression of flying. One 19th-century explorer into the South American interior described how he felt himself going on 'an aerial journey' as a result of drinking *ayahuasaca*, a potent Indian tincture made from a hallucinogenic vine. Modern dope slang reflects something of the same experience: among other things, one gets 'high', goes on a 'trip' and gets 'spaced out'.

The mental imagery induced by drug use and trance became central to many tribes' art. Among the rock paintings in a Chumash Indian shrine at Burro Flats, near Los Angeles, California, there is a series of geometric forms – dots, lines, crosses, circles and concentric rings. Similar patterns are found in rock art all over the world, and can be seen carved into the rock at many megalithic sites in Britain.

The source of these patterns is the human brain. The Tukano Indians of Colombia in South America (who use trance-inducing drugs in religious ceremonies) employ similar imagery as a basis for the decorative work on their pottery and clothing, and freely admit that these are based on the colourful but geometric forms they see under the influence of the drugs. The San (Bushmen) of the Kalahari, too, make no secret of the fact that the patterns and motifs in their own rock paintings are based on what their shamans see when in trance. These patterns were probably the original inspiration for another enigmatic pattern found at endless numbers of sacred sites all over the world: the labyrinth or maze.

Most significantly, the shaman moved from normal awareness to the Otherworld to the endless beating of a magic drum, which was covered in signs and symbols to protect him on his 'journey' elsewhere. He called his drum his 'steed' or 'canoe' on or in which he would travel to the spirit realm. One of the more intriguing discoveries

LABYRINTH AND MAZE PATTERNS FOUND AT ENDLESS NUMBERS OF SACRED SITES ARE PROBABLY INSPIRED BY FORMS SEEN UNDER THE INFLUENCE OF DRUGS.

Below: *A Siberian shaman's drum. His trance partly induced by its rhythmic reverberations, the shaman believed that the drum became a steed or canoe on which he rode to the Otherworld.*

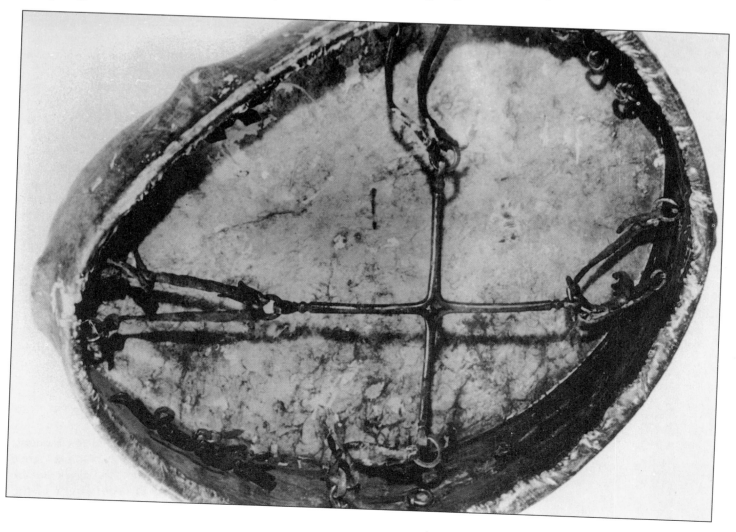

Below: *The ceremonial costume of a Siberian shaman, dating from about 1890.*

made about these drums is that they produce sounds at extremely low frequencies – as few as four cycles per second. These affect the so-called *theta* brain waves, which are somehow involved in the deeper levels of dreaming, trance and meditation.

In the Siberian tribes, the shell of the shaman's drum was, in theory, made from a branch of the world tree (usually, in fact, a birch). Because of this magical link and through his hypnotic drumming, the shaman is 'magically projected into the vicinity of the Tree', as the anthropologist Mircea Eliade put it. In the tribes of central and northern Asia, the shaman would actually climb a birch tree during his trance, to show his spectators that he was indeed ascending the axis of the world and passing into the realm of spirit.

BIRD-MEN THROUGH THE AGES

Once up the tree, he flew. In some tribes, he waved his arms like a bird's wings when he got to the top. During his trance, the Yakut shaman of north-east Siberia also made dance movements and gestures to imitate the flight of a bird.

The image of flight was the unmistakable sign of a shaman in the ancient world, and is still in those cultures that have remained prehistoric and pre-industrial in spirit. The most frequent is the form of a bird perched on a stick (standing for the world axis or tree). From this token, the almost unimaginable antiquity of the shaman tradition becomes evident, for among the Cro-Magnon cave paintings of Lascaux, France, there is one of a bird-stick next to a man in a bird mask, who is apparently in trance. The painting may be a quarter of a million years old.

The Mississippian people, who flourished between about AD 900 to 1500, left many examples of pottery decorated with human–bird figures. Siberian shamans wore bird-claw shoes, and the Hopewell Indian shaman would decorate his robes with bird-claw shapes cut out of mica. In China, Taoist monks were called 'feather scholars', which reveals their original role. In Ireland, the Celtic Druids were believed to be able to take wing through applied magic. While North American shamans most often identified with the eagle, the ancient Indian text *Upanishads* calls the out-of-the-body spirit or soul 'the lone wild gander'; and the image flies from the tropics to the Arctic Circle, for geese figure prominently in Eskimo accounts of magical flight.

COSMIC CROSSING POINTS

The spirits, as we've seen in the accounts of healing techniques, for example, move in straight lines. Thus, the lines on the landscape and the straight flight of the shaman's spirit are almost certainly versions of one and the same thing. Whether the lines on the landscape ('They look like roads, but they are not roads') were put there to guide and protect the travelling spirit – a kind of safety net for the soul – or were put there to celebrate and consecrate shamanic flight, or were a *record* of these journeys in spirit, we shall probably never know.

But these various threads running through magical and religious lore, and the various clues at the ancient sites themselves, all point to the conclusion that the sacred centres were *shamanic* centres, with the life of the Universe – the Earth Goddess, the Sun, the Moon – focused upon them and throwing into relief their significance as crossing points between this world and that of spirit. And it seems clear that the lines radiating from them or linking them were highways of the soul in its out-of-the-body flight. The lines may well have been intended also as markers and guides for the spirits of the dead. The association between death and the ancient places is too strong, and the cultures that built them were too comprehensive in their symbolism, for there to be no connection.

The other mysterious aspects of the sites now fall into place. The pictures on the ground at Nazca, and the effigy mounds in Ohio, were made to be seen during an out-of-the-body experience. Again, we shall probably never know for sure whether they were seen purely in the mind's eye of the entranced and drugged voyager, or if his soul did literally wing its way along the leys and spirit paths laid out on the ground.

The geological abnormalities of the ancient centres too begin to make sense. Not only did the 'earthlight' effects around them, created by the anomalies in the Earth, proclaim them as unusual, but the enhanced magnetism or radioactivity of the stones in turn catalysed the trance of the initiated. Paul Devereux, who pioneered this interpretation of the ancient sites, speculates in *Earth Memory*:

'We can perhaps envisage the megalithic shaman, in an altered state of consciousness, lying or sleeping in head-contact with the stone of power at a site. This might have helped to engender special visions… in the way that [the Welsh holy man] St Byrnach…used the magnetically anom-

alous Carn Ingli to "speak with the angels".'

MAGIC JOURNEYS AND MODERN TIMES

In Europe and much of Asia, the early tribal societies that built the ancient sites developed into more complex forms. Shamans became priests, and the priests became kings. But they did not lose all their old associations with the old shamanic world.

The connection between the straight lines of spirit and the holy office of

Above: *A Taoist abbot, or 'feather scholar' – so-called because of the holy man's reputed ability to fly, an echo of shamanic origins.*

A STRAIGHT WAY CONTINUES TO SYMBOLIZE THE SPECIAL POWER ASSOCIATED WITH RULERSHIP, AND RECALLS SHAMANIC LINES.

Above: *A witch flies above the rooftops. The image is a buried folk-memory of the days when Scandinavian female shamans were said to be able to fly, and were pictured riding the sky on broomsticks.*

kingship can still be seen in a word like 'ruler' in English, which means both a straight-edge and a political chief. The word derives from an ancient Indo-European word, *reg*, which means 'movement in a straight line'. From the same root we also get the Latin *rex* (king) and thence the English 'regal'.

Look about the land, and one will see other relics of shamanic lines in regal institutions. Royalty has always surrounded itself with architecture that bristles with ceremonial ways, boundaries, royal routes and imperial avenues. Even the ceremonial ways of kingless Washington DC are laid out in straight lines. In London, the Mall is the broad way leading to and from Buckingham Palace. A sense that a straight way symbolizes a special power associated with rulership has thus survived.

Buried in the folklore of modern Western societies are other relics of the shaman's magic journey. The cosy image of Father Christmas flying in his reindeer-drawn sleigh through the magic midwinter night is a jolly version of the flight in spirit of Arctic European and Siberian shamans. The tribes there were reindeer herders. Their minds grew wings with the aid of the hallucinogenic fly agaric fungus – whose distinctive red and white cap is the colour of Santa Claus's robes. It may be significant too that Santa Claus lives at the North Pole – the axis of the world.

Another relic of the shaman's magical flight is the witch flying on her broomstick. Medieval witches took 'flying ointments' or 'witches' salves', which were made from hallucinogenic herbs that also created the sensation of flight by generating an out-of-the-body experience. The broomstick is an echo of the world tree; it also recalls the habit (still practised in the Americas) of sweeping clean the spirit paths on the ground to make the space sacred. The archetypal image of the witch may come from a Scandinavian sect of women shamans who practised a form of prophecy, known as *seidhr*, while in trance. They wore feathered garments to indicate their ability to fly when in this altered state of consciousness. They, too, were often pictured flying on broomsticks.

As a final provocative footnote to this labyrinthine tale, there is a strong hint in the Norse mythology that it was actually women who first taught men to 'fly'.

The world is a stranger place than it seems – an *even* stranger place than it *already* seems.

NOSTRADAMUS AND VISIONS OF THE FUTURE

NOSTRADAMUS –
The Greatest Seer of All

Nearly 500 years ago a medieval doctor retreated to his secret study, night after night, to journey into the future. The images that he saw were so terrifying that he concealed his prophecies in an elaborate code. Now that code has been broken, and history has confirmed the accuracy of many of his predictions – but are the final devastating prophecies about to come true?

History credits a man named Nostradamus as being the greatest seer who ever lived. His prophecies, cast nearly 500 years ago, have been interpreted by learned scholars, laymen and sceptics alike as the first – and accurate – drafts of great world events. Nostradamus correctly foretold the Great Fire of London and the coming of Adolf Hitler. He prophesized the death of Henri II of France, the triumph and death of Elizabeth I of England and the French Revolution. If his last prediction is right – that of a war to end all wars – then civilization as we know it could be destroyed in the year 1999. It is the one prophecy that all students of Nostradamus hope and pray is incorrect – but if his record is anything to go by, mankind should surely fear the worst.

Nostradamus was born Michel de Nostradame in St Remy de Provence on 14 December 1503. His father, James, was a lawyer, born into a Jewish family who had converted to the Catholic faith. Michel was a brilliant student who spent his time in between lessons reading books on fortune telling and the occult. His grandfather, who had a great influence over his schooling, also taught him the 'celestial sciences' – astronomy. After studying

Opposite: Nostradamus, a prophet unsurpassed through the ages whose premonitions foretold of the cataclysmic events which would shape our world. Here the master is pictured in a 1666 engraving which formed the frontispiece of a collection of his prophecies.

The prophet lived in an ordered world where the divine right of kings reigned supreme. What mystical powers, then, did he tap into to foresee the French Revolution and with it the storming of the Bastille (below), where enemies of the state were held in appalling conditions?

HIS HAND TREMBLED AS HE WROTE HIS PREDICTIONS: HE WAS RISKING THE TORTURES OF THE HOLY INQUISITION.

Capricorn, the reaper, pictured (below) in a medieval German book of astrology. The signs of the planets and their influence upon humankind were of immense interest to Nostradamus.

humanities at Avignon he went to the University of Montpellier where he read medicine and philosophy. Medicine was to be his first calling and he excelled as a physician. When he was 20 Nostradamus retreated from Montpellier as it was ravaged by the Great Plague laying waste to Europe's cities and villages, but returned two years later, after practising in Bordeaux and Narbonne, to complete his medical degree. It was at this time that he changed his name from Nostradame to Nostradamus, 'Man of Our Lady'.

He left Montpellier for Provence, his home region which was also being decimated by the plague. He soon earned a name for himself as a courageous physician who, regardless of his own safety, began venturing into the worst-stricken areas to aid the sick, but he refused to 'bleed' people, one of the commonest – and cruellest – medical practices of the age. Older and more powerful physicians than Nostradamus expounded the virtues of this nonsensical practice, believing that the illness in an afflicted person's body flowed away with the blood. Instead Nostradamus set about

making compounds and potions to relieve suffering and later noted their compositions in a book.

In 1534 after being invited by a prominent philosopher to stay with him at his home in Agen, Nostradamus met and married a beautiful noblewoman. He had a son and a daughter by her but soon the plague – a virulent strain called '*le charbon*' because sufferers were stricken with great black pustules on their bodies – came to Agen and claimed the lives of his family. Heartbroken, Nostradamus wandered around France for several years; the prime purpose of his travels seems to have been the collection and study of potions and medicines from apothecaries and pharmacists across the land. He also travelled to Italy, where one of the legends about his mystical powers first grew. He saw a young monk leading a herd of swine down a narrow street; as the monk drew level with him Nostradamus bowed down on one knee and addressed him as 'Your Holiness'. Later, the humble swineherd, Felice Peretti, became Pope Sextus V, long after Nostradamus had died.

By 1554, when the plague was thought to be on the retreat, Nostradamus had settled in Marseilles, but that year there were massive floods and the swollen rivers, polluted with infected corpses, carried the disease to every part of the region. Once again Nostradamus found himself working around the clock to ease the suffering of the people. It was remarkable that in his close contact with so many sufferers he never succumbed to the disease himself.

In November 1554 he settled in Salon where he married Anne Ponsart Gemelle, a rich widow. Most of the treasures and rewards which grateful towns had heaped on Nostradamus for his care of plague victims had been given away to the poor, but a comfortable life now seemed a certainty thanks to his wise marriage which provided him with a daughter and three sons, a peaceful home life and no money worries. He converted the top room of his house into a study and began work on his immortal *Prophecies* – the foretelling of the future using all his wisdom, astronomical gifts and occult beliefs. In such an age, when the terror of the (church) Inquisition hung heavily over anyone deemed to be a heretic, Nostradamus was

The sign of Scorpio (above) *of the conspicuous southern constellation lying on the ecliptic – the Sun's apparent path through the Heavens – between Sagittarius and Libra.*

certainly taking chances in committing his predictions to paper. He initially composed the prophetic riddles – quatrains – for his own interest; it was only later that he decided to publish them. However, he made sure that they were extremely difficult to interpret, written as they were in a hotchpotch of high French, Provençal French, Italian, Greek and Latin, and riddled with symbolism. Their time sequence was deliberately mixed up so that their meaning and chronology 'would not be immediately discernible to the unwise'. The latter was probably a built-in safeguard in case the guardians of the rack and the branding iron in the Inquisition became displeased with him.

In a section on Nostradamus in his book of seers entitled *They Saw Tomorrow* Charles Neilson Gattey said: 'Even today, when one first reads the original French edition, one's initial reaction is of perplexed disillusion. The language is enigmatic, at times almost unintelligible, as if written in code. The verses are not in chronological order, and jump about in time and subject. Strange soubriquets of Nostradamus' own coining are used for famous personalities. Everywhere we find mystifying puns and anagrams.' But ever since their publication, the *Prophecies* have

withstood the test of time and proved that Nostradamus was an incredible seer.

By 1555 he had completed the first part of his life's work – an almanac of prophecies that were to chronicle world history from his time until the end of the world. The forecasts were called 'The Centuries'; the word 'centuries' had nothing to do with a span of 100 years – it was because there were 100 verses in each book, of which the author intended to write ten. In the preface to the first, Nostradamus wrote that he was afraid that he would be killed by an angry mob if he committed to paper the future which had been revealed to him in prophetic visions. 'That is why I have withheld my tongue from the vulgar and my pen from paper,' he said. 'But later on I thought I would, for the common good describe the most important of the revolutionary changes I foresee, but so as not to upset my present readers I would do this in a cloudy manner with abstruse and twisted sentences rather than plainly prophetical.' Only some of the Centuries are dated – although Nostradamus claimed he could have given a date to all of them had he so wished. Regarding 1792, for instance, when the French Revolution was at its height, he wrote that the year would be 'marked by a far worse persecution of the

Above: *Catherine de Medici, wife of King Henri II of France. She called upon the wisdom of Nostradamus to foresee the future for her sons. He obliged – albeit diplomatically, for fear that too much truth could have cost him his head.*

THE DARK MAGICAL TEXTS HAD SUCH AN INFLUENCE ON HIM THAT HE DECIDED TO BURN THEM IN CASE THEY FELL INTO EVIL HANDS.

Christian Church than ever was in Africa, and which everyone will think an innovation of the age.' That year, Madame Guillotine was at her bloody zenith across France.

At the beginning of his work he also gave the reader an insight into how he divined his prophecies, again in the form of a quatrain: 'Sitting alone at night in secret study; it is placed on the brass tripod. A slight flame comes out of the emptiness and makes successful that which should not be believed in vain.' He went on: 'The wand in the hand is placed in the middle of the tripod's legs. With water he sprinkles both the hem of his garment and his foot. A voice, fear; he trembles in his robes. Divine splendour; the god sits nearby.' According to Nostradamus expert Erika Cheetham in her authoritative work *The Prophecies of Nostradamus*, he touches the middle of the tripod with his wand and then moistens his robe and feet with the water placed on it. 'This is the same method as was used to obtain inspiration by the Apollonian prophetess at the oracles of Branchus in Classical times,' she said. 'Nostradamus is afraid of the power he evokes when it comes to him; he hears it as well as sees it;

it appears to speak to him and he writes down the prophecies. He is unafraid once the gift has possessed him. This dual aspect of his vision is most important when interpreting the centuries.'

Nostradamus also relied heavily on the impressive library he had built up, containing many rare books and manuscripts on the occult. He was influenced by dark, magical texts which he later decided to burn when they came into conflict with his deep religious beliefs. He claimed that when they burned a 'subtle illumination' was cast over his house, acting as a catalyst for further divination and prophecy. He wrote: 'Many occult volumes, which have been hidden for centuries have come into my possession, but after reading them, dreading what might happen if they should fall into the wrong hands, I presented them to Vulcan, and as the fire devoured them, the flames licking the air shot forth an unaccustomed brightness, clearer than natural flame, like the flash from an explosive powder, casting a peculiar illumination all over the house, as if it were wrapped in sudden conflagration. So that you might not in the future be tempted to search for the perfect transmutation, lunar or solar, or for uncorruptible metals hidden under the earth or the sea, I reduced them to ashes.' While using his psychic, meditative and prophetic powers for the Centuries, he was also a firm believer in astrology, using many astrological charts, constellations, planets and signs, to date the quatrains. His implication in the introduction to the Centuries was that, while future events and their dates are determined by planetary movements, their description needed to be modified by the 'spirit of prophecy'.

He ends his introduction to the prophecies by stating that he is not 'vain' enough to call himself a prophet. He says he is a mortal man, 'the greatest sinner in the world, and heir to every human affliction, but, by being surprised sometimes by a prophetical mood, amid prolonged calculation, while engaged in nocturnal studies of sweet odour, I have composed books of prophecies, containing each one a hundred astronomical quatrains which I have joined obscurely and are perpetual vaticinations from now to the year 3797'.

At the end of 1555, the first three Centuries and part of the fourth were published and the fame of Nostradamus spread across Europe with all the speed of the plague that he had devoted his earlier life to conquering. Much of his celebrity spread by word of mouth, from village to village and city to city, as books were expensive and purely a luxury for the rich. But it was at the highest levels of French society where his prophecies aroused most interest, particularly at the court of the royal family. In a superstitious age, someone like Nostradamus was regarded with a mixture of both awe and fear.

Catherine de Medici, wife of Henri II of France, was an avowed occultist, who had entertained many fortune tellers, seers, prophets and charlatans as she tried to plot the course of her beloved husband's reign. She sent for Nostradamus shortly after the publication of the Centuries – both curious and concerned about several passages which, if they were realized, were ominous for the king. It was Quatrain 35 of the first Century which was most worrying, however, as it seemed to predict his death in battle. It read: 'The young lion will overcome the older one, in a field of combat in single fight; He will pierce his eyes in their golden cage; two wounds in one, then he dies a cruel death.' Nostra-

damus arrived in Paris on 15 August 1556 with specific instructions from Catherine de Medici to interpret it.

Catherine was certain of Nostradamus's powers from the first moment she saw him; an aura seemed to emanate from him, particularly from his eyes, and he was adorned with none of the charms and amulets so beloved of the 30,000-odd occultists who made Paris their home. Initially, she hedged around asking him to interpret the quatrains pertaining to the king, instead asking him advice on cosmetics and alternative healing practices. Curiosity, eventually, led her to seek an explanation of the king's death. Nostradamus explained as delicately as he could that he had no power over the visions he had, that he merely recorded events as they came to him. He was aware that a previous seer to the court, a man named Gaurico, had endured horrific torture for prophecies about the king's demise, but he told her anyway – that the king would die in a duel. In 1559 his prediction came true. In celebration of two royal weddings, jousts, tournaments and feasts spanning a three-day period were held in Paris. On the final day the king jousted with Captain Montgomery of the Scottish

THE LANCE PIERCED THE KING'S THROAT AND THEN HIS EYE; HE DIED IN AGONY TEN DAYS LATER.

Below: *Nostradamus, commanded by Catherine, is depicted here with occult symbols such as the zodiac, a cat and skulls. He is engaged in summoning up pictures of future French kings in a mirror.*

Guard, with both men wearing the emblem of a lion on their chests. When they rode against each other for a third time the splintered end of Montgomery's lance pierced first the king's throat and then knocked up his protective visor, piercing his eye. Mortally injured by the 'two wounds in one', he was carried from the field of combat to die in agony ten days later.

After this, Nostradamus drew up the horoscopes for the royal offspring – children for whom he had already predicted grim fates in the Centuries. Rather than piling on the agony, he diplomatically concentrated on the positive aspects of their lives, predicting that all Catherine's sons would be kings; only François died before he could ascend to the throne.

After his royal audiences he lived in Salon, continuing to work on the Centuries and, upon command, drawing up horoscopes for his many learned and wealthy visitors. In 1564 Catherine, now Queen Regent, went on a royal tour of France with 800 family members, courtiers and attendants. One of her first calls was on Nostradamus, whom she dined with and bestowed upon the privileged title of Physician in Ordinary. It carried with it a small stipend and other benefits; more importantly, it silenced those justices and clergy who mumbled from time to time about heresy and witchcraft being practised by the old sage.

One interesting incident worth recording occurred during this royal visitation in Salon. Nostradamus, whose visions were the root of his prophecies, also occasionally foretold future events by looking at a person or touching them. He attached great importance to birthmarks upon a person's body, believing them portents of greatness. It was while the royal retinue was at Salon that he made a request to view the naked body of a young boy who was with them – ten-year-old Henri of Navarre – but the boy was shy and feared he would be beaten. The old seer crept into his bedchamber that night and examined the boy as he slept, and found the birthmark he was seeking. Catherine still had two sons in line to the throne but Nostradamus was adamant: the child would be king of France. His prophecy was true – Henri of Navarre became Henri IV of France.

After the royal visitation he worked on completing five more Centuries, bringing the total to eight in all, but the completed works were not off the printing press until 1568, two years after he died. Nostradamus made his will on 17 June 1566 and left a large sum of over 3500 crowns. On 1 July he told his local priest to give him the last

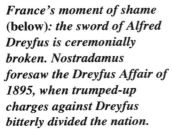

France's moment of shame (below): the sword of Alfred Dreyfus is ceremonially broken. Nostradamus foresaw the Dreyfus Affair of 1895, when trumped-up charges against Dreyfus bitterly divided the nation.

rites as he would not be seen alive again. Sure enough, he foretold his own death, with his body being discovered the next morning, a victim of virulent dropsy. He had penned a quatrain for the occasion: 'On returning from an embassy, the King's gift safely stored, No more will I labour, for I will have gone to God, by my close relations, friends and brothers, I shall be found dead, near my bed and the bench.' He lived for 62 years, 6 months and 17 days. His legacy is a work that, through the ages, has been as relevant for people as it was when he was alive. As a prophet, he had the satisfaction of both seeing his predictions come true in his own lifetime as well as having them quoted in the highest circles. Before his death his fame had spread to England where two of his almanacs were printed in London, but it wasn't until 1672 that *The True Prophecies or Prognostications of Michel Nostradamus, Translated and Commentated by Theophilus de Garencieres*, a doctor of the 'College of Physick' in London, were printed, spreading his prophecies to a much wider and altogether more learned audience.

His last request was to be buried upright – he couldn't bear the thought of people walking over him 'during my final sleep'. Placed into the wall of the Church of the Cordeliers in Salon, it was not to be his final grave. In Quatrain 7 of Century IX he had written that evil would come to any man who violated his resting place. It so happened that during the French Revolution the church was pillaged, with one of the looters desecrating his grave, ripping out his skull and using it for a drinking cup. Sure enough, the vagabond was shot dead as soon as he emerged from the crypt. Nostradamus was re-interred in the church of St Laurent in 1813 where he has been allowed to rest in peace ever since. A tablet nearby says: 'Here lie the bones of the illustrious Michel Nostradamus, whose almost divine pen alone, in the judgement of all mortals, was worthy to record, under the influx of the stars, the future events of the whole world. He died at Salon in the year 1566. Posterity, disturb not his sweet rest! Anne Ponce Gemelle hopes for her husband true felicity.' It was written by his second wife.

Although Nostradamus enjoys fame long after his death, he does remain an

enigma to many. In his scholarly work *Oracles of Nostradamus*, author Charles Ward wrote of him: 'It has been well said that the man and his works are an enigma. Everything in our author is ambiguous; the man, the thought, the style. We stumble at every step in the rough paths of his labyrinth. We try to interrogate, but grow silent before a man of emotionless nerve and of impenetrable mask. What are these Centuries? What is Nostradamus? In them and him all may find something; but no man born of woman can find all. The Sphinx of France is here before us; a riddler, riddling of the fate of men; a man at once bold and timid; simple, yet who can plumb his depth? A superficial Christian, a pagan perhaps at heart; a man rewarded of kings; and yet, so far as one can see, furnishing no profitable hint to them that could make their life run smoother or remove a single peril from their path. Behold this Janus of a double face; his very breath is double; the essence of ambiguity lies wrapped incarnate in him and it moulds the man, the thought, the style.'

A villain of the piece in 'L'affaire', as the French termed the Dreyfus scandal, Pierre Waldeck-Rousseau (above) was identified as such in the Centuries.

THE CENTURIES

Only by reading the prophecies – and the violent world events which they seem tailored to – can the enthusiast of Nostradamus really begin to grasp his astonishing powers. There follow some of the most remarkable events that this remarkable individual foresaw, together with interpretations as to their meanings. Some of his more foreboding prophecies, dealing with cataclysmic events yet to come, are left, appropriately, until the end.

CENTURY I, QUATRAIN 7
Arrived too late, the act has been done. The wind was against them, letters intercepted on their way. The conspirators were fourteen of a party. By Rousseau shall these enterprises be undertaken.
TRANSLATION: This is widely regarded as Nostradamus's foretelling of the Dreyfus scandal which rocked France at the turn of this century. Alfred Dreyfus was a Jewish officer of the General Staff falsely accused of passing on vital military intelligence to the arch-enemy, Germany. Nostradamus mentions letters – and indeed, it was later learned, shortly before Dreyfus was pardoned and released from Devil's Island, that faked documents had smeared him in the first place. The term '*vent contraire*' in the language of Nostradamus is interpreted by scholars as meaning political, anti-semitic reasons for his false arrest. But by far the most interesting part of the quatrain is the mention of Rousseau in the last line. Waldeck Rousseau was perhaps the most virulent, violent Dreyfus accuser. And there were, it is believed, no less than 14 generals, staff officers and politicians involved in the conspiracy to brand Dreyfus a traitor.

CENTURY I, QUATRAIN 18
Because of French discord and negligence an opening shall be given to the Mohammedans. The land and sea of Siena will be soaked in blood and the Port of Marseilles covered with ships and sails.
TRANSLATION: In these few words Nostradamus predicted the most cataclysmic event yet to befall mankind – World War 2. The discord is a reference to the chaos which France found herself in during 1940 which allowed the armies of Italy, allied with Hitler, to march into Africa, where their blood was spilled in the desert. The harbour at Marseilles was in German hands and remained a busy port throughout the war.

CENTURY I, QUATRAIN 26
The great man will be struck down in the day by a thunderbolt. An evil deed, foretold by the bearer of a petition. According to the prediction another falls at night time. Conflict at Reims, London and pestilence in Tuscany.
TRANSLATION: This is a prime example of the 'open to interpretation' tag that applies to so many of Nostradamus's predictions, but several historians believe that he is referring to the twin assassinations of the

Kennedy brothers, John and Robert. Gunshots are the 'thunderbolts' with one dying during the day – JFK – and his brother being murdered five years later in June 1968. The petition mentioned could be a reference to the numerous death threats both received while in public life, and the mention of the three places refers to the anguish that swept the world at the news of the deaths.

CENTURY I, QUATRAIN 60
An Emperor will be born near Italy, who will cost the Empire very dearly. They will say, when they see his allies, that he is less a prince than a butcher.
TRANSLATION: Nostradamus predicted the arrival on Earth of Napoleon I, France's greatest warrior son who was indeed born closer to Italy than France upon the island of Corsica. A squanderer of men and resources in his endless campaigns, he cost France dearly in both – hence the additional reference to butchery. Nostradamus had great success in predictions about Napoleon and the Centuries are dotted with references to him.

CENTURY I, QUATRAIN 64
At night they will think they have seen the sun, when they see the half pig man: Noise, screams, battles seen fought in the skies. The brute beasts will be heard to speak.
TRANSLATION: In this remarkable quatrain Nostradamus foresaw a battle in the skies, a totally unique and unknown experience in

NOSTRADAMUS SAW THAT AT FIRST NAPOLEON WOULD BE HAILED AS A GREAT PRINCE, AND THEN AS A BLOODY BUTCHER OF MEN.

How painful it must have been for a true patriot such as Nostradamus to come to terms with his own prophecy foretelling French humiliation at Waterloo (below). Here is Wellington encouraging British troops before the battle.

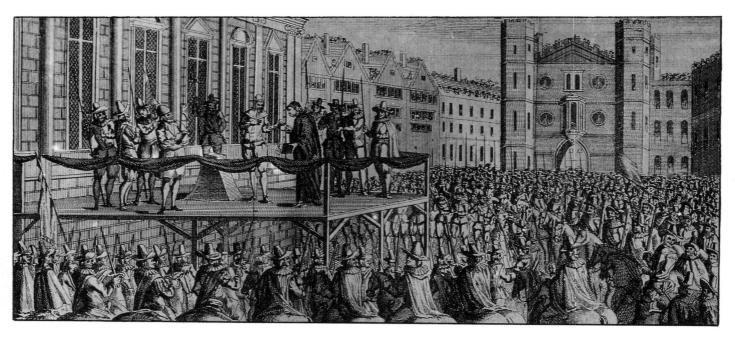

King Charles I (1600–49) on the block (above)*, as predicted in Quatrain 49.*

Below: *An engraving of Oliver Cromwell, who was foretold by Nostradamus.*

the times he came from. 'Sun' means searchlight, piercing the sky; pig-like man perfectly sums up the ghoulish appearance of an aviator in goggles and oxygen mask, distending his face like a pig. 'Brute beasts' are the men, speaking to each other over their voice microphones and the

screams may be, according to Cheetham in her work on Nostradamus, the whine of bombs as they fall to Earth.

CENTURY I, QUATRAIN 97
That which neither weapon nor flame could accomplish will be achieved by a sweet speaking tongue in a council. Sleeping, in a dream, the king will see the enemy not in war or of military blood.

TRANSLATION: This relates to the death of Henri III of France in 1589, a monarch who did not die in combat or jousting, but who was assassinated by a monk who pretended he wanted to pass on a message to him. The reference to the dream means the victim will have a premonition of his death – as was the case. Henri III told his royal circle three nights before his murder that he had dreamed of his violent end.

The preceding quatrains give the reader an idea of the style that Nostradamus employed with his predictions. He ranged over the whole gamut of human affairs and emotions: peace and war, love and hate, religion and disbelief.

QUATRAINS ON ENGLAND

In the following sections more of his predictions are grouped according to individual subjects. England was a source of endless intrigue and curiosity for Nostradamus – he believed that the English were to be envied and closely watched at the same time. Perhaps that is why he foresaw so much of how British society would develop.

CENTURY I, QUATRAIN 23

In the third month, at sunrise, the Boar and the Leopard meet on the battlefield. The fatigued Leopard looks up to heaven and sees an eagle playing around the sun.

TRANSLATION: Nostradamus saw the end of Napoleon at Waterloo, the boar signifying the forces of Prussia which teamed up with those of the leopard – England, for Napoleon referred to the British lion on her armed forces' standards as the English Leopard – for the final crushing blow aimed at Boney's ambitions on the Continent. The eagles are those of Napoleon's standards, the Imperial Eagles. The English Leopard is indeed exhausted, but Napoleon knows the end is near.

CENTURY III, QUATRAIN 80

He who had the right to reign in England shall be driven from the throne, his counsellor abandoned to the fury of the populace. His adherents will follow so low a track that the usurper will come to be protector.

TRANSLATION: This prophecy foretold the fall of Charles I. Nothing could be clearer – the king was driven from his throne and his righthand-man Strafford was beheaded. The Scots, his countrymen, sold the king back to Parliament in 1646 for a sum of £400,000 after which Cromwell – referred to in the French version as 'Le bâtard' – became Lord Protector, not the king.

CENTURY IX, QUATRAIN 49

Ghent and Brussels will march past Antwerp, the Senate at London will put their King to death; salt and wine will be applied contrariwise, so that they will set the whole kingdom in disarray.

TRANSLATION: This is the foretelling of the death of Charles I; ironically Quatrain 49, as the king was executed in 1649. Salt and wine was used as a metaphor by Nostradamus for force and wisdom, and is a good example of the vagueness attached to so many of his predictions. The references to the Netherland cities in the first line concerns a war in the Low Countries.

CENTURY VIII, QUATRAIN 76

A butcher more than king rules England. A man of no birth will seize the government by violence. Of loose morals, without faith or law, he will bleed the earth. The hour approaches me so near that I breathe with difficulty.

TRANSLATION: If the preceding quatrain was obscure, then this foretelling of the coming of Oliver Cromwell into English national life could not be clearer. Charles Ward in his work wrote: 'Here we have a most remarkable forecast. It puts into a clear light what view Nostradamus had formed

Queen Victoria (above) as she appeared in 1876, the empress of a mighty empire upon which the Sun never set. An avowed and ardent royalist, Nostradamus would no doubt have approved of this iron lady of her times.

Below: *Elizabeth I, England's Virgin Queen, whose 'triumphant' reign was spelled out in Quatrain 74 of Century VI.*

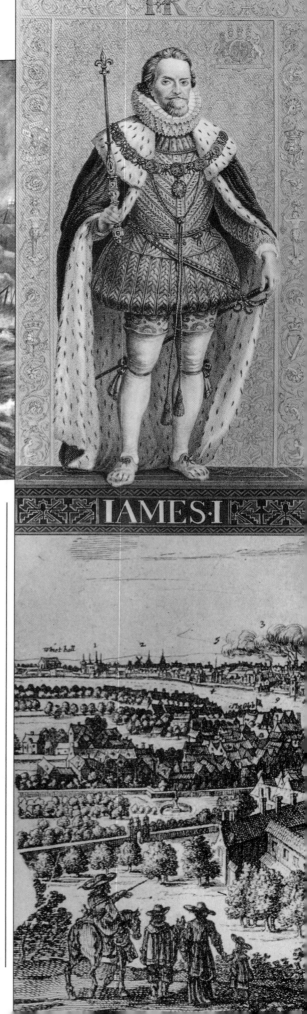

IAMES·I

These floating platforms of Spanish policy and grand design (above) *were broken by the Englishman Francis Drake. But their end had been seen years before by Nostradamus.*

Above right: *James I, whose ascension was foretold in a quatrain which also prophesied massive floods. The master was right on both counts.*

The Great Fire of London as seen from Bankside (right). *Fire consumed the old medieval city for good – and with it much of the splendid architecture of the age.*

of Cromwell. There appears to have been visually present to him the butcher-like face of Cromwell, with its fleshy conch and hideous warts. This seems to have struck him with such a sense of vividness and horror that he is willing to imagine that the time is very near at hand. A full century had, however, to elapse, but he sighs as with a present shudder, and the blood creeps.' It is a departure from the norm in the Centuries in that in it Nostradamus has imparted a sense of the genuine revulsion he felt, giving the reader an idea of how horror-stricken he was when the prophecy came upon him.

CENTURY X, QUATRAIN 100
England the Pempotam will rule the great empire of the waters for more than 300 years. Great armies will pass by sea and land; the Portuguese will not be satisfied.
TRANSLATION: This is the very last quatrain of the last Century but, as stated before, there was no order to the prophecies written down. Most scholars regard this as a statement on the greatness of the British Empire, stretching from Elizabethan times through to the reign of Queen Victoria, when indeed *Pax Britannica* ruled the

waves and the world before modern times sharply reduced her power and influence. Portugal is mentioned because she is Britain's oldest ally in treaties that go back almost 1000 years – although, of course, it was practically half that time ago when Nostradamus penned his prediction. Pempotam is a good illustration of the quasi-classical words that Nostradamus typically peppered his prophecies with – it derives from the Greek *pan*, meaning all, and the Latin *potens*, meaning powerful.

CENTURY IV, QUATRAIN 96
The elder sister of the British Isle shall be born 15 years before her brother; true to her intervening promise, she will succeed to the kingdom of the balance.

TRANSLATION: This means that Mary, elder sister of Edward VI, shall ascend the throne of England. Nostradamus got it slightly wrong here – she was 26, not 15, years older than her brother. She ascended to the throne with the aid of husband William of Orange. The phrase 'kingdom of balance' is one of those pithy comments that often laced the quatrains. In using it, Nostra-damus draws attention to England's continual quest for a balance of power in Europe and the world, so that no state should outgrow another either militarily or politically and thus threaten stability.

CENTURY VI, QUATRAIN 74
The rejected one shall at last reach the throne, her enemies found to have been traitors. More than ever shall her period be triumphant. At seventy she shall go assuredly to death, in the third year of the century.

TRANSLATION: Elizabeth I was long with-held from the throne – and, of course, when she ascended to it she naturally regarded all those who had kept her from it as enemies and traitors. No reign was ever more triumphant than that of Elizabeth as she defied the might of the Catholic Church in Rome, destroyed the Spanish Armada and seized Spanish lands in the Americas. England flourished as she had never done before with righteous pride in great achievements. And, as Nostra-damus predicted, Elizabeth died when she was 70.

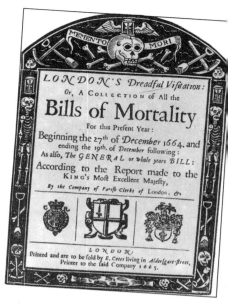

Above: *The Bills of Mortality, a 1665 publication chronicling those who died in an outbreak of plague, one of many that wreaked havoc upon London.*

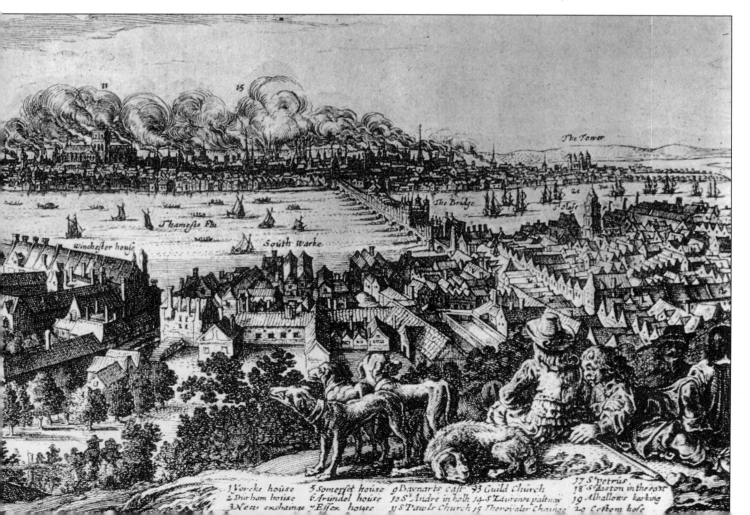

Prince Charles, pictured here in polo outfit (above). The medieval sage was amazingly accurate when it came to describing the trials and tribulations of the House of Windsor. Only time will tell whether he will be the last British king – if he becomes king at all.

'THIS MAY MEAN THAT PRINCE CHARLES WILL BE THE LAST KING ON THE BRITISH THRONE.'

CENTURY III, QUATRAIN 70
Great Britain comprising England, will come to be inundated very forcibly by the waters. The new league in Italy will make war such that all band against any one of the cosignatories.
TRANSLATION: England became Great Britain when Scotland was united with her in 1603 at the accession of James I, who assumed the title 'King of Great Britain'. Historians believe the floods Nostradamus speaks of occurred around the end of January 1607, when the sea breached dykes in Somerset and overflowed the countryside. An old Latin book called *Rerum in Gallia, Belgia, Hispania et Anglia* gives details of the disaster, an almost apocalyptic event at the time.

CENTURY II, QUATRAINS 51, 52, 53
The blood of the just shall be required of London, burnt by fireballs in thrice twenty and six; the ancient lady shall fall from its

high place and many edifices of the same sort shall be destroyed.
Through many nights the earth shall tremble; in the spring two shocks follow each other: Corinth and Ephesus shall swim in the two seas, war arising between two combatants strong in battle.
The great plague of the maritime city shall not diminish till death is sated for the just blood, basely sold and condemned for no fault. The great Cathedral outraged by feigning saints.
TRANSLATION: Historians by tradition have grouped these three quatrains together when analysing their meaning. The first is an astonishingly accurate description of the Great Fire of London, which happened in 1666, the year Nostradamus predicted. St Paul's is, in the original, taken to be the '*Dame antique*' which falls to the flames. The 'just blood' or blood of the just is a reference to the many innocents who died in their wooden homes as the fire, which started in a baker's shop, levelled the medieval city. Nostradamus was no republican; he believed in the divine right of kings and would have seen the fire visited upon London as a fit punishment for the execution of Charles I.

The second quatrain concentrates on the English war with the United Provinces of the Netherlands between 1665 and 1667. 'Cruising' within the narrow channel separating England from Europe, he draws a simile with Aegean waters – Corinth for England, Ephesus for Antwerp.

The third concerns the Black Death, or Great Plague, which devastated London in 1665. 'Maritime city' (due to its dependence on shipping and trade) was a common description of the English capital in use during Nostradamus's day. The outrage he refers to is most probably his own; a confirmed Catholic, he viewed with dismay the protestantism which he foresaw arising in England against the church he loved.

CENTURY IV, QUATRAIN 89
Thirty of London shall conspire secretly against their king; upon the bridge the plot shall be devised. These satellites shall taste of death. A fair-haired king shall be elected, native of Friesland.
TRANSLATION: In 1689 William III – a fair-haired native of Friesland – became king of England after sailing from Holland. It is

interesting to note that when Nostradamus was alive the possibility of a Dutchman taking over the throne of England was as likely as a Soviet politician taking over the White House! Experts estimate that between 30 and 50 opponents of James II conspired to get William on the throne – and that the satellites facing death are his supporters.

CENTURY III, QUATRAIN 57

Seven times you will see the British nation change, dyed in blood for two hundred and ninety years. Not at all free through German support, Aries fears for the protectorate of Poland.

TRANSLATION: The second part is easy enough – Britain going to war for the sake of Poland, as was the case in 1939. It is the first part which vexes historians, wondering when it is that the 290 years starts from. There are some who believe that it is a reference to Prince Charles. Erika Cheetham says: 'This may mean that Prince Charles will be the last King on the British throne.'

CENTURY VI, QUATRAIN 41

The second leader of the kingdom of Annemarc, through those of Frisia and the British Isles, will spend more than one hundred thousand marks, attempting in vain a voyage to Italy.

TRANSLATION: Perhaps rather tenuously, experts believe the reference to Annemarc pertains to Princess Anne and Captain Mark Phillips. At the time of writing England and Frisia had the same ruler – Philip of Spain,

husband to Mary of England and ruler of the Netherlands. In Century IV, Quatrain 27, there is a reference to 'Dannemark' which may be construed as also being about the royal couple – a well-concealed Nostradamus riddle, and one that has yet to be fully understood.

CENTURY VIII, QUATRAIN 82

Thin, tall and dry like reeds, playing the good valet in the end will have nothing but his dismissal, sharp poison and letters in his collar, he will be caught escaping into danger.

TRANSLATION: Her Majesty Queen Elizabeth II was mortified – as was the nation – when the keeper of her royal art collection, Anthony Blunt, was exposed as one of the Oxbridge communist traitor ring which included such notorious agents as Kim Philby and Guy Burgess. He was a trusted official who betrayed his trust at the highest levels.

Above: *The Duke of Windsor and his duchess, formerly Wallis Simpson, the woman for whom he relinquished a crown and an empire.*

Left: *A picture of happiness at the time of their 1973 wedding – Princess Anne and Captain Mark Phillips. The 'Annemarc' quatrain may refer to them but it is still a riddle to experts.*

The great warrior son of France, Napoleon, featured extensively in the predictions. His birthplace is shown **(above)**, together with his retreat from the field at Waterloo **(below)**.

her sister Mary Tudor to the throne. Humble in the days before she became monarch, she nevertheless made up for it with monumental pride during her reign.

CENTURY X, QUATRAIN 19
The day she will be saluted as queen, the prayers coming the day after the blessing. The account is right and valid; once humble, there was never a woman so proud.
TRANSLATION: A reference to Queen Elizabeth I of England, after she succeeded

CENTURY X, QUATRAIN 22
Not wanting to consent to divorce, afterwards recognized as unworthy, the king of the islands will be forced to flee, and one put in his place who has no sign of kingship.
TRANSLATION: As clear as a bell – the abdication of Edward VIII over his love affair with the divorced American woman, Wallis Simpson. He was forced to leave his homeland because of the establishment's disdainful view of the woman he loved. George VI, who was not in line for the throne, finally became king.

QUATRAINS ON NAPOLEON

Nostradamus gave many predictions for Napoleon, the soldier-statesman who took

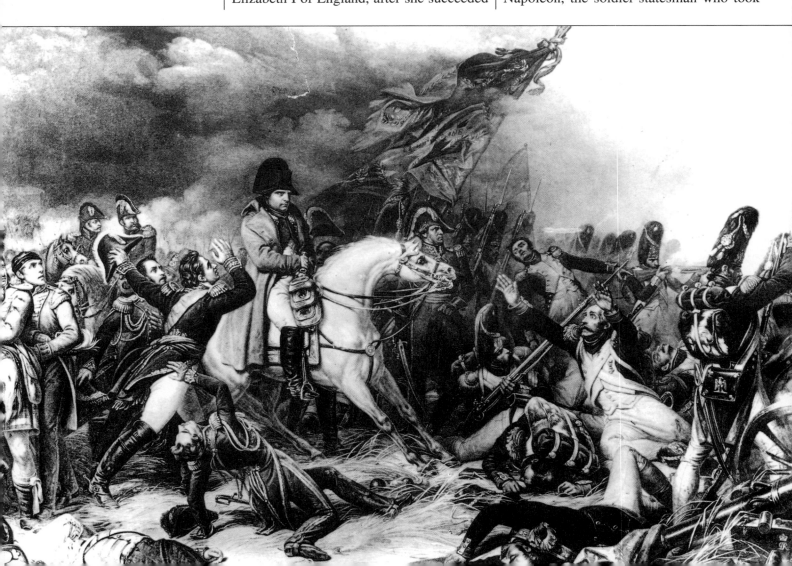

France to undreamed-of heights in his wars of conquest. An avowed royalist, perhaps the prophet saw in him some of the greatness which he believed France lost after the Revolution of 1789 – something he also foretold. There follows Nostradamus's most amazing predictions on Napoleonic rule – quatrains which, no matter which way they are interpreted, leave no room for misunderstanding about this great warrior-statesman whose arrival he predicted.

CENTURY III, QUATRAIN 35

In the Southern extremity of Western Europe, a child shall be born of poor parents, who by his tongue shall seduce the French army; his reputation shall extend to the Kingdom of the East.

TRANSLATION: Napoleon's birthplace was Corsica, his parents poor and his proclamations of greatness ('*la gloire*') for France and her warriors electrified the troops under his command. The last line may refer to his famous expedition to Egypt or his designs upon the throne of Imperial Russia, which ended in defeat and misery in the winter campaign of 1812.

CENTURY IX, QUATRAIN 33

Hercules, King of Rome and Denmark, surnamed the triple giant of France, shall make Italy tremble and the wave of St Mark, first in renown of all monarchs.

TRANSLATION: In his book, Ward argues that Nostradamus in this quatrain not only predicts the arrival of Napoleon but also the whole Napoleonic dynasty. He says: 'There was a Celtic Hercules fabled to draw men by their ears, but this Hercules means the Napoleonic dynasty. As to King of Rome, Napoleon actually assumed that title, and later on he conferred it upon his son by Marie Louise.'

CENTURY V, QUATRAIN 60

It will have chosen badly in the cropped one, its strength will be sapped badly by him. So great will be the fury and violence that they will say that he is butchering his countrymen with fire and sword.

TRANSLATION: Traces of the bitterness and disenchantment which the French began to feel about Napoleon, after the euphoria of his earlier victories had worn off. Here

there is none of the *élan*, the glory: merely a sense of bitterness and recrimination as Frenchmen die on battlefields all across Europe.

CENTURY X, QUATRAIN 24

The vanquished prince is exiled in Italy, escaped by sea sailing past Genoa and Marseilles. He is then crushed by a massive concentration of foreign armies. Though he escapes the fire the bees will be drained to extinction.

TRANSLATION: Following his flight from Elba, Napoleon landed in the south of France, near Marseilles, where he rallied

At the end it was Napoleon's élite guard (above) *who were all that were left with unflinching loyalty to their emperor. They were truly the last symbols of 'la gloire' that he dreamed of for France.*

troops for the final showdown with foreign armies on French soil. It took place, of course, at Waterloo, where the massed legions of Britain and Prussia decimated him. The bees 'drained to extinction' is a clever touch. The bees being Napoleon's emblem, Nostradamus shows that his ambitions have been thwarted, his power spent, yet he is not dead.

CENTURY VIII, QUATRAIN 61
Never shall he in broad daylight, reach to the symbol of sceptre-bearing rule. Of all his possessions none will be of a settled

Below: *In Notre Dame Cathedral the man whom Nostradamus foresaw as an ominous influence on French affairs takes the step from mortal to demi-god when he proclaims himself emperor.*

permanency, conferring of the Gallic cock a gift of the armed legion.
TRANSLATION: This is taken to mean that the Emperor Napoleon will never enjoy a settled seat of firmly established government, but he does bequeath a unique gift to France, one which changed the way nations recruited their forces and the way they fought wars. Until Napoleon's time, armies consisted of professional recruits or mercenaries. Napoleon conscripted huge national armies which effectively made Europe an armed camp – the 'armed legion' of the last line of the quatrain. Some believe there may be a hint in the quatrain in 'settled permanency' to the graveyards of Spain and Portugal where so many of his brave soldiers fell fighting for him.

CENTURY IV, QUATRAIN 26
The great swarm of bees shall rise, that none can tell from whence they came. Night's ambush; the jay beneath the tiles. City betrayed by five tongues not naked.
TRANSLATION: The bees in question stand for the massed ranks of the Napoleonic army, and also his personal emblem which was woven on to embroideries which he carried into battle. Ward believes that the meaning of 'none can tell from whence they came' is a reference to the *bonhomie* and brotherly love engendered by the Revolution – that men are no longer distinct classes, but a single unit united in a common cause. The second part of the quatrain refers to a five-man committee that literally handed Paris over to Napoleon during the coup of 9 November 1797, who were bribed to give way to his consular officers. The coup was planned the night before. In the French, Nostradamus cites the word '*treilhos*' which most interpret as the Tuileries, which became Napoleon's headquarters. Students of Nostradamus are intrigued by this quatrain as it is the only one he wrote in a purely Provençal dialect.

CENTURY VII, QUATRAIN 13
The short-haired man shall assume authority, in maritime Toulon, tributary to the enemy; he will afterwards dismiss as sordid all who oppose him; and for fourteen years direct a tyrant.
TRANSLATION: The English had seized Toulon in the name of Louis XVII and held it for a few months until Napoleon retook

*'Not tonight, Josephine',
goes the old joke; here* (left)
*the emperor sits with his
mistress in an ornate salon
as she is attended by a lady-
in-waiting.*

it. He overturned its government and suppressed free speech in a tyranny which lasted until his overthrow after the battle of Waterloo – a 14-year period. 'Sordid' is generally believed to be a reference to the English, whom Nostradamus believed never had any right to be in France at any time in history.

CENTURY VIII, QUATRAIN 57

From a simple soldier he will rise to the empire, from the short robe he will attain the long. Able in arms, in church government he shows less skill; he raises or depresses the priests as water a sponge.
TRANSLATION: Napoleon was a plain soldier in 1785, consul for life in 1799 and emperor from 1804 until 1814. He changed the formal consular short robe for longer ones. Valiant in battle, he was less skilled in ecclesiastical affairs; nevertheless, he vexed the priests and penetrated into every nook and cranny of their office.

CENTURY I, QUATRAIN 88

He shall have married a woman just before the divine wrath falleth on the great prince; and his support shall dwindle in a sudden atrophy; Counsel shall perish from this shaven head.
TRANSLATION: This is a reference to his infidelity to Marie-Louise of Austria – his wife – with Josephine Beauharnais, his mistress. The shaven head is regarded as an unmistakable reference to Napoleon by Nostradamus experts, relating to the former's close-cropped hair. Counsel perishing from his shaven head alludes to good judgement fleeing Napoleon – perhaps as the result of epilepsy.

Below: *Journey's end for the warrior is Elba – his ultimate exile where spartan living and few home comforts are an unpleasant change from the lifestyle he enjoyed as emperor.*

CENTURY I, QUATRAIN 4
Throughout the universe a monarch shall arise, who will not be long in peace nor life; the bark of St Peter will then lose itself, being directed to its greatest detriment.

TRANSLATION: This is the Emperor Napoleon reviving his pretensions and ambitions to the Holy Roman Empire, but as Nostradamus says, he was doomed to enjoy neither peace, nor life as an emperor, for long. Pope Pius VII first crowned Napoleon as emperor and then became his prisoner when the dictator annexed the Papal States to France in 1809. Religious anarchy existed in France during this time.

Above: *The Russian winter destroyed Napoleon's forces in 1812 as he approached, and then retreated from, Moscow. Nostradamus also successfully predicted the Hitler debacle in Russia a century and a half later.*

Astride Bocephalus, his great white charger (right), Napoleon leads his conquering army to the pyramids, a great wonder of the ancient world.

CENTURY II, QUATRAIN 44

The eagle, drifting in her cloud of flags, by other circling birds is beaten home. Till war's hoarse trumpet and the clarion shrill, recall her senses to the insensate dame.

TRANSLATION: The eagle – the Napoleonic eagle carried by his legions – is in full retreat from the gates of Moscow in the 1812 winter campaign which decimated his legions. The other birds are a reference to the imperial eagles of Russia, Prussia and Austria chasing it all the way back to Paris. The martial music and devastating defeat bring France back to its senses and end in the ultimate defeat of Napoleon.

CENTURY X, QUATRAIN 86

Like a griffon the King of Europe will come, accompanied with those of the north. Of red and white there will be a great number, and they will go against the King of Babylon.

TRANSLATION: The King of Europe is Louis XVII, coming like the mythical griffon, marching with legions dressed in red and white – Austrian and British troops – who will enter Paris, here described as Babylon.

CENTURY VI, QUATRAIN 89

Between two prisons, bound hand and foot, with his face anointed with honey and fed with milk, exposed to wasps and flies, and tormented with the love of his child, his cupbearer will false the cup that aims at suicide.

TRANSLATION: Napoleon, after being consecrated by Pius VII, and anointed with honey and milk, is then imprisoned in Elba and St Helena. The wasps are a reference again to the imperial bees. The two prisons are also taken to mean two wretched states he alternated between after he destroyed his family with his philandering.

CENTURY II, QUATRAIN 99

Roman land as interpreted by the augurs will be greatly molested by the French nation. But the French will come to dread the time of the North wind having driven their fleet too far.

TRANSLATION: In 1812 the ambitions of Napoleon were broken upon the snow-covered steppes of Russia in the campaign that decimated his Imperial Army and his hopes for glory. 'Having driven their fleet

HE DESTROYED HIS FAMILY WITH HIS PHILANDERING.

A cartoon showing the planned Napoleonic onslaught on England (below) – the island of 'shopkeepers' that he was determined to subjugate.

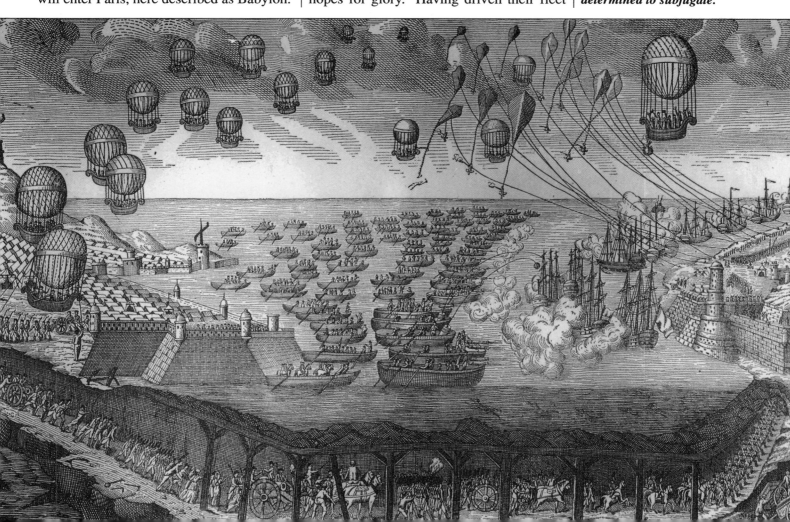

too far' is a clear indication that Napoleon had overextended his forces in his drive on Moscow, the mistake which would be made by that other 'bird of prey', Hitler, nearly a century and a half later. The first part of the quatrain refers to the Vatican States which had been absorbed into the Napoleonic empire in 1810.

CENTURY II, QUATRAIN 29

The oriental will quit his post, to cross the Apennines and see after Gaul. He will transfix the heaven, the mountain ice and snows, striking each of them with his huge magic wand.

TRANSLATION: 'The oriental' is a reference to Napoleon returning to France after his Egyptian expedition, via the Apennines and Alps. Napoleon built marvellous roads through the mountains using his troops, hence the reference to heaven, ice and snows – elements that he kept at bay. His magic wand is nothing more than a huge riding switch that he habitually carried.

CENTURY IV, QUATRAIN 54

Of a name that never belonged to a Gallic king, never was there so terrible a thunderbolt. He made Italy tremble, Spain and the English. He wooed a foreign lady with assiduity.

TRANSLATION: A simple foretelling – one of

Above: *Napoleon at Fontainebleau, from the painting by Paul Delaroche in the Museum of Leipzig. The portrait was painted a year before the emperor's Waterloo defeat.*

A lonely figure, Napoleon strolls in exile upon St Helena (right). *The days of glory are over.*

Left: *The burning ships of Napoleon's Mediterranean fleet at the Battle of Trafalgar. A study of Nostradamus might have dissuaded him from facing the mighty British fleet under Nelson.*

The Iranian royal family (below). The Shah and his queen in the glory days before the Iranian revolution banished the Pahlavi dynasty from the world stage.

several – of the coming of Napoleon, a man with no name like any other. The foreign lady referred to in the last line is believed to be a reference to Marie-Louise of Austria.

CENTURY VIII, QUATRAIN 53
In Boulogne he would make up for his shortcomings, but cannot penetrate the temple of the Sun. He hastens away to perform the very highest things. In the hierarchy he never had an equal.
TRANSLATION: Over the French seaport of Boulogne towers a column dedicated to Napoleon. From its summit on a clear day visitors can see England – and that is all Boney managed to do, even though he intended to launch his invasion from the shores of Boulogne. Westminster Abbey was built on the site of a pagan Sun temple – the high English church which Napoleon never managed to enter. The 'very highest things' he sought to perform included his vanquishing of the Papal States and his attempted conquest of Russia. And he was without equal in his lifetime.

CENTURY IX, QUATRAIN 86
From Bourg la Reine they shall not come straight to Chartres. They shall camp close to Pont Anthony: seven chiefs for peace, wary as martens, shall enter Paris cut off from its army.

Nostradamus warned of a new force in the Middle East. It came in the shape of the Ayatollah Khomeini (above), whose brand of Islamic fundamentalism swept away the Shah.

IRONICALLY NOSTRADAMUS PREDICTED THE TERRIBLE DANGER THAT THE CIA AND THE KGB BOTH FAILED TO FORESEE.

Right: *The monster Adolf Hitler – referred to by Nostradamus as 'Hister'. The war he unleashed was chronicled in many of the Centuries.*

TRANSLATION: After the battle of Waterloo and the final defeat of Napoleon, seven nations were drawn to make peace treaties in which it was hoped Europe could live without war and fear. Austria, England, Prussia, Portugal, Sweden, Spain and Russia – the allied nations against Napoleon – entered Paris on 3 July 1815. The city was stripped of its garrison which was sent to Chartres.

CENTURY I, QUATRAIN 98
The general who led infinite hosts, will end his life far from where he was born. Among five thousand people of strange custom upon a chalk island in the sea.

TRANSLATION: Having mapped out his life – his affairs, his battles, his victories and his defeats – Nostradamus successfully foretold the end for France's greatest warrior son. Death came to him far, far from home, upon the island of St Helena, amid people he neither knew nor whose customs he understood.

QUATRAINS ON GREAT WORLD EVENTS

Nostradamus also gave numerous predictions on Napoleonic successors, including Louis XVIII and Louis-Philippe, but it is perhaps his predictions on great world events, events that have shaped the world we inhabit, that arouse the most interest in him. Some are obscure, others could not be plainer. There follows a cross-section of some of his more incredible, perceptive prophecies.

CENTURY I, QUATRAIN 77
A promontory that stands between two seas; a man who will die later by the bit of a horse; Neptune unfurls a black sail for his man; the fleet near Gibraltar and the Rocheval.

TRANSLATION: Standing between the Mediterranean and the Atlantic is the promontory of rock called Gibraltar. Rocheval is an old French word for Cape Roche. It was between Cape Roche and Gibraltar that the greatest British victory at sea, which determined British policy for a number of years to come, occurred in 1805. In that engagement Lord Nelson, deploying superior skills, destroyed the French fleet. A year later Admiral Villeneuve, one of the French commanders on the day, was strangled at a remote French country inn by someone using the bridle of a horse as a weapon. The black sail

Left: *Geneva, 1926: the League of Nations tries to bring together nations with differing opinions so that war may become a thing of the past.*

The bomb-ravaged streets surrounding St Paul's in London (below). Nostradamus was tragically correct in his prophecy of a new kind of war from the air.

General Winter, the most fearsome opponent of them all, halts and destroys German troops in the advance on the Soviet Union (above).

Opposite: The bright, shining hope of the Western world on his inauguration day in 1961. Nostradamus saw his coming – and his tragic departure.

unfurled on the day of the battle was aboard HMS *Victory*, Nelson's flagship, to commemorate the loss of the commander-in-chief.

CENTURY I, QUATRAIN 70

Rain, famine and war will not cease in Persia; too great a trust will betray the monarch. The actions started in France will end there, a secret sign for one to be sparing.

TRANSLATION: It is bitterly ironic to think that the intelligence agencies of the Western world, including the mighty CIA and KGB, could not predict the end of the Peacock Throne in Iran whereas a man who died half a millennium ago could. In this remarkable vision, Nostradamus saw events unfolding centuries beyond his own time that seemed impossible right up to the time they happened. It was a disbelieving world which watched the Shah of Iran being toppled by the religious leader, the Ayatollah Khomeini, in 1979. Rain, famine and war – and all their ensuing misery – partly caused the Shah to be overthrown, but it was in France that the exiled Ayatollah plotted for years for the religious fundamentalist state to take over from the Pahlavi dynasty. The 'sparing' referred to at the end is interpreted as 'spartan' – certainly a fitting description for the new order which currently reigns in Iran.

CENTURY I, QUATRAIN 34

The bird of prey, flying to the left, before battle is joined with the French, he makes preparations. Some will regard him as good, others bad or uncertain. The weaker party will regard him as a good omen.

TRANSLATION: Throughout the Centuries there are several references to World War 2 and to Adolf Hitler, but this is the first clear portent of the fate to come for mankind. The bird of prey is used by Nostradamus to describe both Napoleon and Hitler – both conquerors of different ages. His reference to the bird flying to the left is a clever one; to the left of France are the Low Countries, through which Hitler launched his mechanized armies in an entirely new form of warfare, the Blitzkrieg, in 1940. The references to the good, bad and uncertain are interpreted as descriptions of the weak and divided French governments in the final days of the Third Republic.

CENTURY II, QUATRAIN 100

In the islands shall be such horrible tumult, that nothing shall be heard except a warlike surprise. So great shall be the attack of the raiders, that everyone shall shelter himself under the great line.

TRANSLATION: This suggests the use of incendiaries and other air-dropped bombs being used on great cities, particularly London, in World War 2, where the inhabitants sheltered from the nightly firestorms in the underground rail system.

CENTURY I, QUATRAIN 47

The speeches of Lake Leman will become angered, the days will drag out into weeks, then months, then years, then all will fail. The authorities will condemn their useless powers.

TRANSLATION: At the end of World War 1 – which, incidentally, Nostradamus also correctly predicted – the combatant nations came together in the belief that a new family of countries was necessary, to bind itself to the aims of perpetual peace instead of future possible wars. The League of Nations first met in Geneva in 1920 – the city which sits on the shores of Lake Leman. With penetrating insight in a few short lines, Nostradamus seems to sum up the futility, the bickering and squabbling which defined the League in its few short years of operation before it dissolved in

The Cuban missile crisis in 1962 brought the world to the brink of nuclear annihilation. And yet it had all been witnessed by Nostradamus five centuries before! Shown here (right) is an intermediate-range ballistic missile base in Cuba.

PROB NUCLEAR STORAGE BUNKER

BATCH PLANTS

PRE-FAB CONSTRUCTION MATERIALS

LAUNCH PAD

CONTROL BUILDING

PROTECTED VEHICLE POSITION

LAUNCH PAD

acrimony before the onset of World War 2. In Quatrain 85 of Century V, Nostradamus further cements his vision of a failed league when he writes: 'Through the Swiss and surrounding areas they will war because of the clouds. A swarm of marine locusts and gnats, the faults of Geneva laid quite bare.'

CENTURY II, QUATRAIN 38
There will be a great number of condemned people when the monarchs are reconciled. But one of them will be so unfortunate that they will hardly be able to remain allied.
TRANSLATION: Shortly before the outbreak of World War 2, a pact was struck between Hitler and Stalin which pledged that each would not attack the other. It was a devastating pact with enormous implications for world peace. No one believed that the architects of the two great

totalitarian states, one fascist, one communist, could work together. However, Nostradamus clearly saw this reconciliation of modern-day monarchs – and the great number of innocents who were murdered on both sides. Finally, the partners in crime fell out in 1942 with Hitler's massive attack on the USSR – his avowed quest since the earliest days of the Nazi party.

CENTURY II, QUATRAIN 24
Beasts wild with hunger will cross the rivers, the greater part of the battlefield will be against Hister. He will drag the leader in a cage of iron, when the child of Germany observes no law.
TRANSLATION: This is the German who observed no law – Adolf Hitler. It was he who loosed his beasts 'wild with hunger' across the river boundaries of Europe and

the USSR, pillaging, murdering and destroying everything in his path. Dragging leaders in a cage of iron is a reference to old medieval practices of humiliating defeated rulers. Hitler humiliated the conquered lands under his swastika in a more sophisticated manner. Critics have argued among themselves over the years whether Nostradamus actually meant a man called Hister or whether he knew he was called Hitler and disguised his true identity, as he was wont to do in so many of his predictions. One thing is certain: the Führer himself was convinced that Nostradamus meant him and great propaganda was made from this quatrain in the years before he embarked on his crusade which would end in millions of deaths.

CENTURY II, QUATRAIN 1
Towards Aquitaine, by British assaults, and by them also great incursions. Rains and frost make the terrain unsafe, against Port Selin they will make mighty invasions.
TRANSLATION: In 1915, utilizing a plan

drawn up by Winston Churchill, the allies embarked on a perilous expedition which, had it succeeded, could well have shortened World War 1, with all its misery and death, by several years. The allies launched an assault on Turkey – the port of Constantinople was known as Selin in the time of Nostradamus – hoping to bypass the Western Front, with all its misery of frost, rain and snow. Again, this is a remarkable example of the powers of Nostradamus. The plan was scoffed at by the high command – even more so in hindsight when the bloodied remnants of the British and empire forces retreated after being held at bay by the Turks at the Dardanelles straits.

CENTURY II, QUATRAINS 56, 57
One whom neither plague nor sword could kill will die on the top of a hill, struck from the sky. The abbot will die when he sees the ruin of the people in the shipwreck trying to hold on to the reef.
Before the battle the great man will fall,

Above: *A Russian soldier sits in the fetid, waterlogged bunker that was the last headquarters – and the suicide location – of Adolf Hitler in May 1945. But Nostradamus suggests that Der Führer may have lived after the collapse of his Third Reich.*

the great one to death, death too sudden and lamented. Born imperfect, it will go the greater part of the way; near the river of blood, the ground is stained.

TRANSLATION: Historians and enthusiasts of the occult have pored over these two quatrains for many years. Most concur that they refer to the killing of John F. Kennedy, although opinion is divided. Nostradamus chronicler Erika Cheetham says: '*Mort trop subite* in the original probably implies an assassination and *nay imparfaict* a person born with a physical deformity. Senator Kennedy was born with a congenital illness. Many of John F. Kennedy's critics agree that he had a great deal of charisma but wonder whether his political judgement would have been sound had he lived to serve another term of office. "It will go the greater part of the way" may well refer to Kennedy's stand against Khrushchev's attempt to set up missile bases in Cuba. The Russian fleet did, after all, get the greater part of the way from Russia. It was after this confrontation that Kennedy was killed at Dallas.'

CENTURY III, QUATRAIN 58
and CENTURY IX, QUATRAIN 90

Near the Rhine from the Noricum Mountains will be born a great man of the people, born too late. He will defend Poland and Hungary and they will never know what became of him.

The Vichy traitors (above). As well as seeing the rise of Hitler, Nostradamus chronicled the treachery of Pétain and Admiral Darlan.

Right: *Israel's prime minister David Ben Gurion, (centre left, wearing jacket), is at the dockside in Haifa in 1948 to see the last British soldier leave the Holy Land's soil.*

A leader of Great Germanies who will come to give help which is only counterfeit. He will stretch the borders of Germany, and will cause France to be divided into two parts. Living fire and death hidden in globes will be loosed, horrible and terrible, by night the enemy will reduce cities to dust.

TRANSLATION: In these two quatrains Nostradamus again gives clear, undisguised warnings of the advent of Adolf Hitler and the terrible revenge he will exact on mankind. The globes he refers to are obviously a reference to bombs falling on cities like London and Berlin, the product of his vicious war. Defending Poland and Hungary – he actually attacked them – could be part of Nostradamus's usual trick of trying to be cryptic about actual events. The final line is interesting in the first quatrain; it could imply that Hitler LIVED after the fall of Berlin. Certainly there has been much dispute about whether or not he and mistress Eva Braun died in the ruins of the bunker as the Russians closed in.

CENTURY III, QUATRAIN 71
Those besieged in the islands for a long time will take strong measures against their enemies. Those outside, overcome, will die of hunger, by such starvation as has never occurred before.

TRANSLATION: This is Nostradamus's way of painting a portrait of embattled Britain at war, blockaded by the U-boats as she builds up her war machine and the resolve of the leaders and the people for total victory over the axis powers grows stronger. The references to those outside and the starvation they suffer is seen as a twofold thing: the starvation and deprivation in conquered Europe and in the concentration camps, and also the starvation of the soul, deprived as it was of love, compassion and religious beliefs under the edicts of the Third Reich.

CENTURY III, QUATRAIN 75
Pau, Verona, Vicenza, Saragossa, swords dripping with blood from distant lands. A very great plague will come with the great shell, relief near but the remedies far away.

TRANSLATION: In 1976 in Seveso, Italy, occurred one of the worst man-made disasters in history. A massive chemical plant explosion destroyed wildlife, contaminated drinking water and agricultural land and caused women to give birth to deformed babies. The cloud of gas drifted across a large section of Italy – but, interestingly enough, the towns that Nostradamus wrote about were not affected, nor was the plan to combat the disaster formulated in them. Much of the land is still unusable, proving that the remedies are indeed still far away.

CENTURY III, QUATRAIN 100
The man least honoured among the French will be victorious over his enemy. Strength and lands he explored in action, when suddenly the jealous party dies from a shot.

TRANSLATION: Recognizing the coming of Charles de Gaulle, a man virtually unknown in France before the collapse of the Third Republic, was a remarkable feat. Strength, in terms of political power and prestige, was gathered during his years in exile as the war raged in various countries, and the envious one dying from a shot is thought to be the traitorous appeaser of the Germans, Admiral Darlan, killed on 24 December 1942. Like Hitler and Napoleon, the quatrains are peppered with references to De Gaulle, supporting many believers' contentions that Nostradamus excelled in prophesying the coming of great men upon the world stage.

A peek at freedom. Through a crack in the Berlin Wall (above) an eastsider gazes through to the West in the days before it was torn down for good.

THE PROPHECY IMPLIES THAT HITLER LIVED AFTER THE FALL OF BERLIN.

Right: *The hero of Verdun, Marshal Philip Pétain, was the traitor of Vichy in World War 2. He agreed to co-operate with the Nazis.*

The mighty Rhine (below), the 'Great River' which Nostradamus referred to in his prophecy about the French Maginot Line.

CENTURY III, QUATRAIN 97

A new law will occupy a new land around Syria, Judaea and Palestine. The great barbarian empire will crumble before the century of the Sun is finished.

TRANSLATION: No one could have foretold in this century, let alone in his day, the creation of the state of Israel in exactly the spot where it would eventually be born in the wake of World War 2, but that is precisely what Nostradamus accomplished. However, part of the prophecy remains unfinished. Nostradamus tags the Arab countries around Israel as 'barbarian' and warns that they will be finished by the end of the 20th century – the century of the Sun.

CENTURY IV, QUATRAIN 32

In those times and areas where the flesh gives way to fish, the common law will be

made in opposition. The old order will hold strong then be removed from the scene entirely, all things common among friends put far behind.

TRANSLATION: Communism falls. Nostradamus did not specify in which country, but it is interesting that the system has effectively collapsed in the USSR. Dried fish, as opposed to fresh meat, was a staple of the grumbling peasants under the communist regime. 'All things common among friends' – i.e., communism and the community spirit it was intended to engender among the proletariat – are broken. In other quatrains Nostradamus foretells an alliance that Russia will make, possibly with the USA. Some already believe that this has happened, interpreting 'alliance' as the business deals that are now taking place due to the fall of the old order.

CENTURY IV, QUATRAIN 61
The old man, mocked and deprived of his position by the foreigner who will suborn him. The hands of his sons are devoured before his face, he will betray his brother at Chartres, Orléans and Rouen.

TRANSLATION: With this quatrain Nostradamus paints one of his clear pictures – about Marshal Pétain, the former hero of Verdun who disgraced his nation in World War 2 by becoming the puppet head of Vichy France, the vassal state of Nazi Germany. During his time as premier he was referred to contemptuously by his subjects as 'The Old Man'. The three French cities mentioned were all liberated by the Allies on the same day, and held strong connections with the old France of Nostradamus's times. Interestingly, each one is the site of some of France's most celebrated and mystical cathedrals, all of which were visited by Nostradamus during his travels and from where he drew divine inspiration for the prophecies.

CENTURY IV, QUATRAIN 80
Near the great river, a great trench, earth excavated, the water will be divided into fifteen parts. The city taken, fire, blood, cries and battle given, the greater part concerned with the collision.

TRANSLATION: Before World War 2 France poured the greatest part of her military

The Maginot Line (above). *Upon this line of pillboxes and forts France gambled her national security – and lost in 1940 when Hitler's panzers merely went around the side of it.*

Right: *The ruins of Paris after the Commune uprising of 1871. The city Nostradamus loved was virtually destroyed.*

Charles de Gaulle, saviour of France **(below),** *in London in 1940 following the shattering news that France and Germany had signed an armistice.*

resources, and her national faith, into a static defence line named after a World War 1 engineer called André Maginot. The line stretched from near the Rhine – 'the great river' – across her north-eastern borders, petering out at the start of the Ardennes forest, which the French high command deemed too thick for armour or artillery to operate in. Ironically, in an earlier quatrain, Nostradamus had already predicted this by pointing out that France's enemies would advance through countries to her left – i.e., the low countries of the Netherlands and Belgium. The collision he refers to is the clash of armies throughout the war.

CENTURY IV, QUATRAIN 100
Fire will fall from the sky on to the royal building when the light of war is weakened. For seven months a great war, people dead through evil, Rouen and Evreux will not fail the king.

TRANSLATION: Nostradamus here predicted the Franco-Prussian War of 1870–71 which sowed the seeds of permanent bitterness between the peoples of France and Germany. The war lasted PRECISELY seven months, during which time a fierce siege of Paris laid waste to many royal buildings. The reference to the Normandy towns of Rouen and Evreux is because they did not become republican along with the rest of France after the war, preferring instead to support a restored monarchy.

CENTURY V, QUATRAIN 45
The great empire will soon be desolate, transformed near the forest of the Ardennes. The bastards will be beheaded by the oldest, Aenodarb will rule, the hawk-nosed one.

TRANSLATION: This foretells the fall of France in 1940, coming as it did via the German advance through the Ardennes forest which the French generals perceived as impenetrable. The bastards are believed to be the two senior French commanders who thoroughly botched battlefield attempts to stem the onrushing tide of German armour, although they were not beheaded, merely captured. The hawk-nosed one is a reference to General de Gaulle, although no one has found a satisfactory explanation for the classical name Aenodarb.

CENTURY V, QUATRAIN 94
He will change into the Greater Germany, Brabant and Flanders, Ghent, Bruges and Boulogne. The truce feigned, the great Duke of Armenia will assault Vienna and Cologne.

TRANSLATION: Again, this is a quatrain concerning Hitler and, more specifically, his designs of conquest upon the world. The 'feigned truce' is seen as the lame excuse he gave to the world upon his invasion of Poland – that he was merely aiding 'ethnic Germans' persecuted by the Poles. The Duke of Armenia is seen as the Russians who, towards the end of the war, invaded Germany from the south and east.

CENTURY VI, QUATRAIN 72
Through feigned fury of a divine emotion the wife of the great one will be badly violated. The judges wishing to condemn such a doctrine, the victim is sacrificed to the ignorant people.

Above: *Gregori Rasputin, the 'Mad Monk' of the Russian imperial court, whose dominance of the Czarina Alexandra led ultimately to the demise of the Romanov family.*

The Great Dictator, Benito Mussolini (above). *His brand of Fascism would lead Italy into ruinous, bloody war.*

TRANSLATION: In this Nostradamus has summed up the plight of the Czarina Alexandra, wife of Czar Nicholas, who became spellbound by the evil monk Rasputin. Rasputin exerted a terrible grip on the Russian court, and thereby Russian life, due to his hocus-pocus about her son's haemophilia which she believed. The 'ignorant people' are the masses with whom the Romanov family were so utterly and so completely out of touch, which led to the Russian Revolution, their downfall and murder.

CENTURY VI, QUATRAIN 31
The king will find that which he desires so greatly; when the Prelate will be wrongfully taken. The reply to the Duce will make him angry; in Milan he will put several to death.
TRANSLATION: The foretelling of the rise to power of Mussolini – together with the title of Duce which he conferred upon himself. In Milan several of Mussolini's opponents were exiled while the Prelate, taken to be the Pope, finds himself in a Catholic country surrounded by the forces of the anti-Christ.

CENTURY VIII, QUATRAIN 80
The blood of innocents, widow and virgin, with many evils committed by the Great Red One, holy images placed over burning candles, terrified by fear, none will be seen to move.
TRANSLATION: In 1917 the Romanov dynasty, which had ruled Holy Russia, was swept away in a great revolution that used the colour red for its flag. The blood of innocents could pertain to the children of the royal household, who were massacred along with czar and czarina, or the many millions that died in the ensuing terror after the Bolsheviks took power. Organized religion, bedrock of the czarist regime, was also outlawed in the new order as prescribed by the followers of Lenin. Some interpret the last line as being about the massacre of the royal family at Ekaterineburg in 1917. 'None will be seen to move' may mean that Nostradamus saw that all were murdered, giving the lie to a woman who, for years afterwards until her death in the late 1980s, claimed she was the Princess Anastasia who escaped from the execution site.

CENTURY IX, QUATRAIN 16
From Castel Franco will bring out the assembly, the ambassadors will not agree and cause a schism. The people of Riviera will be in the crowd, and the great man will be denied entry to the great Gulf.

Below left: *Is this the Grand Duchess Anastasia, who somehow escaped the massacre that befell her parents and siblings? Or is she in fact an impostor who lived a lie all her life?*

TRANSLATION: This is another of those extraordinarily perceptive prophecies in which the master makes no attempt at disguising his portent for the future. In this he warns of the coming of Franco and the Spanish Civil War. The reference to 'the great man being denied entry' refers to Franco's inability to cross the Mediterranean when he was exiled to Morocco. Gattey writes: 'Ingenious commentators have surmised that the personages named are the late General Franco and his predecessor, the dictator Primo de Rivera, and that the verse also refers to the struggle for power between the two men. The last line alludes to Franco's exile in Morocco, or to his meeting on 12th February 1941 with Mussolini on the Riviera, when he refused to permit the troops of the Axis to pass through Spain and attack Gibraltar. The "great Gulf" is the Mediterranean.'

Nostradamus foresaw the Spanish Civil War and Franco's dictatorship in the earlier Quatrain 54 of Century III. He wrote:

One of the great ones shall fly into Spain which will then bleed with a long

Right: *Another of the great European dictators so successfully foreseen by Nostradamus. Here General Franco makes a tour of the party faithful.*

Divining new methods of war in all their grotesque horror seemed to be a special gift belonging to Nostradamus. Here (below) are men of the East Lancashire Regiment in a trench at Givenchy in World War 1.

wound. Armies will pass by the high mountains, destroying all, after which he will reign in peace.

CENTURY IX, QUATRAIN 11
They will come to put the just man wrongfully to death, publicly in the midst he is extinguished. So great a plague will be born in this place that the judges will be forced to flee.

TRANSLATION: This tells of the execution of Charles I of England – while giving an insight again into Nostradamus's belief in the divine right of kings. Charles was beheaded in 1649. The second part of the quatrain is the Great Plague of London which came in 1665. Nostradamus believed that the plague was God's retribution against the men who had overthrown the king.

CENTURY *IX, QUATRAIN 55*
The dreadful war which is prepared in the west, the following year pestilence will come, so horrible that neither young, nor old, nor animal will survive. Blood, fire, Mercury, Mars, Jupiter in France.
TRANSLATION: Another two-in-one quatrain in which he successfully foretells World War 1 – the war in the west, or Western Front – and the massive influenza outbreak across Europe which followed it, w˙ ˙ch claimed more lives than the fighting. ˙e planetary references refer to their position at the time the prediction would come true – again, correctly.

CENTURY *IX, QUATRAIN 77*
The kingdom is taken, the king will plot while the lady is taken to death by these sworn by lot. They will refuse life to the queen's son and the mistress suffers the same fate as the wife.

TRANSLATION: Erika Cheetham believes this to be one of his more 'impressive' quatrains. She writes: 'After the [French] royal family's imprisonment, Louis XVI was executed in January 1793. He was condemned by the convention who elected these powers to itself. However, the queen, who was not executed until the following October, had a newly created Revolutionary tribunal elected to judge her, which was selected by lot. This was an institution unknown to France in Nostradamus' day. The third line tells the fate of Louis XVII. Whether he died or lived abroad is irrelevant; his kingdom was denied to him. Finally, the most interesting line of all. While the queen was imprisoned in the Conciergerie, the old mistress of Louis XV, Mademoiselle du Barry, was taken for a while to the prison of Sainte Pelagie.'

Above: *The end for Marie Antoinette, extravagant bride of the king of France. Here the Dauphin is torn from her before she is led away to her own execution.*

'PESTILENCE WILL COME, SO HORRIBLE THAT NEITHER YOUNG, NOR OLD, NOR ANIMAL WILL SURVIVE.'

New warfare; the Japanese attack at Pearl Harbor (above). It crippled America's Pacific fleet in 1941, but ultimately led to Japan's unconditional surrender in 1945.

Opposite: *Halley's Comet, the extra-terrestrial orb which Nostradamus refers to in several quatrains through the Centuries.*

CENTURY IX, QUATRAIN 100
A naval engagement will be overcome by night; fire in the ruined ships of the west. A new code, the great coloured ship, anger to the vanquished and victory in a mist.

TRANSLATION: This describes the attack on Pearl Harbor, 7 December 1941, in which the greater portion of the American Pacific Fleet was destroyed in a surprise attack launched before dawn by a Japanese carrier-borne force. The new coding is believed to refer to aircraft launched from ships, a new kind of war which eventually led to the Allies' victory over Japan.

THE SHAPE OF THINGS TO COME

What does the future hold for us, as defined in the writings of Nostradamus? Even the most hardened sceptic must concede that the old sage has had some remarkable successes in interpreting the ages. There follows a selection of some prophecies yet to be realized – culminating in those which could spell doom for mankind if the sleeping seer of Salon got them right.

CENTURY II, QUATRAIN 91
At sunrise a great fire will be seen, noise and light extending to the north. Within the globe death and cries are heard, death awaiting them through weapons, fire and famine.

TRANSLATION: Erika Cheetham believes this to be the portent of a great war between Russia and the USA. Although the threat of nuclear confrontation has abated since the fall of the Berlin Wall and the collapse of communism, many observers think that the

situation is still too volatile to predict lasting peace. If this can be linked with Century II, Quatrain 46, it is ominous indeed. That one states:

After great misery for mankind an even greater approaches when the great cycle of the centuries is renewed. It will rain blood, milk, famine, war and disease. In the sky will be seen a fire, dragging a great trail of sparks.

TRANSLATION: Halley's Comet is obviously the fire in the sky with the sparks trailing behind. It is due to appear again at the end of the century – hopefully without the rain of 'blood, milk, famine, war and disease', which some think could be a third world war.

CENTURY IV, QUATRAIN 99

The brave, elder son of a king's daughter will drive the Celts back far. He will use thunderbolts, so many and in such an array, few and distant, then deep into the west.

TRANSLATION: Celts are taken to mean the French. Not being part of NATO, does Nostradamus predict a new tyrant within Europe ready to use thunderbolts – possibly nuclear or chemical missiles – to seize the unprepared French?

CENTURY V, QUATRAIN 90

In the Cyclades, in Perinthus and Larissa, in Sparta and all of the Peloponnesus, a very great famine, plague through false dust. It will last nine months throughout the whole peninsula.

TRANSLATION: Nostradamus is usually very specific about plagues or famines. Here he talks of 'false dust', i.e., possibly man-made, which has led many to believe that this could be a reference to chemical or biological warfare. The Balkans have long been a troublespot in the world – World War 1 was sparked off over them and, more recently, the bloody civil war between Bosnia and Serbia has been fought over parts of the area.

CENTURY VI, QUATRAIN 5

A great famine, the result of a pestilence that will extend its long rain the length of

Endless suffering – Canadian engineers, part of a UN peacekeeping contingent (below), *in the killing fields of Bosnia.*

the Arctic pole. Samarobrin one hundred leagues from the hemisphere; they will live without law, exempt from politics.

TRANSLATION: Samarobrin has yet to be defined, but most analysts concur that Nostradamus is back to his theme of a chemical fallout on the Earth, possibly emanating from far out in space. Some argue that he foresees a manned space station, where people will indeed live without politics and normal laws, and whose use is corrupted to rain down death on the people below.

CENTURY VI, QUATRAIN 97
The sky will burn at forty-five degrees, fire approaches the great New City. Immediately a huge, scattered flame leaps up when they want to have proof of the Normans.

TRANSLATION: If this one is true then New Yorkers must fear a massive aerial bombing at some point which will destroy most of the metropolis. New York County actually lies between the 40° and 45° parallel in the USA. The last line is typically muddled and no one seems to have come up with a satisfactory explanation of his reference to 'the Normans'.

CENTURY VI, QUATRAIN 24
Mars and the Sceptre will be in conjunction, a calamitous war under Cancer. A short time afterwards a new king will be anointed who will bring peace to the earth for a long time.

TRANSLATION: Seen by most as another reference to war towards the end of this century – but this one more hopeful, with the promise of a new peacemaker to give Earth some respite.

CENTURY VIII, QUATRAIN 9
While the eagle is in unison with the cockerel at Savona, the eastern sea and Hungary. The army at Naples, Palermo, the marches of Ancona, Rome and Venice a great outcry by the Barbarian.

TRANSLATION: Here Nostradamus warns of a Moslem invasion of Italy, naming key Italian cities as targets for the hordes. Italy, home to the Church of Rome, would make a key target for religious fundamentalists seeking to exert domination over the Christian church. And with the rise of

Islamic fundamentalism around the world it is not too far-fetched a prophecy.

CENTURY VIII, QUATRAIN 81
The new empire in desolation will be changed from the Northern pole. From Sicily will come such trouble that it will bother the enterprise tributary to Philip.

TRANSLATION: This tells of a civilization moving southwards, shifting the centre of power in a world region – possibly North America – leading some to believe it will occur after a nuclear holocaust as people look for new life and sustenance in

Above: *The Statue of Liberty at the entrance to the New York harbour. If Nostradamus has got it right the Big Apple will one day burn under a massive aerial bombardment.*

unaffected zones. The references to Sicily and Philip imply that the war might emanate from there or Spain – once ruled by King Philip. This might link up with Century VIII, Quatrain 9, concerning the Moslem invasion of Italy. If Moslem fundamentalists rule this part of Europe perhaps Nostradamus is implying that nuclear war may be triggered in the future.

CENTURY IX, QUATRAIN 83

The Sun in twenty degrees of Taurus, there will be a great earthquake; the great theatre full up will be ruined. Darkness and trouble in the air, on sky and land, when the infidel calls upon God and the saints.

TRANSLATION: Twenty days after the Sun moves into Taurus is 10 April, so Nostradamus gives us the date of a catastrophic earthquake – one which modern-day scientists believe must apply to the San Andreas fault, and more specifically to the destruction of San Francisco, which all experts say MUST happen – it is merely a question of when.

CENTURY X, QUATRAIN 67

A very great trembling in the month of May, Saturn in Capricorn, Jupiter and Mercury in Taurus. Venus also in Cancer, Mars and Virgo, then hail will fall greater than an egg.

TRANSLATION: Nostradamus displays his extensive knowledge of the planets in this quatrain, describing a rare event in the heavenly bodies when all fall into place in a set pattern. Astrologers say the planets will not be in conjunction in this manner until May 3755. Then the world can expect massive earthquakes, followed by enormous hailstones.

CENTURY X, QUATRAIN 72
In the year 1999 and seven months there
will come from the skies the Great King of
Terror. He will bring back to life the great
King of the Mongols. Before and after war
reigns happily.

TRANSLATION: It is perhaps fitting – if not
sombre – to end a study of Nostradamus
upon his most melancholy, unfulfilled
prophecy. He tells of an Asian anti-Christ,
steeped in the traditions of the warrior
hordes of the Mongols, visiting death and
destruction upon the face of the globe.
Most experts believe that this new demon
will be an anti-Christ, committed to tearing
down the values of Judaeo-Christian
society as we know them. If Napoleon and
Hitler were the two other anti-Christ
figures that Nostradamus draws in some of
his prophecies, then this will be the third
and final one.

He makes a further reference to this in
Century VIII, Quatrain 77. In that he writes:
The anti-Christ very soon annihilates
the three, seven and twenty years his war
will last. The unbelievers are dead, captive,
exiled: with blood, human bodies, water
and red hail covering the earth.

This implies that the third anti-Christ,
after Napoleon and Hitler – the one yet to
come – will be annihilated, but that it will
take 27 years of fearsome war to do so. The
reference to red hail could mean atomic
fallout, such as that which blanketed the
Japanese cities of Hiroshima and Nagasaki
after the dropping of the atom bombs
towards the close of World War 2.

Although Nostradamus signals the end
of civilization as we know it, there could be
hope still. In Century I, Quatrain 48, he
gives the actual end of the world as much
later. He writes:

**THE THIRD ANTI-CHRIST IS
YET TO COME...IN THE YEAR
1999.**

The ruins of San Francisco
after the tremendous earth-
quake of 1906 (left).
Nostradamus's logic mirrors
that of earthquake specialists
– that the city will once again
be destroyed by earthquakes
and fire. It is merely a
question of when.

Right: *Perhaps more than any other symbol of our age, the mushroom cloud explosion of an atomic bomb has burned itself into mankind's collective soul.*

Twenty-seven years after the reign of the moon passes, seven thousand years another will hold his monarchy. When the sun shall resume his days past, then is my prophecy accomplished and ended.

Erika Cheetham translates his prophecy thus: 'According to Roussat the cycle of the Moon lasted from 1535–1889, which places the date of the first line as 1555, the publication date of the first part of the Centuries. Nostradamus seems to envisage another 7,000 years from that date to the cycle of the sun when all will be accomplished. It is as though Nostradamus believes the Centuries are written at the start of a new era lasting 7,000 years.'

Even after the third anti-Christ, then, there is still hope for humanity.

VISIONS OF THE FUTURE
Prophets, Psychics and Seers

THE ORACLE OF DELPHI

THE ATHENIANS WERE PREPARED TO PAY DEARLY FOR THE ANSWERS TO THE PROBLEMS THAT BESIEGED THEM.

For 1000 years mankind sought guidance from the gods of Olympus at the shrine of Apollo at Delphi.

Below: *The great scholar Homer, seen here meditating upon the* **Iliad.** *He was one of the great chroniclers of the Oracle of Delphi.*

Oracles are shrines where gods are said to speak with mortals through the mouths of priests – and none is more famous than that of the Pythia of Delphi, a shrine constructed by the ancient Greeks in homage to the god Apollo. Here was the most influential oracle of the classical world, built on the slopes of Mount Parnassus, north of the Gulf of Corinth, where people came to commune with their gods and be guided by their wisdom.

The cult of Apollo spread rapidly throughout the ancient world – he was regarded as the best and brightest of the ancient Greek gods as the deity of music, archery, prophecy, healing and animals, and he was identified with the Sun. Legend has it that Jupiter, seeking dominance over the central point of the Earth, despatched two eagles to fly in opposite directions over the globe and they met at Delphi, which the gods then called the Navel of the Earth. Fumes were seen issuing from a cave near the site, laying the foundations for the idea that the spot was mystical and linked with the gods in Olympus. It acquired its Pythian forename from the legend of Apollo slaying the Python, a snake-like dragon.

The oracle was run by priests who interpreted the incoherent ramblings of the Pythia, a middle-aged woman dressed as a young maiden who sat on a tripod inhaling fumes of chopped herbs and spiced oil. It's not known why a certain woman was chosen, but she became the conduit between the priests and the gods, with citizens of Greece paying for the privilege of learning their fortunes. It lasted for 1000 years: after the Greeks the Romans and even conquerors from the Orient believed in its mystical properties. Socrates, the great philosopher, wrote of the profound changes which overcame pilgrims who journeyed to it.

In the 5th and 4th centuries BC it cost an Athenian two days' wages to ask the oracle questions. Mediums – there was always a minimum of three working a shift system – were on hand to work morning to night on the allotted days that consultations with the gods were allowed. Knowledge seekers made written requests to the Pythia and she went into a trance-like state after inhaling the herb and oil mixture. When the incoherent mutterings spewed forth, they were interpreted by the priests for the customer. Apollo's influence over the ancient Greek world – a world of civility, modera-

Left: Apollo Killing the Python, *as painted by J.M.W. Turner and displayed in the National Gallery, London. The dragon and the god were both principal players in fortune telling at the oracle.*

tion and conservatism – is regarded by historians as being particularly important. These values were passed on to the pilgrims at Delphi, making the shrine a moral as well as a metaphysical force for its believers. Carved in a pillar of a temple at Delphi are the maxims of the ancients which governed Greece: 'Know thyself', 'Nothing in excess', 'Go surely', and 'Ruin is at hand'.

Historians believe the first seekers of truth at the oracle wanted merely to learn if their hunting would be good the next day or if their crops would ripen. As time went on the oracle assumed an ever-larger role and the direction of the gods was sought in all the affairs of state. Answers were frequently ambiguous – which left them wide open to interpretation but guaranteed that they could never be accused of being wrong!

The summoning of Olympian guidance at Delphi lasted until well into the Christian epoch. Apollo is said to have delivered his last advice in the year AD 362 to the Emperor Julian who sought to restore pagan gods and worship to his Byzantine empire. Julian said that when he sought advice from Apollo the message came back: 'Tell the king that the curiously built temple has fallen to the ground, that bright Apollo no longer has a roof over his head, or prophetic laurel, or babbling spring. Yes, even the murmuring water has dried up.'

Below: *Socrates, the philosopher, whose humanitarian and scholarly wisdom was embodied in a thousand years of Greek learning.*

ST MALACHY – Predictor of Popes

Right: Pope Pius V, pontiff from 1566 to 1572. Malachy called him 'The Angel of the Wood' in his amazing prophecies on the popes.

Nine hundred years ago an Irish monk predicted the line of popes that would lead the Roman Catholic church up to and beyond modern times.

Pope Innocent III (below), one of the greatest medieval figures. His ecclesiastical reforms were far-reaching.

S. PIVS V. Michael drin'. creat' die 7. Ian Ghisilerius, Alexan- uarij an. 1566. Sed it an.6.men.3.dies 24. Obijt die 1.Ma ij an.1572. Vac. Sed.dies 12.

Using symbolic titles, set down in Latin, Malachy O'Morgair – monk, bishop and later saint of the Catholic Church – bequeathed to the world an astonishing set of prophecies in which he successfully predicted the succession of Roman pontiffs from Celestine II in 1143 to the present day. A learned scholar, a man of outstanding wisdom, virtue and humanity, his stunning prophecies were not even discovered until 400 years after his death.

He was born in Ireland in 1094, and was given the Gaelic name Mael Maedoc ua Morgair. Ireland was a wild, dark place in those times, the only physical and spiritual havens being the monasteries which dotted her bleak landscape. His father, Mugron, was a professor at Armagh, the country's seat of piety and learning, and from his earliest days Malachy – the name which he adopted when he entered the church – was drawn to Christianity. He studied under the Abbot of Armagh and in 1119 was ordained as a priest. He became Abbot of Bangor in 1123. With this rise in his status he embarked upon clerical reforms.

Ireland's ecclesiastical system was in a state of chaos. The church was still basically a tribal hierarchy, based on the system set up by St Patrick. Paganism was rife in the countryside (mainly due to marauding Danes). The clergy was corrupt, the churches in disrepair, the people left in a state of religious limbo between heresy and Catholicism. Malachy made it his task to reform the church. He was responsible for bringing in the Roman liturgy, Christian marriage rites and the Latin mass.

In 1140 he journeyed to Rome and, *en route*, stopped at a French monastery at Clairvaux, where he befriended Abbot Bernard – later St Bernard – who subsequently wrote a contemporary biography of Malachy's life. So impressed was Malachy with the Cistercian way of living, as practised by Bernard and his brothers, that he requested Pope Innocent II at the Vatican to relieve him of his bishopric to become a simple disciple at Clairvaux. The pope refused, saying that there was much work for him still to do in Ireland. While he was in Rome the pope announced that Malachy was to be papal legate over all Ireland. Returning to his country with renewed vigour, Malachy brought paganism to an end and order to the church.

Malachy was intrigued by mystical theology – as was St Bernard – and he demonstrated some amazing prophetical attributes. One story has it that he was able to foretell what he was to be given to eat on a given day three months hence. He even gave a grim prediction regarding himself: that he would die at Clairvaux on his next visit there. Sure enough, on 2 November 1148 while resting there, *en route* to Rome, he passed away surrounded by the entire community. In 1190 he was canonized by Pope Clement III, and became the first Irish-born saint.

His life was well chronicled by St Bernard, and other essays on his life and times have dealt with his good works and his teachings, but no contemporary mention was ever made of the prophecies. It wasn't until 1559, when the Benedictine historian Anrold Wion mentioned them in his work *Lignum Vitae*, that the world knew of their existence. In 1871 the Abbé Cucherat in France put forward his theory that Malachy had visions between 1139 and 1140 during his first papal visit. He said that he committed these visions to paper and handed the manuscript to Pope Innocent II. Innocent II then placed the manuscript in the archives where they remained undisturbed for four centuries. It is still not entirely clear how they eventually surfaced into the public domain. What is patently clear, however, is

both their appeal and their accuracy.

Malachy did not come straight out and say 'so and so will become pontiff'. Instead he used a practice later made famous by Nostradamus, of wrapping up his visions with quirky Latin and secular images. His phrases were short – no more than four words – but within them, say the interpreters of the prophecies, lay the clues to the papal succession. The first, for instance, he called '*Ex Castro Tiberis*', which translates into 'From a castle on the Tiber'. Guido de Castello (or 'castle') was the first pontiff who ruled from 1143 to 1144. The second he titled '*Inimicus Expulsus*', or 'The enemy expelled' which translated into Lucius II, pontiff from 1144 to 1145. Lucius II was born Gerardo Caccianemici. '*Cacciare*' in Italian means to expel and '*nemici*' are the enemies. In his reign Lucius II suffered severe head injuries as he attempted to expel a foreign army from Rome. The third pontiff was Eugene III, called '*Ex Magnitude Montis*' by Malachy, meaning 'From the great mountain'. His place of birth was Montemagno and he ruled from 1145 to 1153.

The list of the popes as predicted by Malachy, with the descriptions he attached

Above: *Pope Pius XII, formerly Cardinal Eugenio Pacelli, whom Malachy foresaw as 'An angelic shepherd'.*

Above: *Pope John Paul II at the Mass held at Coventry on the third day of his visit to Britain in 1982.*

to each, continues with Anastasius IV, 'Abbot from Suburra' and Adrian IV, 'From a white country'. Adrian IV was born Nicholas Breakspear and was the only English pope to date; England was known as Albion, the white country.

A little research will reveal how Malachy's descriptions link with the popes who followed: Alexander III, 'From the guardian goose'; Victor IV, 'From the loathsome prison'; Paschal Transtiberina, 'The road beyond the Tiber'; Calixtus III, 'From the Hungary of Tuscia'; Lucius III, 'The light at the door'; Urban III, 'A sow in a sieve'; Gregory VIII, 'The sword of Lawrence'; Clement III, 'He shall go forth from the school'; Celestine III, 'From the Bovensian territory'; Innocent III, 'A signed count'; Honorius III, 'A canon from the side'; Gregory IX, 'The bird of Ostia'; Celestine IV, 'The Sabinian lion'; Innocent IV, 'Count Laurence'; Alexander IV, 'The standard of Ostia'; Urban IV, 'Jerusalem of Champagne'; Clement IV, 'The dragon crushed'; Gregory X, 'The man of the serpent'; Innocent V, 'A French preacher';

Adrian V, 'A good count'; John XXI, 'A Tuscan fisherman'; Nicholas III, 'The modest rose'; Martin IV, 'From the office of Martin of the lilies'; Honorius IV, 'From the leonine rose'; Nicholas IV, 'A woodpecker among the food'; Celestine V, 'Elevated from the desert'; Boniface VII, 'From a blessing of the waves'.

For modern times Malachy predicted Pius IX, 'The cross from a cross'; Leo XIII, 'A light in the sky'; Pius X, 'The burning fire'; Benedict XV, 'Religion laid waste' (this is a particularly interesting one – Malachy saw that, indeed, with the coming of this pope in 1914, his reign was overshadowed by the holocaust of World War 1 which destroyed the Christian menfolk of Europe in endless slaughter); Pius XI, 'Unshaken faith'; Pius XII, 'An angelic shepherd'; John XXIII, 'Pastor and mariner'; Paul VI, 'Flower of flowers'.

In 1978 Pope John Paul I, Albino Luciani, was elected. Malachy had given for this Holy Father the clue of 'Of the half Moon'. A half-moon was over the world when he died 33 days later. Later that same year Pope John Paul II was elected, for whom Malachy had written 'From the eclipse of the Sun'. As the 263rd pastor of the Holy Church, students of Malachy believe that this is a reference to Karol Wojtyla's ability to eclipse the work of previous popes, which in his remarkable career he has managed to do.

The next pope listed by Malachy is described as *'Gloria Olivae'*, or 'The glory of the olive'. The olive branch has always been associated with peace and Benedictines are also known as the Olivetans, which may well account for this reference. Apart from that it is impossible yet to say who the next pope will be.

Malachy lists the last pope – although he does not specify whether there will be any between 'The glory of the olive' and this one – as *Petrus Romanus*, 'Peter the Roman'. He concludes the prophecies saying: 'In the final persecution of the Holy Roman Church there will reign Peter the Roman, who will feed his flock among many tribulations, after which the seven-hilled city will be destroyed and the dreadful judge will judge the city.' As an omen of what may happen to Rome one day, it is a sombre one.

MOTHER SHIPTON – Prophetess of Tomorrow

While she was in a state of trance, Yorkshirewoman Mother Shipton foresaw the future, and was able to predict all of the major technological developments that were to come.

Mother Shipton was a legendary British prophetess, born in the reign of King Henry VII and credited with foretelling the deaths of Cardinal Wolsey and Lord Percy, as well as painting a remarkable portrait of the shape of things to come in the modern world. Her most famous rhyming couplets depict an H.G. Wells-type world that was remarkable for its accuracy:

Above: **A Punch and Judy show, similar to the ones that travelled all over Britain in the 18th and 19th centuries.**

'Carriages without horses shall go,
And accidents fill the world with woe.
Around the world thoughts shall fly,
In the twinkling of an eye.
The world upsidedown shall be,
And gold be found at the root of a tree.
Through hills man shall ride,
And no horse be at his side.
Under water men shall walk,
Shall ride, shall sleep, shall talk.
In the air men shall be seen,
In white, in black, in green.
Iron in the water shall float,
As easily as a wooden boat.
Gold shall be found and shown,
In a land that's now not known.
Fire and water shall wonders do,
England at last shall admit a foe.
The world to an end shall come,
In eighteen hundred and eighty one.'

It was later learned that the final lines, about the end of the world, were an unscrupulous

A glorious chapter in British history (left)*: the victory of the British longbowmen over the French knights at the Battle of Agincourt, 1415.*

Above: *London's burning – the great prophetess Mother Shipton was among the seers who foretold the demise of the medieval capital.*

THE HIDEOUS OLD HAG PREDICTED THE MAJOR TECHNICAL INNOVATIONS OF OUR WORLD TODAY.

Mary, Queen of Scots (right), *whose execution on the block was predicted four years in advance by John Dee.*

addition to her premonitions by a publisher hoping to cash in on her fame in a publication of her works in the last century, but in one short poem, Mother Shipton captured all of the major technical innovations that humanity would perfect over the coming years. She spoke of cars – and the accidents they caused – the telegraph system, motorcycles, diving suits and submarines, flying machines, gold in South Africa and the harnessing of energy for humanity's benefit. It was the Victorian bookseller Charles Hindley who, in 1862, published the latter verses in a pamphlet that was itself a reprint of a 1684 booklet entitled *The Life and Death of Mother Shipton*.

The information is sketchy on Mother Shipton – certainly, her life, simple as it was, never achieved the scrutiny of countrymen like John Dee. The wife of a Yorkshire carpenter, born in 1488 at a place known as the Dropping Well, near Knaresborough, Yorkshire, she was baptized Ursula Southell, changing her name when she married Toby Shipton. She was, by all contemporary accounts, an ugly woman. An account written of her prophecies in 1797 describes her thus: 'Her stature was larger than common, her body crooked, her face frightful, but her understanding extraordinary.' A hunchback, by all accounts, some believe that the Punch and Judy shows beloved of British children at seaside resorts and fêtes have Mr Punch modelled on Mother Ship-

ton. However, it is for her prophecies, rather than her physical traits, for which she is best remembered.

Mother Shipton did not conform to any accepted occult or mystical practices for her prophecies. Rather, she went into trance-like states for hours and would wake up to tell friends and family who had been waiting for her predictions what had occurred. In such a manner she successfully foretold the success of King Henry's routing of the French at Agincourt, Cardinal Wolsey's arrest for treason, the Caesarian birth of Edward VI, the reign of a maiden queen – Elizabeth I – and the beheading of a widowed one, Mary, Queen of Scots. She also, like Nostradamus, successfully predicted a 'great fire consuming London'.

In 1641 a pamphlet appeared entitled *The Prophesie of Mother Shipton, in the Raigne of King Henry the Eighth, Foretelling the Death of Cardinal Wolsey, the Lord Percy and Others, As Also What Should Happen in Insuing Times*. Four years later the famous astrologer William Lilly published a collection of *Ancient and Modern Prophecies* which included what he called 'Shipton's Prophecy' of what would happen in the world.

She died in 1561; undoubtedly, had she been more highly born, more of her remarkable life would have been chronicled. As it is, little survives as testimony to her strange powers.

JOHN DEE –
Unscrupulous Rogue or
Brilliant Astrologer?

Tudor scholar John Dee
became personal
astrologer to Queen
Elizabeth I before appar-
ently losing his powers
and falling from favour.

Charlatan, rogue and impostor – or
brilliant mathematician, astrologer
and crystal gazer, true sage and
worthy of the praise that his believers
heaped on him? Researches into this
intriguing man have left the argument
unresolved after almost four centuries.

Dee, born in 1527 to a noble Welsh
family in Mortlake, received a fine
education. At the age of 15 he went to
Cambridge University where his zeal for
study astounded his contemporaries.

After graduating he plunged into

> **DEE TOLD THE QUEEN SHE
> WOULD DIE CHILDLESS:
> FURIOUS, SHE HAD HIM
> THROWN INTO A DUNGEON.**

D.ͬ Dee *avoucheth his* Stone *is brought by Angelicall Ministry.*

*John Dee – the man upon
whom Shakespeare is said to
have based the character of
Prospero. Dee was truly
'connected' to the high and
mighty – but the debate
about his talents still rages.*

Above: *Philip of Spain. He became one of the crowned heads of Europe happy to entertain John Dee and retain his services as a fortune teller.*

Elizabeth I (right), *who appointed Dee 'hyr astrologer' and had a high opinion of his powers.*

childless while Elizabeth's own future was a bright one. Unfortunately for him, a spy in her camp sent word of his account to Mary and he was arrested and spent two years in jail on the charge of 'trying to take the life of the monarch through magic'.

Following Elizabeth's accession he was appointed 'hyr astrologer'. His first task was to predict a suitable day for her coronation. He chose 14 January 1559. The weather was fine and sunny – reinforcing the queen's view of his powers.

He travelled extensively abroad, buying massive libraries of occult and astrological works, and greatly increased his scientific and mathematical knowledge. Indeed, he is credited with foreseeing the invention of the telescope by studying the refraction of light, and suggested its military use.

He returned to a house at Mortlake-on-Thames provided for him by the queen. Here he became famous for his astrology and his prophecies. He found the lost basket of clothes of a neighbour after having a prophetic vision in a dream. He also helped a butler locate his master's missing silver in the same way. He began crystal gazing – the practice of staring into the point of light at the centre of a sphere of glass – from which

astronomy, deciding to pursue the study of the stars in Holland and Belgium. He returned to England with newly devised astronomical instruments, and also with books on magic and the occult.

He began casting horoscopes and was much influenced by Geronimo Cardano, the Italian physician and astrologer. He amassed a vast library of works on astrology and mysticism and was soon commissioned by Queen Mary I to read horoscopes for her and her future husband, Philip of Spain. Through his cousin Blanche Parry, maid of honour to Princess Elizabeth, he came into contact with the future queen. He drew up her horoscope and compared it to that of Mary. Mary, he told her, would die

bounce back telepathically received ideas, hallucinations or images transmitted by supernormal means. However, he had minimal success with gazing and decided to use the services of mediums.

Edward Kelly joined his household as a crystal 'scryer', or reader, at a salary of £20 per year after summoning the angel Uriel to appear in the ball for Dee. Kelly is widely regarded as the person who chiefly devalued the scholarly Dee's reputation with his hocus-pocus and his mystical incantations in which he summoned up the spirits of the dead. But there appears to have been something to him; believers in Dee feel that his interplay with the angels was genuine and that he attained telepathy and spiritualism with a nether-world never previously reached. Dee laboriously wrote down the conversations he had with numerous angels summoned forth by Kelly.

In the margin of one book, four years before she was executed, Dee drew an axe next to the name of Mary Queen of Scots – and got the date of her execution right. He also predicted 'the sea full of ships' after Uriel revealed plans about a foreign power preparing a 'vast fleet against the welfare of England'. Queen Elizabeth was grateful to Dee for warning her of the Spanish Armada.

In 1583 Dee brought Prince Adalbert Laski, representative of the King of Poland, to Mortlake to observe his angel-summoning sessions with Kelly. During one seance an attendant to the prince burst into the room uninvited, much to the displeasure of Dee and Laski. Dee said the angel told him that within five months the boy would be 'devoured by fishes'. Sure enough, five months later, the boy drowned at sea. Laski stayed on in the house searching for the mythical formula which turned base metals into gold before he departed with Dee and Kelly on a six-year odyssey to the Continent. While abroad they earned the patronage of counts and princes, an offer to reside in Moscow from the Russian royal family, and a rebuke from the pope about their 'unchristian' activities.

Elizabeth, missing 'hyr astrologer', consulted him about how to defeat the Spanish Armada which he had foreseen. Her military advisers urged her to attack the Spanish ships while still in foreign ports, but he said a consultation on her horoscope had shown that the Spanish fleet must be defeated in English waters. The advice was heeded and he returned to England in a splendid coach provided by his monarch, but the relationship with Kelly was shattered over his command that an angel had informed him that Dee was obliged to share his wife with him!

In England, Dee's fortunes rapidly went downhill. His library had been ransacked by a mob during his absence abroad and he was facing poverty. He tried to recapture his earlier successes from the crystal ball, but nothing seemed to work. Eventually, Elizabeth tired of him and in 1595 she gave him the Wardenship of Christ's College in Manchester, a post he held for ten years before he returned to Mortlake, where he died in 1608.

Richard Deacon, who has made an authoritative study of John Dee, said: 'Some writers have depicted him as the foolish dupe of Kelly. Others have suggested that both he and Kelly used crystal gazing to obtain money fraudulently from Laski. But if it was through greed that Dee exploited the crystal then why reject the Czar's magnificent offer?' Deacon thinks that Dee was a spy for Elizabeth, passing back intelligence on his last mission – perhaps bolstered with astrological readings – to her court. He concludes: 'Dee…was a sincere seeker after knowledge, a mystic at heart but a scientist in his mind, and in many respects a pioneer in a variety of scientific fields.'

The destruction of the Spanish Armada (above). Queen Elizabeth is understood to have obeyed the warning of her seer, who said the fleet must be destroyed in British waters.

THE ANGEL HAD INSTRUCTED DEE TO SHARE HIS WIFE WITH KELLY.

CAGLIOSTRO – Prince of Quacks?

Showman or seer, charlatan or sage? Historians once differed immensely on the qualities of Count Alessandro Cagliostro (right), but now he is recognized as a genuine seeker after truth.

'IN SPITE OF POSSESSING ALL THE CHARACTERISTICS OF A CHARLATAN, HE NEVER BEHAVED AS SUCH.'

Below: *A brutal and enduring symbol of the French Revolution. Madame Guillotine was never unemployed during the dark days of 'the Terror' which followed the overthrow of the House of Bourbon.*

Famed in France as the 'Divine Cagliostro', this versatile count conducted experiments in a search for the key to the secrets of the Universe.

Sometimes branded a showman – and cruelly dubbed a 'Prince of Quacks' by Thomas Carlyle – Count Alessandro Cagliostro was an enthusiast of the occult and the mysterious. He was a genuine seeker after knowledge, who strived to unravel the 'heavenly magic' which he believed held the key to the secrets of the Universe.

Little is known of his early life and education. He arrived in London in 1776 with his young wife, Sarafina, whereupon he made contact with Freemasons' groups intent on turning base metals into gold. He held seances, summoned up spirits, and on three occasions at least predicted the winning numbers of a lottery. His main interest, however, was divining the affinity between the Church, Freemasonry and other religions.

His first supernatural experiments are chronicled as having taken place in 1779. Using an Egyptian method of clairvoyancy he had discovered, he hypnotized a child, causing him to see visions and utter prophecies. As the subject was induced into a trance-like state, Cagliostro strove for his 'heavenly magic' by summoning angels to speak for him with God.

In one Egyptian rite ceremony Cagliostro employed the nephew of the Countess Elsa von der Recke. Cagliostro had earlier asked the husband of the Countess what sort of vision he would wish the boy to have. He suggested it be of his mother and sister who were some kilometres away in another village. Ten minutes later the boy – having no idea who he would see under Cagliostro's 'spell' – cried out that he saw his mother and sister, and that his sister was holding her 'hand to her heart as if in pain'.

Cagliostro later sent an emissary to check on the family. It was discovered that the sister had recently suffered such violent heart palpitations that she thought she was dying! It is worth pointing out that Cagliostro was privately wealthy and never charged money for any of these seances.

Soon afterwards he moved across France, before arriving in Paris where he was lauded as the 'Divine Cagliostro'. Here, fresh from his successes, he assumed the role of a master magician and held many seances in which phantoms and angels were invoked in glass vases of water. This led to an introduction to King Louis XVI where he performed the same spectacular feats at Versailles.

Cagliostro also possessed seemingly remarkable powers of healing. There exist numerous accounts of the potions and elixirs which he dispensed to the sick. He was also one of the earliest believers in the powers of crystal healing. With his massive library of books, which included pharmaceutical and herbalist works, it is likely that many of his potions were used in tandem with the crystals. And again, he refused all payment for his services.

Cagliostro moved on to prophecies. At a masonic meeting held at the home of a noted occultist he expounded the theory of Gematria – that all letters of the alphabet

have a numerical value and that a person's future could be foretold from the total of the digits his or her name represented. For the king he forecast a violent end to his life as he neared 39; for the queen, Marie Antoinette, he said she would become 'prematurely wrinkled through sorrow', would languish in prison and then would be beheaded on the scaffold. For her close companion, the Princess de Lamballe, he said she would die on the corner of the street named Rue des Ballets. ALL of these predictions turned out frighteningly true.

And there was more – he predicted that a Corsican would end the Revolution and that his name would be Napoleon Bonaparte. Although a victorious general at first, Cagliostro said Napoleon would finish his days 'pacing the circle of a melancholy island' – an accurate reference to his exile to Elba.

Cagliostro's downfall came when he was falsely accused of stealing a necklace worth hundreds of thousands of francs. He spent nine months in the notorious Bastille before being found not guilty in a trial which inflamed the passions of the poor against the nobility, and upon his acquittal he was ordered to leave France by the king himself. It was 1786, three years before the French Revolution would sweep away Europe's old orders forever. He returned with his wife to England where he published a pamphlet predicting the Revolution, the storming of the hated Bastille gaol, and the downfall of the French monarchy.

Seeking fulfilment and peace elsewhere,

Above: *Napoleon at the Battle of Wagram, July 1809. Cagliostro prophesied his coming, marking him down as the man who would end the Revolution.*

Left: *Louis XVI, king of France from 1754 to 1793, granted permission for Cagliostro to summon up the spirits of dead ancestors – in the great Hall of Mirrors at the Versailles palace!*

Right: *This mosaic was found at Pompeii in 1874. It includes a number of symbols of a secret society akin to Freemasonry.*

HE WAS SUBJECTED TO HORRIFIC TORTURES BUT HE REFUSED TO DENY THE TRUTH OF HIS PREDICTIONS.

The storming of the Bastille **(below),** *hated symbol of monarchist rule. It was liberated by the mob.*

the couple moved to Rome. Here, free-masonry was banned but Cagliostro wanted to recapture his fame and fortune. He held one illegal seance with some Rome noblemen before he was arrested. At the seance in 1789 he used a young girl as the conduit with the spirit world. She uttered words about a mob armed with sticks, racing towards a place called Versailles: she had accurately predicted the start of the Revolution which did not take place for a further three weeks. The French ambassador, the Cardinal de Bernis, was among those present at the seance; he was outraged at the prediction that his lord and master was about to be destroyed. 'I am sorry, my Lord Cardinal,' said Cagliostro. 'But the prophecy will be realized.'

The vengeful ambassador told the Inquisition about him and Cagliostro was placed under close supervision before being arrested on 27 December 1789. He endured horrific tortures before being tried and found guilty of heresy, sorcery and Freemasonry. The pope commuted his sentence to life imprisonment, the same fate prescribed for his wife. She died in captivity in 1794, he a year later following a fit. Had he lived for two more years the French, under the warrior Napoleon whom he foresaw, would have liberated him.

CHEIRO – Prophet of the Politicians

From an early age Cheiro had astounding powers of prediction. Later he travelled widely and was consulted by the world's leaders.

Cheiro, born William John Warner, is probably the most successful of clairvoyants from the last century.

Born on 1 November 1866, he found himself at an early age blessed with strange gifts. He found he could easily read the palms of his classmates and teachers. Later, after his father was ruined by a disastrous land deal – as Cheiro had foretold – he read the palm of a stranger on a train. He told the man he was another Napoleon, with a great destiny, but that he would meet his own 'Waterloos' in the shape of a beautiful woman. Years later the man, Charles Stuart Parnell, was brought down in the divorce of Katherine O'Shea.

Cheiro travelled to India, where he delved into transcendental meditation and out-of-body experience. He stayed for three years before inheriting a fortune from a relative, and then returned to London.

One of his successes was in helping to solve a murder in the East End. Police called upon him to 'read' a bloodstained palmprint left on a door jamb at the scene of the killing. Cheiro said that the palmprint was that of the murdered man's illegitimate son, whose existence was not known at that stage by the police. Three weeks later the son was arrested and charged with the murder. Cheiro soon became bored with London and took himself off to the temples of the Nile where he acquired the severed hand of a mummified princess. The hand travelled with him constantly after he returned to London to try to become a full-time teacher of occult studies. The name Cheiro, from the Greek word *cheir* for hand, came to him in a premonition and he became permanently known by it.

Arthur James Balfour, later the Tory prime minister, was one of his first clients, and he brought along with him a wealthy and fashionable clientele, but fortune telling, as defined by law, was illegal under laws dating back to Henry VIII. Police warned him to cease his practice within a week or face prosecution, but thanks to influential friends he managed to keep going. He went on to read the palms of several members of the nobility. A famous reading occurred in the home of a friend, Blanche Roosevelt, who insisted on him reading the hands of someone through a curtain. He said: 'The left hand is the hand of a king, but the right that of a king who will send himself into exile.' The owner of the hand asked when, and was told, 'A few

HE 'READ' THE BLOODSTAINED PALMPRINT AND IDENTIFIED THE MURDERER.

Oscar Wilde (below). *The dandy wit and playwright had his hand read by Cheiro without revealing his identity. Cheiro foretold that he had the hand of a man 'destined to send himself into exile'. Wilde ended up in Reading gaol.*

Above: *Czar Nicholas Romanov and his son Alexis in 1911 – six years before the Revolution which would sweep away their dynasty's rule of all the Russias.*

Arthur Balfour (above right), *in a photograph by W.D. Downey, was a patron of Cheiro, and he brought to this remarkable man a wealthy and élite clientele.*

years from now, at about your fortieth year.' Cheiro later learned he had foretold the future for Oscar Wilde.

Cheiro moved to the USA in 1894 and became an instant hit after reading the palmprints of several prominent Americans. One of them was of a man who had recently been arrested for murder. Without knowing the man, a Dr Meyer of Chicago who was poisoning his patients with potions, Cheiro predicted that he would die peacefully in prison after many years behind bars. On the eve of his execution Cheiro again read his hand – and said that he would be reprieved. The next day the Supreme Court commuted his sentence to life imprisonment. He died in jail 15 years later.

Another stunningly accurate prediction was to a Mrs Leiter of Chicago who gave him a print of her daughter's hand. He prophesied that the girl would marry a man from another country and then 'lead the life

of a queen in the East, but she will die young'. Mary Leiter became Lord Curzon's wife and later Vicereine of India. Tragically she died young.

Cheiro spoke all over the USA, saying that a baby an hour old has lines on its hands that foretell its future. Eventually, richer but bored, he returned to England, fed up with the questions from clients that mostly demanded to know how they could be richer and when it would happen.

Even King Edward VII consulted Cheiro at the Belgrave Square house of an American society friend. At the reading Cheiro told the king that the numbers six and nine would be the most significant in his life. He died in his 69th year. Cheiro also accurately foretold the month the king's coronation would take place: August 1902.

King Leopold II of the Belgians was another client who consulted Cheiro – but the news was grim. Cheiro said the king's death in 1909 would be caused by serious problems with his digestive tract. He died on 17 December that year, the cause of death given as 'the complete breakdown of the digestive organs and intestinal obstruction'. Another reading for the Czar of Russia was foreboding but true: 'He will be haunted by the horrors of war and bloodshed…his name will be bound up with some of the most far reaching and bloodiest wars in history, and in the end, about 1917, he will lose all he loves most by sword or strife in one form or another, and he himself will meet a violent death.' Cheiro had predicted the end of the Romanov dynasty and the Russian Revolution.

Georgi Rasputin, the evil monk who held so much sway over the czarina, was also a client. Cheiro told him that he would be a power for evil, holding enormous sway over others. He told him he would die by bullets and would finally be dumped in the Neva River – exactly, as it turned out, how Rasputin did meet his end.

Herbert Kitchener, the great Lord Kitchener of Sudan, consulted him on 21 July 1894 at the War Office. Cheiro said he would be in great danger in 1916, caused by a storm at sea. Kitchener died that year on board a vessel bound for Russia that struck a mine.

Cheiro went on to predict the election result for a Conservative MP in a marginal seat, the Wall Street Crash of 1929 for a businessman and saved the Shah of Persia from an assassination attempt. He did not, however, manage to predict the crash of his own fortunes, which came when he made a disastrous business deal involving the purchase of an American newspaper.

After World War 1 Cheiro foretold the treaty in 1926 between Soviet Russia and Germany, the General Strike in Britain in May 1926, the breaking out of civil war in China and an earthquake in the Channel Islands. All came true. In 1927 he published a book of world predictions, stunning in their accuracy. He foretold the return of the Jews to Palestine in a state they would call Israel, World War 2 and the spread of communism throughout the world. In 1930 he went to live in Hollywood with the intention of becoming a scriptwriter, but he wrote only one screenplay – about Cagliostro – and it was never made. He ran his own school of metaphysics there until his death in 1936.

> **HIS TRAGIC PREDICTIONS HAD AN UNFORTUNATE KNACK OF COMING TRUE.**

Left: *Lord Kitchener, chief of the general staff at the outbreak of World War 1. He consulted Cheiro, who told him he would be in great danger in 1916. That year he died at sea* en route *to Russia.*

WOLF MESSING – Stalin's Psychic

A Polish Jew had such powers of mental gymnastics that he acquired the patronage of no less a person than Josef Stalin.

Josef Stalin, history's bloodiest dictator, at one time placed his faith in Wolf Messing, who was undoubtedly Russia's greatest-ever seer. Messing, who discovered his gifts as an 11-year-old boy, is regarded by many as one of the great psychics of this century.

Born a Polish Jew near Warsaw on 10 September 1899 Messing was a subject then of Imperial Russia and its last czar, Nicholas II. He ran away from school when he was 11 and boarded a train for Berlin with no ticket. He was caught by a brutal ticket collector who asked him repeatedly for his ticket; Messing ended up handing him a scrap of paper from his pocket – and thereby performed his first conscious act of mental gymnastics. He recalled: 'Our gazes crossed. How I desperately wanted him to accept that scrap of paper as a ticket!... I mentally suggested to him: "It is a ticket... it is a ticket...it is a ticket..." The iron jaws of the ticket punch snapped. Handing the "ticket" back to me and smiling benevolently he asked me why I had been sleeping under the seat when I had a valid ticket. It was the first time my power of suggestion manifested itself.'

After suffering grinding poverty and chronic malnutrition in Berlin, Messing gradually managed to carve himself a living as a mind-reader in city theatres. By placing himself into a light trance he found he could concentrate on the thoughts uppermost in a person's mind. He earned the grand sum of five marks a day.

Right: *The Kremlin in Moscow. It was here that Stalin put the unique talents of Wolf Messing to the test.*

Soon his mind-reading abilities brought him into the orbit of the truly great men of his day – Albert Einstein and Sigmund Freud. There is a famous story of how Freud told Einstein that he would 'think' a command for Messing to interpret. On a given day all three were seated in Freud's Vienna salon and Messing, now 17, went into a trance. Soon, he sat upright, walked across to a pair of scissors lying on a desktop, picked them up and proceeded to clip three hairs from Einstein's moustache. Messing had interpreted the mental orders with absolute precision.

Messing toured South America and the Far East during World War 1 and returned to his birthplace, now in an independent Poland, in 1922. After compulsory military service he took up travelling throughout Europe, again performing his mind-reading stunts to amazed audiences. One of his most appreciated performances was the ability to drive a car while totally blindfolded as he received telepathic instructions from a chauffeur about directions.

It was with the coming of Hitler and World War 2 that Messing fled to Moscow – even though the racial policies of Stalin were often just as harsh as those of Hitler. In 1939 he found himself in a squalid apartment in the capital – and in a quandary about how to make a living.

Stalin had banned those who practised extra-sensory perception and other psychic arts, his paranoia leading him to distrust anyone with powers he could not understand. Messing did obtain work as the last act in various nightclubs but on more than one occasion found himself as a guest of the police or the KGB for a night.

Finally, one night, after he was arrested at a club in the town of Gomel, he was presented to someone of 'immense authority'. That person was Stalin himself, and at the meeting he was cordial, asking Messing questions about his life in Poland and the situation there. A few days later Messing was collected by the KGB and subjected to a special test, on Stalin's orders, of his abilities. The 'test' consisted of asking an official of the state bank to hand over 100,000 roubles, presenting him with a piece of blank paper at the same time. Messing said: 'It was essentially a re-run of the test I had on the train.'

There followed several audiences with Stalin in which Messing spoke of his foreboding that Hitler planned war on the

Left: Sigmund Freud – the man who, more than any other, came close to unlocking the secrets of the mind.

BY CONCENTRATING DEEPLY HE COULD READ ANYBODY'S MIND – EVEN THE MURDEROUS STALIN'S.

Below: Josef Stalin, the Kremlin overlord who liked to test Wolf Messing's abilities. More attention to Messing might have shortened the war and saved untold thousands of lives.

Above: *Adolf Hitler. The Messianic leader of Nazi Germany had a closet interest in the occult – but Wolf Messing delivered warnings about him to his arch-enemy Stalin.*

Right: *Wolf Messing, psychic extraordinaire, shown here in the 1950s giving one of his stage shows in Russia. He was a man of quite astonishing powers.*

USSR. Messing told Stalin that he had had a vision that war would come in June 1941. On 22 June that year the full weight of Hitler's mechanized armies fell against the USSR.

During the war years Messing was allowed by Stalin to perform his mind-reading feats in morale-raising public appearances. Later that year he was summoned to the Kremlin where Stalin asked for a personal display of his powers. He recalled: 'He said he did not think anybody could make a fool of him and that I would not be able to leave the Kremlin without a pass signed by him... He telephoned the guards to say I could not leave without a pass and ordered his private secretary to follow ten paces behind me.

'I entered my deepest state of trance that I can ever recall. Several minutes later, I walked right out on to the street past the guards, who remained standing at attention and looking up at the window of Stalin's study. "Maybe I should blow him a kiss, " I thought mockingly.'

Stalin looked upon Messing as his personal seer, and he was forever inviting him to his private apartments in the Kremlin. But the 'Man of Steel' did not heed his advice on the war. Stalin seems to have regarded him more as a personal pet, but it was a powerful patronage and one that Messing was keen to engender for as long as possible.

In the 1950s Messing underwent extensive testing at the hands of Soviet scientists, on Stalin's orders, to probe the workings of his extraordinary mind. Until then belief in the paranormal was attacked in Soviet society as being 'bourgeois, materialistic and pseudoscientific' but with Messing they decided that electrical impulses in the brain were acting as radar signals which he bounced off similar strong thought patterns from individuals whose minds he endeavoured to read. Messing was less scientific and said: 'All I know is that I was born with this gift and have always been able to utilise it.'

In his later years Messing toured the USSR, deriving most pleasure from performances of his powers in small villages, where he also gained a reputation as a faith healer. In the early 1970s his health began to fade and he died from a heart attack in 1972, by which time his fame was so widespread within the USSR that he was accorded a hero's burial.

KARL ERNEST KRAFFT and the Hitler Horoscopes

At first at risk of harass-ment by the Nazis, Krafft attracted the attention of the leaders of the Third Reich by predicting an attempt on the life of Hitler.

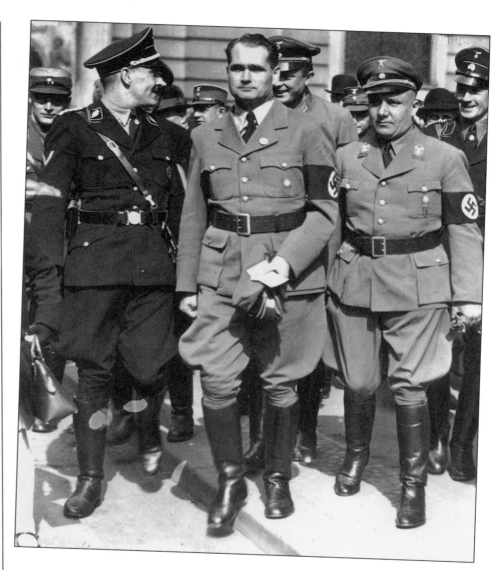

Deputy Führer Rudolf Hess (centre) was an occult enthusiast. When he flew to Scotland the times became harder for Nazi seers like Karl Ernest Krafft.

Many dark forces shaped and defined the Third Reich during its 12 years. But lurking in the background was a little-known astrologer called Karl Ernest Krafft. Historians now believe that if Hitler had listened to Krafft more closely, the final outcome of the war might have been very different indeed.

Born in 1900 in Basle, Krafft was a brilliant young man with a genuine gift for figures and statistics, but his greatest love was the study of the planets and astrology. After graduating from university in mathematics, for the best part of ten years he worked on a massive book entitled *Traits of Astro-Biology*. This expounded his own theory of 'Typocosmy' – the prediction of the future based on the study of an individual's personality, or type. By the early 1930s, when Hitler had come to power, Krafft enjoyed a unique status among occultists and prophets in Germany. But ironically, it was the Nazis – later to become his greatest patrons – who at first posed the biggest threat to him. Occultists, like Freemasons, were among those harassed and vilified by the Nazis.

However, while publicly the state may have persecuted astrologers, privately men like Hitler, his right-hand-man Rudolf Hess and the SS chief Himmler were all in favour of consulting them. Krafft moved directly into the orbit of the higher echelons of the Nazi élite in November

1939 when he made a remarkable pre-diction. He predicted that the Führer's life would be in danger between 7 and 10 November. He wrote, on 2 November, to a friend called Dr Heinrich Fesel who worked for Himmler, warning him of an attempt on Hitler's life. Fesel filed the letter away, unwilling to become enmeshed in something which he felt could become extremely dangerous.

On 8 November, a bomb exploded at a Munich beer hall. There were many injuries, but the man who was targeted, Adolf Hitler, was unscathed. When newspapers reported the near-catastrophe

Above: *Joseph Goebbels, supreme propagandist of the Third Reich, liked to twist the prophecies of Nostradamus and others into showing Nazism in a favourable light.*

Fesel despatched a telegram to Hess, drawing attention to Krafft's prediction. Krafft was instantly arrested and brought to Gestapo headquarters in Berlin for questioning. Questioning soon proved that he was innocent as far as the attempt on Hitler's life went. After his release he was summoned to the offices of the Reich propaganda ministry, run by Josef Goebbels. Goebbels had recently taken to poring over the historic prophecies of Nostradamus, trying to squeeze from them the maximum amount of propaganda to portray the Third Reich in flattering tones. Krafft, he felt, had the weight and authority to begin work on deciphering the often cryptic quatrains. In January 1940 the Swiss astrologer began work on a pro-German evaluation of Nostradamus.

Krafft was convinced that the prophecies of Nostradamus boded well for the Third Reich. Tens of thousands of pamphlets based upon his interpretations of the quatrains were circulated in various languages and he soon came to the attention of the Führer. In the spring of 1940 he gave a private horoscope reading for Hitler to an aide, but he never met his leader. Later he boasted to friends that he mentioned that the time for an attack on the USSR was some way off. Hitler, who was impatient to launch Operation Barbarossa (the conquest of the USSR) after he had dealt with the West, in fact delayed his operations in the east until the following June. The stunning success of the early days of Barbarossa convinced him that Krafft had great powers.

British intelligence became so concerned at the thought that their opponent's war was being conducted by a mystic that they, for a time, hired the services of the astrologer Louis De Wohl to divine the kind of prophecies that Krafft was divining for the Nazis. De Wohl was quietly dropped after several months, having failed to procure any hard evidence about Krafft's work.

Krafft warned the Reich leaders that for victory to be certain, the war MUST end for Germany in 1943; in this, it turned out, he was entirely correct. By the end of 1942 Germany was at the zenith of her victories, but after that date the full might of the allies, with the USA behind them, could not fail to eventually swamp the Fatherland.

Left: *Rommel, the Desert Fox. When Krafft was shown astrological charts of both him and Montgomery he declared the British field marshal to be made of stronger stuff.*

IF HITLER HAD TAKEN KRAFFT'S ADVICE, HE MIGHT HAVE WON THE WAR.

Below: *Montgomery of Alamein, who truly did have the mettle, in the end, to take on Rommel and drive him all the way out of Africa.*

Krafft's star was still in the Nazi ascendancy when Rudolf Hess made his astonishing flight to Scotland in 1941. Hitler was outraged. He knew that Hess was the biggest occult supporter of them all and, in his fury, ordered a massive purge of astrologers, occultists and other sages. Even Krafft was caught up in this and he languished in prison for a year before being released. This time he was sent to work on horoscopes of allied generals and admirals. One of his predictions when seeing the charts of both Rommel and Montgomery, adversaries in the desert war, was: 'Well, this man Montgomery's chart is certainly stronger than Rommel's.' History proved him to be correct.

Krafft's health began to fail and he developed a persecution complex. He wrote to a senior official predicting that British bombs would very soon destroy the propaganda ministry in Berlin – another true statement. The letter was passed on to the Gestapo who viewed it as treasonous. He was incarcerated in foul conditions, contracted typhus and eventually died on 8 January 1945.

JOAN QUIGLEY – the Power behind the President

For six years socialite and astrologer Joan Quigley played a major part in world events.

When the story first broke about Joan Quigley's involvement with the Reagan administration in the White House, the impact was shattering. If what was being alleged was true, then for close to six of the eight years that Ronald Reagan ruled as the world's most powerful man his destiny – and therefore humanity's – was linked to Quigley's interpretations of the Universe in her role as an astrologer. Not since medieval times has a soothsayer had so much influence in power-politics.

Quigley was an educated, soft-spoken spinster who lived on San Francisco's luxurious Nob Hill and was considered a major player on the city's social scene. But what drove her was her love for, and her gift of, interpreting the stars.

Plotting future events by the alignment of the heavens was at first an escape for Joan, and then something of a permanent challenge. In the late 1960s and early 1970s she began reading the horoscopes of wealthy Republican friends.

She was introduced to the Reagans in 1973 and soon Nancy Reagan was calling her up on a regular basis. Quigley claimed: 'From 1973 on I drew up horoscopes for both the then governor and Mrs Reagan annually. When I first saw Ronald's horoscope I knew it was world class.'

Reagan became the single most powerful individual on earth with his triumph at the polls in 1980. His rule would lay the foundations for the most cataclysmic changes in world history since the end of the war and herald the beginning of the end for the USA's old arch-enemy, the USSR. During Reagan's first 15 months in office Joan Quigley had little influence, but after he miraculously survived an assassination attempt in March 1981, she became a force to be reckoned with within the corridors of power. For a fee of 3000 US dollars a month she would soon be running the affairs of a superpower – or if not running them, certainly having a major say in them.

Later Joan would recall: 'Nancy was interested in everything, not just the president's safety. She was interested in her image. She wanted me to improve it.' In effect, Quigley became an ex-officio cabinet member. In regular telephone conversations, Quigley would hammer out every nuance of the president's schedule. Nancy became obsessed with working out when would be the most propitious time for him to under-take any aspect of his job. By her own

Below: *Joan Quigley. The world was shocked to learn of her star-gazing in the White House, which subjugated the most powerful man in the world to the will of the cosmos.*

JOAN QUIGLEY – THE POWER BEHIND THE PRESIDENT

admission Quigley was a powerful force: 'For over seven years I was responsible for timing all press conferences, most speeches, the State of the Union addresses, the take-offs and landings of Air Force One. I picked the times of Reagan's debates with Carter and Mondale and all of his trips. I delayed the president's cancer operation and chose the time for Nancy's mastectomy.' Using what she calls 'analysis' on the data provided by astronomers, and charts calculated by computers, here's what Quigley also takes credit for:

• Overturning Nancy's initial hostility to Gorbachev. Quigley says her examination of Gorbachev's horoscope proved to her that his Aquarian planet sign was in such harmony with Reagan's that they would share a 'beautiful vision'. Quigley credits herself with forcing Reagan to drop his 'evil empire' rhetoric against the Soviet leader.

• Defusing the crisis over the visit by the Reagans to a cemetery in the German town of Bitburg in May 1985 that contained the graves of Nazi SS officers. She completely threw the scheduling into disarray by saying that the planets were only favourable for a visit at 2.45 pm instead of two hours earlier as planned. 'The Bitburg visit was brief,' she said. 'And the controversy soon died down. I defused it for him.'

• Foreseeing also in 1985 the president's need for surgery. She says that on 10 July his

horoscope proved conclusively that he needed an operation for cancer. The doctors that day found out and wanted to operate immediately, but she told Nancy that an operation wouldn't be successful until noon on the 13th. Nancy obeyed her and Reagan did not need further cancer surgery during his entire time in office. But Quigley said: 'Had they not listened to me they would have risked not removing the cancerous growth completely.'

• Staging the announcement in Washington of a controversial Supreme Court Justice. Right-winger Anthony Kennedy's election was not a popular one with moderates and liberals, so Quigley says she used a unique astrological device to pick the exact right time for Reagan to announce his choice. Nancy, she says, went along with her advice and Anthony Kennedy was later installed without fuss or rancour.

• Smoothing over the fuss about Irangate. She claims that between January and August

Nancy Reagan (left), forceful wife of President Reagan. It was at her insistence that astrological charts dominated many aspects of his presidency.

1987, when the scandal about the arms-dealing-for-hostages was at its zenith, she re-organized Reagan's schedule to make it 'practically impossible' for hostile media representatives to get to the president with embarrassing questions.

• Securing the president's safety while

Above: Ronald Reagan, 40th president of the United States and the first ever to have his daily schedule worked out around the signs of the horoscope.

Above: *Mikhail Gorbachev – another world leader with whom Ronald Reagan had a great many dealings. He couldn't have known that his capitalist counterpart was running the White House according to the stars!*

Libyan dictator Colonel Ghaddafi (**right**). *Quigley claims that she advised on the most auspicious time for the US to attack the desert despot in 1986.*

airborne. She says that many times she contacted Nancy while Air Force One was transporting President Reagan around the world, dictating flying patterns and landing and take-off times. She remains convinced that his life could have been in jeopardy if her advice had not been heeded.

• Advising him on the most momentous single act of his presidency – the bombing of Libya because of Colonel Gaddafi's continued sponsorship of world terrorists.

Quigley's interpretation of the pageantry of the zodiac may have been vital to Nancy, and even to the president, but it was viewed by professionals within the White House as calamitous. Donald Regan, the chief-of-staff who blew the whistle on the entire affair in 1990, says her stargazing created a hammerlock on business. On his desk he was forced to keep a colour-coded calendar to chart the president's 'good', 'bad' and 'iffy' days and on at least one occasion she gave him a list in which large chunks of time were marked 'stay home' or 'be careful'. Regan claims Quigley chose the most auspicious time for the Aquarian Ronald to meet the Piscean Gorbachev.

'I wanted secrecy more than Nancy,' she said. 'That's why I stayed so much in the background.' However, Regan's book about the stargazing years set the media hounds on the trail and Quigley claims she was forced

to go public to protect her own reputation. It caused a rift with Nancy Reagan, but she says she could not lie, not even for the former First Lady.

Quigley also takes the credit for what she calls 'PR by astrology' – smoothing the image of the 'great communicator' and his sometimes frosty wife, but perhaps her greatest claim of all is that she kept Reagan ALIVE. She points out: 'From William Henry Washington on, every president elected in a zero year has died in office except for Reagan. I think I had something to do with that. In fact, I know I did.'

After she no longer worked for Reagan she was so upset about the rift with Nancy that she pledged never, ever to read the horoscopes of an American again.

After she quit working for the Reagans she tried to drop back out of the public limelight, although occasionally she would offer up some predictions on public figures whose horoscopes she was already acquainted with. A year before the abortive August coup in Moscow by hardliners she said this about Gorbachev: 'He's going to have more troubles from his generals and more food shortages. There is going to be a loss of power for him.'

Quigley hasn't made any dramatic predictions for the end of the century in seven years' time. She does, however, offer up one Hollywood prophecy: that volatile couple Ryan O'Neal and Farrah Fawcett might not be together by the year 1999.

J.Z. KNIGHT AND JACK PURSEL – Channellers of Wisdom

Thousands of her supporters follow the teachings of Seattle housewife J.Z. Knight, who claims to be the channel for a warrior from ancient Atlantis.

In a remote mountain ranch in Washington State the faithful adherents of 'channelling' gather like pilgrims every weekend for £500-per-time mind-sessions with the most famous channeller of them all. Judy Z. Knight was a Seattle housewife until she was visited in 1977 by the spirit of a long-dead warrior from the long-lost continent of Atlantis. His name was Ramtha and ever since he has been sending his prophecies and his wisdom to numerous believers – among them *Dynasty* star Linda Evans and Hollywood legend Shirley MacLaine.

The concept of channellers is as old as the centuries – only the term is relatively new. It describes practitioners of prophecies who turn over control of their bodies to spirits of the dead, or to extra-terrestrial beings, who in turn proffer their wisdom, coupled with portents of things to come. J.Z., as she is known to her devotees, has become wealthy and influential through her connection to Ramtha – a Cro-Magnon man, 35,000 years old. The channelling movement offers an exotic way towards spiritual fulfilment and Ramtha is credited by thousands of people as having totally changed their way of living. His 'teachings' seem to consist of bits and pieces of Buddhism, Hinduism and Christianity.

'Ramtha helped me find happiness,' said Hollywood celebrity Linda Evans. 'For me, he has been a powerful teacher. And J.Z. is one psychic who has certainly changed my life.'

Evans first heard Ramtha speak through J.Z. Knight in 1985. She took a day off from the set of soap opera *Dynasty* and drove to a Ramtha seminar near Los Angeles. She said, 'I had been exploring psychic phenomena for close to 20 years, but when I first heard his voice speak I felt it was adding wonderful bridges that I had never come across.

'In the beginning I was totally suspicious. I wanted proof that the channelling wasn't just trickery. I wanted to protect myself. I didn't want to be misled after all I had been through in my personal

*Below: **J.Z. Knight** – rich, successful and powerful, thanks to her 'channelling' with the spirit of a long-dead warrior from the lost kingdom of Atlantis.*

Right: *Seattle housewife J.Z. Knight, channeller of the ancient Atlantean Ramtha.*

life. But he holds you in the moment – holds a truth or emotion until you can totally feel and know it. He puts the information in front of you to see. He made me see first off that I could no longer put all the blame on my husband John Derek for leaving me. I had to take responsibility for my part.'

Why did Ramtha decide to impart his knowledge to a Seattle housewife? J.Z. – married five times and recently involved in a messy divorce – said: 'I have no idea why he chose me. I am the medium for him. He speaks and the words come out of my body, but it is not me speaking. It is his voice. When it happened I had mixed feelings. I knew that there would be days that would not belong to me any more. I am his tool. But I have learned so much wisdom from him, which others have too, that I never regret that day.'

Just what does Ramtha offer, other than self-enlightenment, contentment and advice for people to look inside themselves for the clues to the secret of the

Shirley MacLaine (below), *one of a long line of celebrity clients who have given channelling respectability and status in the US.*

Universe? At any given session, channelling disciples will ask many wide-ranging, worldly questions – and Ramtha always gives an answer. A man at a seminar in 1990 asked what the best investment for his cash was. Ramtha told him to buy Taiwanese dollars (at the time, a sound investment bet). He predicted the San Francisco earthquake of 1989 and takes credit – through J.Z., of course – for predicting the worldwide recession of 1992. Literally thousands of people have taken the advice of his central philosophy for the 20th century – that people must abandon the cities for a more rural life. That rural life for many is in the surrounding countryside near to J.Z. Knight's home where Ramtha instructs them to 'keep to high ground' and store up to two years' food supplies in the basement for the coming unspecified catastrophe.

Shirley MacLaine is another big-name celebrity who has consulted with Ramtha on numerous occasions as part of her quest for 'new age enlightenment'. She insists that Ramtha is the summoning of a powerful, relevant force that needs to be listened to and reckoned with. MacLaine, who believes she has been, at various times in the past, a Peruvian Inca child, a Mongolian maiden and an Indian princess, says that Ramtha has provided her with many valuable lessons.

'I just knew he had been my sibling in a previous existence in Atlantis,' said MacLaine. 'He was profound.' Profound, too, is the acceptance that Knight has gained with her ancient guru from among both sceptics and students of the paranormal in the USA. Although at times the media have portrayed Knight as everything from wily cult leader to harmless psychotic to dangerous manipulator, those who have examined Ramtha's teachings find that, for the most part, his wisdom is sound and his predictions true. Arthur Hastings, who studied dozens of channellers for his book *With the Tongues of Man and Angels*, said: 'I am deeply impressed.' Even Charles Tart, author of *Open Mind, Discriminating Mind*, who questions the value of channellers, agrees: 'No high-minded entity, including Ramtha, has ever come up with a carburettor design that would help improve gas mileage, something that would concretely help civilisation. Still, much of what he says makes good common sense.'

If J.Z. Knight is the most famous, and richest, channeller, Jack Pursel from Palm Beach, Florida, runs her a close second with a celebrity client list every bit as good. He summons up Lazaris, a disembodied spirit – not a warrior-god like Ramtha – who calls himself 'the consummate friend'. Lazaris appears to channel his thoughts and predictions through former insurance adjuster Pursel, who quit his climb up the corporate ladder after being visited by the un-incarnate spirit six years ago. Celebrities Sharon Gless, Michael York, Barry Manilow and Lesley Ann Warren – all have credited Lazaris with helping them.

Gless, who won an Emmy award for her role as a New York cop in the *Cagney and Lacey* show, even thanked Lazaris in her acceptance speech when she received the award! Like Ramtha, he works on the basis of inner love and a re-evaluation of the Universe to improve life and health, rather than specific predictions. But at seminars, almost identical to those held by Knight, Lazaris is summoned to speak where he offers wisdom on such practical matters as health care and finances. One woman suffering from pancreatic cancer credits him with saving her life after telling her to recuperate in a yellow room. Another, a man, claimed Lazaris accurately predicted a fall in certain share prices.

Like Knight, Pursel can give no reason why this force in the spirit world should have chosen to visit him. He added: 'If we can add to the sum total of knowledge, though, in the world, and its happiness, surely that can't be a bad thing, can it? He has a great deal of wisdom for us all to share.'

Barry Manilow (below) *subscribes to the teachings of Lazaris, a disembodied spirit summoned up by Floridian channeller Jack Pursel.*

JEANE DIXON – the Celebrities' Clairvoyant

For 70 years devout Roman Catholic Jeane Dixon has predicted private and national events with outstanding accuracy.

Below: *Jeane Dixon is perhaps America's most successful and respected clairvoyant, with a career spanning many years and many influential clients.*

Jeane Dixon is one of the most remarkable clairvoyants who has ever lived, a prophet of outstanding perception and accuracy who in her lifetime has literally changed the lives of the world's most powerful people as well as the views of those who often refuted her powers. She correctly predicted the deaths of John F. Kennedy, the airplane deaths of Hollywood actress Carole Lombard and United Nations secretary-general Dag Hammarskjold, and the suicide of Marilyn Monroe. A devout Roman Catholic, she believes that her gift of second-sight comes directly from God as part of his 'divine plan' for each and every one of us.

Born Jeane Pinckert in Wisconsin in 1918, she moved to California with her parents as a toddler. As a five-year-old she said to her mother that her father would be bringing home a black and white dog that day. Her father brought a puppy home as a surprise and was baffled about how she knew about it. On another occasion she told her mother that she would shortly be receiving a 'black letter'. Two days later a black-bordered envelope announcing the death of a relative in Germany arrived through the post. It was when she was eight years old that a gypsy travelling near her home came upon her and told her mother: 'Your child is blessed with great sensitivity and wisdom.' The gypsy left the young Jeane with a crystal ball, which she went on to use as a means of concentration so that her mind became re-ceptive to telepathic visions of future events. That gift all those years ago led to her title today of 'Seeress of Washington'. She keeps none of the money she earns from her books and lectures, preferring instead to contribute it to her non-profit-making Children to Children foundation.

As a little girl she was soon doling out advice to family and friends after gazing into her crystal ball, but it wasn't until she was married during World War 2 and living in Washington that she began crystal reading with intensity. She started doing psychic readings for servicemen at parties, but once word of her abilities began to spread she moved into a higher circle of diplomats, congressmen and other dignitaries. She was invited twice to the White House for private

consultations with President Roosevelt, but she has never revealed what she foretold for the great wartime leader.

She went on to predict major events with stunning accuracy. With the exception of 1960 she correctly foretold the outcome of each presidential election in America since 1948; she foretold the partition of India, the assassination of Mahatma Gandhi and the coming of Red China. But it was in 1963, with the murder of John F. Kennedy, that she achieved international fame. It was back in 1956 that Dixon predicted that a Democratic president 'with thick brown hair and blue eyes' would be assassinated by a man whose name began with an O or a Q. Dixon said the vision of this president's death had first come to her in 1952 when she prayed before a statue of the Virgin Mary in Washington's St Matthew's Cathedral. Dixon has always said that her premonitions came to her in three ways – by crystal gazing, by handling the treasured possession of a person or in direct messages from God. The last was the case in the prophecy of the murdered president.

It was four years until her vision was revealed to an American journalist. In 1959 she told a communist official visiting Washington from an Iron Curtain country – his name is not revealed but his identity authenticated by Dixon biographer Denis Brian – that the next president of the USA would be called Kennedy and that he would be assassinated in office. As 1963 approached, many people in the Kennedy circle were warned on numerous occasions about his impending doom, including one of

his secretaries and a secretary to his sister. Shortly before his fateful trip to Dallas, Texas, on 22 November 1963 she tried to get him to cancel his visit as the man with the name beginning with Q or O came to her in a vision. The warnings were ignored and Lee Harvey Oswald snuffed out the life of the best and brightest politician in the world with a high-powered rifle.

After his death she became known throughout the globe; her reputation was further enhanced the following year with the publication of a biography which chronicled her remarkable gifts. By 1966 she was an established international celebrity – and about to make another world-shattering prophecy.

America's manned space flight programme was within three years of putting men on the moon when Jeane suddenly had an awful premonition about the fate of the astronauts aboard an Apollo rocket. Jeane had become friendly with a woman named Jean Stout, wife of the chief of missions operations at the Office of Manned Space Flight. In December 1966 she lunched with Mrs Stout in Washington when she suddenly had a premonition that something terrible was about to happen to the Apollo programme. Holding her hand Jeane Dixon said: 'There's something strange about the floor of the capsule. It seems so thin that it almost resembles tinfoil. I am afraid that a tool dropped on it or a heel pushed firmly against it would go right through it. Under

John F. Kennedy (left). *The slaying of this president was one of many tragic premonitions of Jeane Dixon which came true.*

Below: *Carole Lombard was warned by Dixon not to take a certain plane. She ignored her – and paid for it with her life.*

Above: *The sex goddess to end them all. Her tragic death was foretold by Dixon.*

Robert Kennedy (right), *the senator who shared the same fate as his brother – and whose death was also foretold by Jeane Dixon.*

She has gone on to successfully predict the deaths of Martin Luther King, Marilyn Monroe and Robert Kennedy. When some of her prophecies have failed – like World War 3 which she forecast would break out in 1958 – she says that the basic information from God was correct and that she was merely wrong in her interpretation of the signals she received.

It is the prophecies that Mrs Dixon has written down for the end of the century that interest most observers. She predicts a great war with Russia in the Middle East and then a mighty war with China – an apocalyptic clash between good and evil which will result, by the year 2025, in China's conquest of most of Russia, Finland, Norway, Denmark, Libya and much of central Africa. On the good side, she predicts that western Europe will not feature in China's war plans and that salvation for the world will come after the war in the shape of the Second Coming of Christ.

'When that time comes,' she said, 'and it will come, we will all be united in the Brotherhood of Christ under the fatherhood of God.'

the floor I see a great clump of tangled wires...I see a terrible fiery catastrophe. And it will cause the astronauts' deaths. I sense their souls leaving the blazing capsule in puffs of smoke...' On 27 January 1967 an uncontrollable blaze snuffed out the lives of three astronauts as they tested the Apollo capsule at Cape Kennedy. Electronic malfunction was cited as the cause of the disaster.

Hollywood was naturally drawn to Jeane Dixon like paperclips pulled to a magnet. She read for the Reagans – long before Ronald Reagan as president would become reliant on a seer called Joan Quigley to chart his days for him – and Bob Hope. The famous comedian once tried to test her skills by asking how many strokes he had made during a game of golf earlier that day – but he didn't mention the name of his partner on the links. Without hesitation, she replied: 'You took 92 strokes and Eisenhower took 96.' She was correct on both counts. She once told a client, actress Carole Lombard, not to travel by plane for a six-week period. Lombard chose to ignore her and died in the wreckage of her aircraft.

MYSTERIES OF THE MIND

AN EYE TO THE FUTURE

The young aristocrat's dreams had proved correct in the past. If he trusted his erratic gift this time he stood to win a fortune – or lose one.

After serving gallantly in World War 2, the young aristocrat, the Hon. John Raymond Godley, went up to Balliol College, Oxford. On the night of 8 March 1946, he dreamed that he was reading the next day's evening paper. Among the racing results he noted that a horse named Brindal and another named Juladin had both won their respective races at odds of 7–1.

The next day he met a friend and told him about the dream. The pair checked two daily papers, and found that Brindal was running in the 1 pm race at Plumpton that afternoon, while Juladin was running at Wetherby in the 4 pm race. Godley's dream, however, had been optimistic: Brindal's starting price was 5–4, and Juladin's 5–2. He put money on Brindal, which won, and then put his winnings on Juladin, which also won. Several of Godley's friends, hearing about his dream, had put money on one or other of the horses too.

Rather than being elated at the accuracy of his precognition and the pleasure of winning his bets, Godley was actually rather worried at the outcome. In the next few weeks, his mornings were disturbed by people asking him if he'd had any good tips in his dreams. This bothered him: he reasoned that if he did have such a dream again, and his friends put money on his premonition – and *then lost their money*, he would be mightily, and rightly, unpopular.

But no more dreams came for nearly a month, by which time Godley was safe at his father Lord Kilbracken's isolated home in Ireland for the Easter vacation. On the night of 4 April he again dreamed of reading a list of winners; the only name he recalled on waking was Tubermore. The family house was so remote that the papers arrived days late, so Godley used the telephone to discover that a horse called Tuberose was running in the Grand

When he was a student at Balliol College, Oxford (above), in 1946, John Godley had the first of a series of dreams that could have turned into a bookies' nightmare: he accurately foresaw the winners of two races, one at Plumpton (opposite) and the other at Wetherby. Such dreams continued intermittently over the years and included several winners of the Grand National (below).

Right: *Mr What wins the Grand National in 1958 – as John Godley's dream had foretold. But this was the last occasion on which Godley's unlikely gift was to make him any money.*

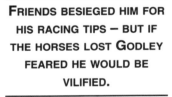

FRIENDS BESIEGED HIM FOR HIS RACING TIPS – BUT IF THE HORSES LOST GODLEY FEARED HE WOULD BE VILIFIED.

National that day. The name was near enough to the dream horse for Godley and his family to back it. The evening news on the radio told them Tuberose had won.

The next time Godley dreamed of a winning horse, the following July, the image that came to him was not of a newspaper, but of a telephone booth at the Randolph Hotel in Oxford, from which he was checking the result of a race with his bookie; the time after that – a year later, in July 1947 – he dreamed he saw the winner come in, and even recognized the jockey. In both cases his dreams came true, and he made money.

Godley's gift was erratic and irregular in its appearances, but it rarely let him down – until, in 1958, he had his last successful punter's dream winner (and bookie's nightmare). He won £450 (the equivalent today of about £7000) on an outsider in the Grand National. After that, he dreamed of no more winners.

John Godley's gift was at once typical of precognition in general, and highly unusual. It was typical in that the information he received about the future was often not strictly accurate. The names of the real-life horses were frequently slightly different from those he dreamed – his biggest win ever, and his last, came from a horse named Mr What, running in the Grand National, but the name he dreamed was 'What Man'. Typical too was the spasmodic fashion in which these dreams arrived, and the abrupt way they stopped. Godley could hardly have made a living out of his premonitions,

for they simply did not come often enough.

What is peculiar about them is their consistency when they did come, and their highly specialized nature (when they began, Godley was only mildly interested in racing) – and they are most unusual in *continuing* to occur. Most precognitions of such a specific kind come once or twice in a lifetime. Even 'professional' psychics, whose premonitions are usually much more general in nature, rarely have such runs of precise, repetitive and particular visions from the future.

A CLOSE SHAVE WITH DEATH

Precognition in general, however, is a recognized branch of extra-sensory perception, and like all parapsychological phenomena raises endless questions – both about the mysterious mechanics of how the human mind can read the future, and about the nature of time itself. Both these problems arise when people foresee disasters.

One of the best-attested and documented instances of a precognition of a disaster was first made known to one of its victims at a cocktail party. The night before he was due to fly home from Shanghai in January 1946, Air Marshal Sir Victor Goddard of the Royal New Zealand Air Force was invited to a gathering hosted by the British Consul-General, G.A. Ogden. In the midst of the general chatter, Goddard was suddenly distracted by someone behind him saying, 'Too bad about Goddard.

Terrible crash.'

Goddard turned round in amazement. The speaker – a Royal Navy officer named Gerald Gladstone – recognized Goddard and froze. 'I'm terribly sorry – I mean,' he stammered, 'I'm terribly glad.' Then Gladstone (he was later to be Admiral Sir Gerald Gladstone) explained that he had had an unbidden, overwhelmingly powerful vision of Goddard in a DC-3 ('Dakota'). In his vision, the plane ran into a snowstorm, flew over mountains and then crashed in failing light on a shingly shore. All aboard were killed. The passengers, apart from Goddard, included three civilians: two Englishmen and a girl.

Goddard was no stranger to psychic experiences and did not mock Gladstone's vision. But he felt he had no need to worry. He was indeed about to fly the first leg of his journey, to Tokyo, in a DC-3, but he was taking only two of his staff officers.

But by the end of the party he had gathered three further passengers. The Consul-General, G.A. Ogden, had an urgent message requesting him to be in Tokyo as soon as possible for a meeting; Goddard offered him a seat on his plane. A London *Daily Telegraph* reporter, Seymour Berry, then begged a lift. Finally, Tokyo sent a further request – for a secretary to take minutes of the meeting. Miss Dorita Breakspear became the third civilian on the flight.

Goddard's DC-3 – named *Sister Ann*, it was Supreme Allied Commander, South-East Asia, Lord Louis Mountbatten's personal aircraft – took off for Tokyo next morning. At about 3 pm, it began to run into snow, and the radio failed. When the *Sister Ann* finally crossed the coast of Japan, the crew was confronted unexpectedly by mountains. The plane was low on fuel, and clearly well off course. The pilot decided to look for somewhere to land the plane as safely as possible.

True to Gladstone's premonition, there was a snowstorm raging as the plane came out under the cloud cover. Ditching in the sea, whipped up by the storm, was out of the question. But below them they saw a small village, and a strip of shingly shore. Goddard was now sure that every detail of Gladstone's vision would come true.

The pilot made three attempts to land on the narrow beach. The last succeeded, but the plane spun across the shingle, its undercarriage collapsing. When it came to rest facing the sea, Goddard was amazed to

GODDARD REALIZED THAT EVERY DETAIL OF THE PREMONITION HAD COME TRUE, AND AS THE PLANE CRASHED ONTO THE SHINGLE, HE KNEW THAT HIS DEATH WAS INEVITABLE.

find himself still alive – as were all the other passengers and crew. They had landed on Sado Island, some 200 miles north of Tokyo, and on the other side of the Japanese mainland from the capital.

Gladstone's distressing vision had been right in all respects but one: those on board had lived to confirm the details of his premonition. Crucial though the difference was to those who survived, some

Someone, somewhere, will always have an accurate premonition of major events. The sinking of the liner **Titanic** *in April 1912 (above) and the Allied campaign in France after D-Day (below) were foreseen by a host of people.*

parapsychologists would argue that this does not invalidate Gladstone's experience as a genuine precognition.

The theory behind this assertion is easier to understand when you realize that a certain kind of premonition of disaster is *always* incomplete.

A number of people, for example, cancelled their passage on the ill-fated *Titanic* after premonitions that the ship would sink. One, a Mr Conan Middleton, had two dreams in which he saw the liner floating capsized. Another, Colin Macdonald, would have taken a step up in his career had he taken the job of second engineer that he was offered on the doomed ship. None of these glimpses of the future actually *prevented* the disaster that overtook the *Titanic* on the night of 12 April 1912, although the chances are that precognition did alter the future for those who had them, and acted on their hunches and refused to sail: roughly seven in every ten people on board died after the ship hit an iceberg in the North Atlantic.

PHANTOM ORDERS

To take a more recent instance of a premonition of disaster that saved the life

of the percipient, Mr Chris Ross of Hove, Sussex, described in the early 1980s what happened when his father was driving a truck loaded with ammunition in a convoy across France some time after D-Day in 1944. For the duration of the journey, the men had been ordered to sleep in their trucks during rest stops. In the first such stop, Ross's father had been asleep for an hour or so when he was woken up by someone shouting an order: 'Get that truck out of here, quickly!'

The soldier did as he was told, automatically – then stopped after a few hundred yards, mystified at the fact that he alone had started up and pulled out. The next thing he saw was a pair of Messerschmitt fighters flying straight at the parked convoy through a gap in the nearby hills. After they had done their brief but nasty work, three trucks were out of action and several men lay dead.

Ross then found himself being quizzed by the unit's commander about why he had driven off – it was impossible for him to have seen the two enemy planes coming. Ross replied that he had simply obeyed the order he'd heard – only to be told that no such order had been given. When the two men returned to the convoy, they found a bomb crater precisely where Ross's ammunition truck had been parked. The phantom order – or premonition – had prevented the bomb hitting the ammunition truck and, no doubt, killing many more men than the convoy actually lost.

Nonetheless, there was nothing Ross could have done to stop the Messerschmitts attacking; his premonition (which, one presumes, was cannily interpreted by his subconscious to take the form most likely to get an unquestioning response) and his prompt action certainly saved lives. But Ross did not, in a sense, foresee the future: he saw what *would* inevitably happen if he did not act in a certain way, and quickly.

Something like Ross's dramatized flash of intuition must have occurred to the anonymous young man described by Mr E.J. Branwell in a letter written in the early 1980s. One day in the late 1970s, Branwell was in Peter Robinson's department store in Oxford Street, London, when he saw a young man appear as if from nowhere, running furiously toward an 'up' escalator between two floors of the store. On the

escalator were two women and a child in a pushchair, riding to the next floor. The young man leapt up the escalator, and as he got to 'within three steps' of the group, the pushchair slipped and the child fell out – into his arms. The witness noted that other people who saw this happen were amazed at the speed of the young man's reaction; but, he asked pointedly: 'How can you have a reaction to something that hasn't happened?'

Some forms of precognition, then, are not precise pictures of the future, as if the course of coming events is inevitable and immutable, like John Godley's (sometimes hazy) precognitions of winners of horse

Above: *A Messerschmitt ME-109 of the type that fired on a convoy of British Army trucks in 1944 – and whose attack was foreseen by one of the convoy's drivers.*

ROSS OBEYED THE ORDER INSTINCTIVELY — ONLY TO FIND HE'D LEFT HIS CONVOY BEHIND AND THE MESSERSCHMITTS WERE MOVING IN FOR THE KILL.

races. These premonitions are intimations of potential events, whether involving their percipients or others. But the *general* pattern of events is unchanged. The *Titanic* still sailed from Southampton, and sank; the Messerschmitts still flew, and a number of British soldiers died as a result, unaware of their approach; the child still fell from its pushchair at Peter Robinson's store.

Gladstone's 'vision' of Goddard's death was *itself* no different from these examples: he foresaw the *potential* results of a crashed aircraft and some very accurate details of the circumstances of the crash. He begged Goddard not to fly to Japan the next day; Goddard felt safe in doing so – even though, as it turned out, detail by detail of Gladstone's precognition emerged as accurate. Precisely why he may have been wrong about the final, critical detail – the death of the passengers and crew on board that plane – we shall consider later.

POINTLESS WARNING

Crises in the future are clearly significant in generating premonitions – and perhaps for obvious reasons. We mark our lives by crises – the highs and lows of getting on with living. Few people are not touched emotionally to some degree by major disasters, however distant their connections with those dead, maimed or fortunate enough to escape.

But by that token, everyone 'ought' to have premonitions of major events affecting their own and others' lives; and yet most of us go through life with not an inkling of the personal disasters that will befall us as individuals, let alone the horrors that may confront hundreds or even thousands of our fellow humans caught up in a plane crash, an earthquake, or some similar calamity. The arbitrary, infuriating and mysterious nature of premonitions (and of ESP in general) is nowhere more obvious than in the very obscurity and uselessness of some of them.

Mrs Marjory Walker of Harrietsham, Kent, was struck in 1950 by an extraordinarily vivid dream that she had while on holiday that year. 'I dreamed,' she recounted, 'I was looking at a scene in a busy London street, complete with tramlines [then a feature of the London scene], vehicles and a crowd of people who were gathered around a body on the ground. Next I found myself looking at the right-hand column of the front page of the *Daily Express*. It read: "Stuart Andrew Walker, aged 8 1/2 years [the name and age of one of my sons], falls to death from the balcony of his parents' London flat."'

Some time later, the *Daily Express* featured a report of a child's death in precisely the place Mrs Walker had foreseen it, and with a picture of exactly the scene she had dreamed. But the report read: 'Hilary Page's 2 1/2-year-old daughter, one of twin girls, falls to her death from the balcony of her parents' flat.'

'Why,' asked Mrs Walker reasonably enough, yet with obvious pain, 'should I have a dream so similar to an actual tragedy, yet about the wrong child so that I could not warn the family in time…why did I have that dream at all when it proved of no use to anyone?'

What makes this story additionally curious is that Mrs Walker's second son (not the one who featured in her dream) in due course became a successful businessman and bought the company owned by Hilary Page (who had invented the Kiddicraft range of educational toys). So there was a connection between the two families lying in the future: although Mrs Walker's premonition was garbled and useless, it does suggest that there was some kind of attraction across time between them that expressed itself in this particularly frustrating way.

MAGIC RITUALS

Still more frustrating – and perplexing – are those few instances of premonitions that amount to major prophecies – and that no one at the time registers as such. The most often quoted instance of seemingly accurate prophecy of this kind is the vast body of obscure quatrains published by the French physician and clairvoyant Michel Nostradamus (1503–1566).

Nostradamus reputedly gathered the material for these verses by 'scrying' nightly in his study. He began each session with a magic ritual, setting a bowl of water in a brass tripod on his desk, touching the tripod with a wand and dipping the wand into the water, after which he touched the tip of the wand to his robe. He would then settle down to record what he saw and heard – visions that came to him, he said, 'by the subtle spirit of fire', in a fragmented form and accompanied by a disembodied voice that, he believed, was the Divine Presence in limbo (the region of the afterlife that, in Roman Catholic doctrine, houses the souls of the unbaptized).

The peculiar obscurity of the results of this ritual has been ascribed to Nostradamus's fear of the Inquisition, which had paid him some unwanted attention in the past; to avoid any suspicion of dabbling in witchcraft he wrote in a patchwork of Greek, Latin, French, and local Provençal dialect, and liberally sprinkled his visionary text with what later interpreters construed as anagrams. Other obscurities – a famous one is the similarity between the name 'Hister' and the name 'Hitler' – have been put down to the corruption of details so common in premonitions.

Nostradamus has been credited with a truly astonishing range of accurate predictions. According to Marion Zimmer Bradley's *Encyclopedia of Mystical & Paranormal Experience* these include foreseeing the Napoleonic wars; the history of the British monarchy from Elizabeth I to Elizabeth II – including the abdication of Edward VIII; the American revolutionary and civil wars; the rise and fall of Hitler; the assassinations of US Presidents Lincoln and Kennedy; and even the rise of the Ayatollah Khomeini in Iran. He predicted air and space travel, the use of submarines in warfare, and the development of the atomic bomb.

Some of Nostradamus's quatrains indeed appear to be startlingly precise and accurate about events that were to occur long after the publication of his verses. He did, for instance, predict the date of the French Revolution, and described a particular event that would follow: 'By night will come into Varennes through the forest of Reines two married people, by a circuitous route, Herne the white stone, the black Monk in grey, the elected Capet; and the result will be tempest, fire, blood, slice [*tempeste, feu, sang, tranche*].'

On 20 June 1792, Louis Capet – King Louis XVI, who was in fact elected to the throne he had inherited by the revolutionary Constituent Assembly – and his wife Marie Antoinette disguised themselves (he in grey, she in white) and fled from Paris in an attempt to reach their army of supporters near Rheims (Reines). The royal pair took a circuitous route to Rheims by way of Varennes – which was where they were arrested. The attempt at flight discredited Louis entirely, and led directly to the Reign of Terror in which the 'slice' of the guillotine played so prominent a part. That tireless instrument of death indeed ended Louis's and Marie Antoinette's own lives in the summer and autumn respectively of the following year.

Below: *Nostradamus, whose predictions in obscure verse have been the object of fascinated study for over 400 years.*

Above: *Inflation of the German currency reached almost surreal heights in the 1920s – an event prophesied by an obscure French civilian captured on the Western Front in August 1914, when the German empire was at its most powerful.*

All this is very impressive; but the accuracy and truth of Nostradamus's words are apparent only *after* the events they describe have occurred. And some details still trouble even the sympathetic modern reader: who, or what, is Herne the (white) stone? By what stretch of the imagination could King Louis XVI be called a black monk? Apart from these nagging points, there is little in the quatrain itself that unambiguously says that the King of France and his wife would be caught trying to escape from Paris in 1792, and predicts the invention and the industrious application of the guillotine.

This is not to say that Nostradamus did not foresee these very events: but he did

not say so very clearly. The difficulty we are left with is how to determine, from his somewhat less than limpid language, exactly what Nostradamus may have been predicting would happen during any particular period that still remains in the future; and when the details seem clear, the dating of them is frequently not.

The quatrains are so obliquely written that no one has actually been able to use them as predictions until events have already occurred to bear them out. Before 1990 it would have been hard to point with any certainty to what he may have foreseen concerning, for example, the former Soviet Union in the early 1990s. This will not stop those who wish to from finding a suitable set of lines that seems to predict the fall of the Soviet empire – but it will be hindsight, not Nostradamus's precognition, that reveals them.

TERRIFYING ACCURACY

Far more specific, and far more astonishing in their clarity and precision, are the prophetic words of another Frenchman, reported in the 'Rill letters' from World War 1.

Andreas Rill was by training a carpenter; he came from Untermuhlhausen in Bavaria. In August 1914 he was on active service with the German army, and his unit was billeted in a Capuchin monastery near Colmar, Alsace. From here he wrote two letters to his family about the extraordinary predictions that a French prisoner had made while being questioned by Rill and his fellow-soldiers.

Rill described the prisoner – who does not seem to have been a soldier, but a French citizen who simply got in the way of the Kaiser's army – as 'a strange holy man who said incredible things'. Much

The anonymous Frenchman foretold the rise of Hitler (above, with Mussolini) and his defeat (left – British, US and Soviet troops celebrate the fall of Berlin in 1945), along with a host of other startlingly accurate details of the Nazi regime.

later, in the 1980s, Rill's son Siegmund told investigators that his father had maintained that the Frenchman had told him that he had once been a rich man and a Freemason, but had given away his wealth and joined the monastery. Among this visionary's predictions were the following:

• The war they were fighting would last five years.

• Germany would lose the war.

• A revolution would follow the war in Germany.

• Everyone in Germany would become a millionaire; indeed 'there would be so much money that it would be thrown out of windows and no one would bother to pick it up' [Andreas Rill commented that this was 'ridiculous!'].

• During this time the Antichrist would be born, and around 1932 would become a tyrannical dictator over Germany for approximately nine years.

• In 1938, preparations for war would begin.

• The war would last three years and end with the downfall of the dictator – 'the man and his sign will disappear'.

• After the war, things 'that are simply inhuman' would be discovered about the dictator's regime.

• In 1945 Germany would be 'pressed from all sides and totally plundered and destroyed'.

• Foreign powers would occupy Germany, but the country would recover economically.

• Italy would fight against Germany in this war [i.e. World War 1] but with Germany in the next war.

The accuracy of these predictions is astonishing. World War 1 lasted only four years and three months, but in August 1914 the word on everyone's lips, on both sides, was that it would be over by Christmas. As everyone knows, the Germans lost, and there was a revolution in Germany. Phenomenal inflation in the early 1920s made everyone in Germany a 'millionaire'. 'Around 1932' is not a bad guess for the establishment of Hitler's power: the Nazi party swept to power in elections held in January 1933. World War 2 lasted longer than three years, although it was clear that Germany could not win it by the end of 1942.

The natural conclusion of a sceptic would be that the letters were forged after World War 2. But Dr Hans Bender of the Freiburg Institute in Germany had them examined by forensic scientists for signs of fraud or later changes, and they found none; while Rill's son – who was born in 1906 – recounted how the predictions in his letters were well known around Unter-muhlhausen between the wars. Dr Bender's researchers also cross-checked other details of the letters with existing records and concluded they were authentic.

But who was the mysterious French prophet?

Dr Bender's investigators used the war journal of the unit in which Andreas Rill served to establish that in August 1914 part of Rill's company had billeted at a Capuchin monastery in Sigolsheim, six miles from Colmar. Another key fact was that in 1918, Rill's unit had returned to the Colmar area and had been stationed in Turckheim, some eight miles from Sigolsheim. Rill took the opportunity to walk the distance in the hope of seeing the visionary again, but on arriving there he was told that the Frenchman had died earlier in the year.

Checking the monastery's records – and those of all the Capuchin houses in the area – the researchers found no record of a French monk who had died in 1918, but they did discover that at Sigolsheim an official *guest* – known as a Frater Laicus Tertiarius – of the monastery there had died that year, and before Rill's visit. A rich man (who may well have given his wealth to the order) and one who was also a Freemason would not have had difficulty in being accepted as a permanent guest with the order, the investigators believed. Although they were unable to establish that this was precisely the man they were looking for, they felt satisfied that the Rill letters were indeed authentic.

In this extraordinary case we are confronted yet again with predictions that are startlingly accurate, mingled with others whose details are imprecise or at least less accurate than others. And some of the French prophet's precognitions – which we have not dwelt on here, and they were markedly fewer than his accurate pre-dictions – were simply wrong. But so too have details in the other cases we have looked at here been wrong. Is there any explanation for this? Or any explanation for cases like that of Mrs Walker, whose premonition was, as we said, garbled and useless, although it was accurate in many points of detail and did indeed concern someone who, in the future, would play a major part in the life of one of her sons?

SIGNALS FROM THE FUTURE

To account for precognition of any kind we are forced to speculate about the nature of time. The only possible explanation for accurate precognition is that it is possible, by some inexplicable means, to see into the future. But the real question is: which future?

There is no reason, the experts tell us, to believe that there is only one possible future. Both physicists and theologians would agree on that point. The physicists go one stage further, and suggest that time may constantly be splitting up into different 'timelines' and, indeed, even into separate universes *all the time*. To some extent we may each of us be living in a private universe, but one that is intimately related – indeed barely distinguishable – to the universes of most other people.

A precognition of a future event may be 99 per cent accurate and yet its key feature not come true – as in the case of Admiral Gladstone's vision of Air Marshal Goddard's death. Some scientists would argue that Goddard did die – but not in this timeline or in this universe. What Gladstone saw was an event from a parallel universe, obviously one that shared most of the features of the one in which this story is told. In that parallel reality, Gladstone's precognition may be celebrated as an all too accurate picture of what was to come. In yet another reality, the precognition will have been forgotten, because Goddard took his flight alone, as he had assumed he would, and landed safely in Tokyo.

But if these different realities do exist, it would be surprising if the more similar ones did not suffer from a certain amount of 'cross-talk' – like the dim echo of a different conversation, running parallel to our own, that we hear occasionally on the telephone, or as the left-hand channel of a stereo picks up sound that is intended for the right-hand loudspeaker.

The signal from the future – from this

timeline or any other – is not strong, however, and the information that individuals pick up can be strangely distorted. But the 'parallel universe' hypothesis might itself explain this lack of clarity – in radio or hi-fi terms, this high signal-to-noise ratio. Until we find a way of crossing these barriers, it is unlikely that many precognitions will be as useful as John Godley's were to him.

Above: *The late Dr Hans Bender. A team from his research institute in Freiburg, Germany, verified the authenticity of the prophetic 'Rill letters' and almost succeeded in identifying the author of their astonishingly accurate predictions.*

A MEETING OF
MINDS

The professor's telepathic gifts told him that his daughter's life hung on a thread, but he was powerless to do anything to help her.

Ernst Cassirer, who died in 1945 at the age of 70, was one of the 20th century's most humane and creative philosophers. He was also psychic, in one specific way: he always knew, without being told, when his daughter Anna was ill. On three or four occasions, she told psychical researcher and scholar Lawrence LeShan, during the years she was at boarding school in Germany, Cassirer woke up in the middle of the night and insisted on telephoning her school. Each time, he was told that Anna had been taken ill and was in the school sanatorium. He never, she said, called in this way when she was well – which was most of the time.

In 1919 Cassirer became professor of philosophy at the University of Hamburg, and remained there until Hitler came to power in Germany in 1933. During this time Anna grew up and left home to study in Berlin. While she was a student, Cassirer came to visit her; they spent an evening at a party together, and the next day Cassirer caught the train back to Hamburg. The express made only one stop on the journey, at Wittenberg. As it pulled in, Cassirer grabbed his suitcase, jumped off the train, and at once telephoned his daughter's lodgings in Berlin.

'What happened?' he demanded of the housekeeper. 'What is the matter with Anna?'

He was told she had been taken to hospital. Cassirer called the infirmary at once, and learned that only an hour after he had caught his train home, she had begun to haemorrhage. She was now in emergency surgery.

Cassirer's experiences are good instances of telepathy at work. And they are typical, too, of telepathy in Western societies – which for the majority of us seems to occur most often as a spontaneous response to a crisis. A few gifted individuals do seem able to 'tune in' to other minds at will, and some have tried to train and develop these powers. But they are few and far between – and far less common in the industrial West than they are in so-called 'primitive' tribal societies.

Why this should be the case may offer some clues as to *what* telepathy is, even if the mystery of how it works remains unsolved. And it may help explain why laboratory experiments into telepathy have not been consistent or entirely successful.

MIND READING

Frederic Myers, like his famous near-contemporary Matthew Arnold, was an erudite inspector of schools and a poet; born in 1843, he was also one of the founders of the Society for Psychical Research. It was he who coined the term 'telepathy', defining it as 'the communication of impressions of any kind from one mind to another independently of the recognized channels of the senses'.

Since the SPR was founded in 1882, there have been literally thousands of experiments in psychology laboratories around the world, all dedicated to establishing the reality of telepathy. The

The free and easy movement of a Masai dancer (opposite) *contrasts with the formality of a Western city such as Hamburg* (above), *where Ernst Cassirer, philosopher and occasional telepathist, lived before World War 2. Does the human mind have a built-in capacity for telepathic communication – one that flourishes in so-called 'primitive' societies but only occasionally bursts forth in 'civilized' cultures?*

experiments have become more and more sophisticated over the years, but the data that have been collected from them have failed to convince mainstream scientists that telepathy actually exists at all. The parapsychologists who have designed and conducted these experiments would disagree, but even the most dedicated and 'believing' of them would agree that none of this work has got anyone closer to understanding *how* telepathy works.

The reasons for this strange and unsatisfactory state of affairs are various. Not least among them is the stubborn conviction among many orthodox scientists that *all* paranormal phenomena are simply 'impossible' because they break the known laws of science. The logic, such as it is, of this argument runs approximately as follows: science has no way to explain these things, and the known laws of nature seem to exclude them. Because science can't accommodate or account for them, they do not happen.

The flaw in the argument is obvious enough: because there is so much evidence that paranormal events do happen – but not to order – it's clearly the laws of nature, as presently understood and stated, that are lacking. And such a mulish attitude is

Above: *Frederic W. Myers, one of the founders of the Society for Psychical Research. The aim of the SPR has always been to approach psychic phenomena in an objective, scientific spirit.*

Right: *The Yugoslav psychic Velibor undertakes a parapsychology experiment, monitored by the researcher who discovered him, Ainul Kebir. Velibor has succeeded many times in 'reading' letters and numbers contained in sealed envelopes.*

hardly fitting for a scientist, of all people – since the very basis of scientific endeavour is supposed to lie in the hope of discovering more about nature than we already know. In science laws are made to be broken; they are, as the old saw has it, for the guidance of wise men and the obedience of fools.

But investigations into the paranormal have always run up against one major difficulty and that is the notorious inconsistency of its effects. Telepathy, like other forms of extra-sensory perception (ESP), is no exception to this rule. Even very sensitive individuals don't receive information from other people's minds 100 per cent of the time, even when notably successful 'senders' are deliberately and carefully trying to transmit their thoughts to such a person. Nor do they always pick up the information with 100 per cent accuracy when they *do* receive it.

A good illustration of how blurred telepathic communication is can be had from the experience of George Gilbert Murray (1866–1957). In his day Murray was regarded as the world's greatest scholar of ancient Greek, but he also had a consistent and genuine telepathic talent, which he did his best to develop in 'guessing games' with his family. Murray did not limit himself to single objects, words or images on which someone else was concentrating: he could pick up entire quotations, episodes from public or family history, or scenes from books. In his study *The Paranormal* Dr Brian Inglis quotes what he calls a 'typical' example of one of Murray's successes, when the 'sender' was thinking of a scene in the French novel *Marie Claire*. Murray's response ran:

'This is a book – it's not English, not Russian – it's rather a – I think there are nuns in it – there are a lot of people – either a school or a laundry – and one of the nuns is weeping – I think it's French. Oh, it's a scene in *Marie Claire*, near the beginning – I can't remember it, but something like that – it's in the place where she goes – one of the nuns crying – a double name – no I can't get the – Marie Thérèse –.'

The name of the weeping nun in the scene from the book was in fact Marie Aimée. Whether that error was the result of Murray's memory of the book being at fault, or was a matter of garbled

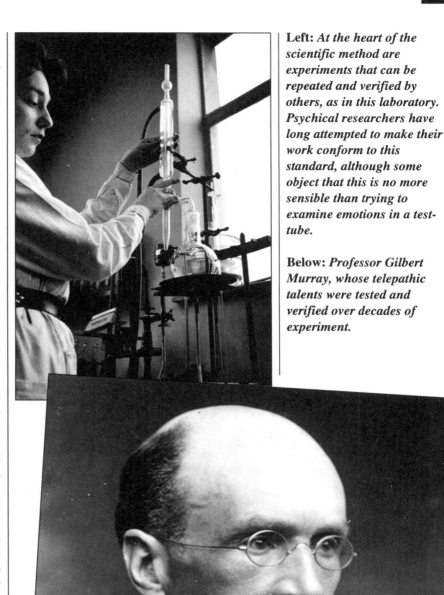

Left: *At the heart of the scientific method are experiments that can be repeated and verified by others, as in this laboratory. Psychical researchers have long attempted to make their work conform to this standard, although some object that this is no more sensible than trying to examine emotions in a test-tube.*

Below: *Professor Gilbert Murray, whose telepathic talents were tested and verified over decades of experiment.*

transmission, it is certainly typical of telepathy that even the best 'hits' are slightly awry.

And Murray did not have hits all the time, by any means. The results of some 50 years of his practice in these games were eventually published by the Society for Psychical Research, and they show that Murray was correct in only one-third of his 'guesses'. The other results included either failures in detail or attempts that did not work because guesses were simply not offered by Murray (another third), and the remaining third were ambiguous. Even so, such a high proportion of successes, especially given the elaborate kinds of target ideas that Murray was trying to pick up, is way above what anyone could explain away as 'chance' or 'coincidence'.

Murray did not, by any means, always have to have some prior knowledge of the subject he was offered in order to pick it up – even when it might be something as obscure as a scene from a book. Dr Inglis quotes an instance of this, but notes another curious aspect of it. Murray's impression was partly formed by the way his daughter had pictured the scene when it was chosen as a target for him.

The particular target was a scene from a book by Alexandre Aksakov, in which children were being taken by their parents to visit their grandparents. Murray did not identify the author, but he got the gist of the scene correctly – and added that the family was, he thought, crossing the River Volga. In the particular scene in question, they were not, but that image *had* been in his daughter's mind when the target was chosen, and does feature frequently in the book. The only explanation Murray could provide for this was, simply, that he had read his daughter's mind – in other words, it was her thoughts about the target that he had picked up, not the target itself.

MENTAL BLOCKAGE

Experiments in telepathy in the industrialized West are one thing; but some peoples living in constant and intimate contact with nature – and not in any sickly, patronizingly romantic sense, but through the sheer necessity of survival – seem to take telepathic communication for granted. This suggests that all of us may well have a telepathic ability, but that the ingrained habits of mind encouraged in industrialized societies – habits of will, of conscious, logical thinking rather than lateral or intuitive thinking – make it more difficult to get access to that ability.

Some specific instances of the *normality* of telepathic powers in traditional societies, as recorded by surprised Westerners, may serve to illustrate the difference between the two ways of looking at the world – and may illuminate the nature of the West's mental blockage when it comes to telepathy and associated forms of ESP.

HYPNOTIC DRUMS

In April 1962, the London *Times* carried a report of a bizarre telepathic relationship between an African family in the remote Singida province of Tanganyika (now Tanzania) and the local lion community. The family's ability to control lions was well known in the district, and villagers began to protest when the number of livestock killed by lions – but shared with them by their human controllers – reached new heights.

Colonel Mervin Cowie, the director of Kenya's national parks, told *The Times*: 'Recently one of the "lion-controllers" was gaoled by a chief after villagers protested…The man told the chief that unless he was freed by nightfall he would get his lions to kill the chief's cattle. The chief refused. Next morning fourteen of his cattle lay dead.'

FOOLISHLY THE CHIEF REFUSED TO FREE THE MAN WHO COULD CONTROL LIONS; WHEN THE DAWN CAME, THERE WERE FOURTEEN FRESHLY KILLED CATTLE CORPSES IN THE AFRICAN VILLAGE.

Below: *A Russian village on the banks of the River Volga, in Russia, which featured in a key experiment by Gilbert Murray.*

In his memoir *Africa Drums*, published in the 1930s, Richard St Barbe Baker, a conservator of forests in Kenya and in Nigeria during the early years of the 20th century, recalled a number of occasions when Kenyan tribesmen appeared to have received telepathic communications. For example, Baker describes how he was on a field trip in the foothills around Mount Kenya and around noon one day pitched camp. He continues:

'Lunch was served by a boy, who observed that Bwana Katchiku had died, this man being a well-respected farmer who lived some two hundred and fifty miles from the camp. When asked how he knew, the boy replied that N'degwa, one of the elders of the tribe about sixty years old, had "seen" it. He sent for the older man…

'"What is this? [Baker asked the elder when he arrived] Bwana Katchiku dead, you say? How did you learn of this?"

'"*N'iona*, I see it," was his astonishing reply.

'"When?" I demanded.

'"Now," he said. Somehow I knew he was speaking the truth, nor was there any reason for him to do otherwise.

'"I am sorry," I told him. "It is too bad…"

'"Yes, that is so," agreed N'degwa. "It is a bad business."

'N'degwa retired, but I made a mental note of the time and place. I pondered on the word *N'iona* – I see – which could not possibly be confounded with *S'kia* – I hear.

Left: *Kenyan warriors, like those who demonstrated extraordinary powers of clairvoyance to forester Richard St Barbe Baker. To the Africans, there was nothing unusual about their ability to see distant events in their minds.*

Below: *The Reading Jazz and Blues Festival in full swing in 1971. The power of music both to lull and stimulate at the same time creates a liberated state of mind similar to that created by hypnosis – which, it seems, brings out latent psychic powers.*

Above: *Laurens van der Post, who noted many instances of psychic communication among the San (Bushmen) of the Kalahari desert.*

THE OLD BUSHMAN KNEW THAT PEOPLE WERE HEADED IN THEIR DIRECTION — AND THAT THEY WERE IN TROUBLE.

'Seven days later a runner arrived at my camp with the news that Bwana Katchiku had died, at a distance of two hundred and fifty miles from camp.'

Note that Baker challenges (in best logical, Western fashion) the old man, as if he expects him to be lying, or to have *heard* the news, not seen it directly. But, as he admits, it became clear that the news had not already arrived; N'degwa had not heard about the farmer's death from a messenger of any kind. And in time, Baker came to accept this faculty among the native Kenyans, and even speculated that the hypnotic effect of drums released the ability to transmit and receive messages by mental energy alone.

This may not be the only stimulus that induces telepathic abilities. Baker himself also came to believe that Western people had lost the facility to practise telepathy because in the West 'the rhythm of life was conspicuous by its absence' and 'an air of worry and anxiety in competition' had replaced 'the serenity of the forest or wayside market'. But the paradoxical combination of simultaneous exhilaration, relaxation, and well-being that music can so famously induce (witness the recurrent hysteria about rock'n'roll, which threatens almost everything the constipated Western mind has erected like a moat about its wilful consciousness) is not dissimilar from the peculiar state of swooning alertness that is typical of hypnotic trance, or the blissful awareness that meditation can bring.

MYSTERIOUS MUSICAL POWERS

Psychical researcher Joe Cooper, discussing Baker's African experiences in his book *Telepathy*, refers to the similarity between the effect of prolonged drumming and what he calls the *concentration* of hypnosis, and a resulting state of 'mental assonance'; but this is surely wrong. The drumming may have been concentrated, but its effect is surely different. It is the conscious, thinking, dominating mind that concentrates – and makes a bad hypnotic subject (and an awkward dancer). Whereas it is the unconscious, relaxed, accepting mind that achieves assonance (that is, harmony – a musical term!) with the world

about it, which does not exclude either music or other human minds.

Cooper is probably wrong too in ascribing another Kenyan 'vision' that Baker witnessed to precognition. The instance was as follows, in Baker's words:

'I had a headman called N'duma. For my entertainment he had arranged for an evening with the drums. Two young men… incessantly played on their drums for about a couple of hours until even I became almost hypnotized with the monotony.

'Suddenly N'duma exclaimed, "Master, I see you are going for a journey. You are going up to my country. You are going to Meru."

'At that time I had no intention of going to Meru. It was out of my district and there was, as far as I knew, absolutely nothing to take me there.

'"What makes you say that, N'duma?" I asked.

'"*N'iona*," was the reply, meaning simply, "I see it."'

A week later, Baker received orders to travel to Meru, which was some 200 miles from his station at the time. Cooper's – and Baker's – interpretation is that the headman was 'seeing' a future journey: but it seems more likely that N'duma was actually telepathically aware of the order being made, not the future event.

Another Western veteran of Africa, Laurens van der Post, has equally extraordinary stories to tell of the almost casual fashion in which the Bushmen of the Kalahari – a people whom he especially knows, loves and respects – treat telepathic experiences. In *The Heart of the Hunter*, Van der Post recounts how in the midst of an utterly silent, midday desert an old Bushman suddenly announced that there were people coming their way. There was no sign of any such thing, but the Bushman – and his interpreter, too – insisted that they could 'feel them coming here' (tapping at their chests), and that they were in trouble. And so it turned out to be. Van der Post's group gave the famished group food and water, and helped them on their way.

Another instance involved nothing more dramatic than an ostrich approaching: but the Bushman who became aware of the bird, while it was still out of sight, was also aware (because he felt the same sensation in his own body) that the creature was scratching the back of its neck with its foot. This echoes another African who commented, sensing the presence of a zebra, that he knew it was nearby because 'I feel his stripes on my back' – such was his empathy with the animal.

It is perhaps worth noting – in view of both Richard St Barbe Baker's comments on the significance of drum music among the Kenyan tribesmen he worked with, and the still more obvious fear that 'primitive'

Van der Post cites instances of San people not merely seeing but identifying with approaching animals such as ostriches (below) and zebras (above), although the creatures were invisible to the physical eye. One told Van der Post that he knew a zebra was nearby because he could 'feel his stripes on my back'.

This was for youth, Strength, Mirth, and wit that Time
Most count their golden Age; but t'was not thine.
Thine was thy later yeares, so much refind
From youths Droſſe, Mirth, & wit; as thy pure mind
Thought (like the Angels) nothing but the Praiſe
Of thy Creator, in thoſe laſt, beſt Dayes.
  Witnes this Booke, (thy Embleme) which begins
With Love; but endes, with Sighes, & Teares for ſins

IZ:WA:

Will: Marshall ſculpſit.

Above: *The frontispiece of John Donne's poems, published in 1649. In 1610, Donne had a disturbing and entirely accurate vision of his wife and their stillborn child.*

HER HAIR WAS HANGING AROUND HER SHOULDERS AND A DEAD CHILD LAY IN HER ARMS.

music like rock'n'roll (which has many African characteristics) generates in certain orthodox Western minds – what Van der Post has to say about the place of music among the Bushmen (who, he was surprised to find, had no drums) in his book *The Lost World of the Kalahari*:

'Music was as vital as water, food, and fire to them, for we never found a group so poor or desperate that they did not have some musical instrument with them. And all their music, song, sense of rhythm, and movement achieved its greatest expression in their dancing. They passed their days and nights with purpose and energy, but dancing too played the same deep part in their lives, as [it did for] the Bushmen of old in legend and history.'

Does the liberating effect of music and a nearness to the subtleties of the natural world – and music, after all, is no more than the human reflection of both the stately and the intimate rhythms of nature – bring out the latent psychic abilities of humankind? It is a question that those who have organized the crude and impersonal guessing games that have so long passed for 'research' in telepathy might do well to address.

EXCRUCIATING PAIN

While laboratory research into telepathy has failed to prove the existence of ESP to the satisfaction of scientists – and has even involved fraud on a few occasions – everyday experience of telepathy by ordinary people persists in defying rational explanation and continues to provide the most convincing evidence that such a

faculty does indeed exist. And accounts of telepathy go back a very long way.

The English poet and cleric John Donne (1572–1631) was not, perhaps, an ordinary man, but a genius for poetry does not necessarily imply any predisposition toward psychic talents. In his biography of Donne, Sir Izaak Walton recounts that in 1610 or so the poet (who was also a courtier) was sent to France on a diplomatic mission; his wife remained at home, since she was pregnant. When Sir Robert Drury, the English ambassador in Paris, went to meet Donne, he found him 'so altered as to his looks as amazed Sir Robert to behold him'.

Donne finally managed to account for his condition. 'I have seen a dreadful vision,' he explained. 'I have seen my dear wife pass twice by me through this room, with her hair hanging about her shoulders, and a dead child in her arms.'

Drury reluctantly agreed to send a messenger to England to discover what, if anything, was ailing Donne's wife. Twelve days later, the man returned to report that he had found Mrs Donne, as Walton put it, 'very sad, and sick in her bed; and that after a long and dangerous labour, she had been delivered of a dead child. And, upon examination, the abortion proved to be the same day, and about the very hour, that Mr Donne affirmed he saw her pass by him in his chamber.'

As with precognition, and as we noted above, telepathy seems most often to occur spontaneously as a reaction to a crisis, but

Below: *Scene in the Lake District, where Arthur Severn had an accident experienced by his wife.*

Above: *Building the Blue Nile dam in the Sudan in the 1920s. Such projects are typical of the Western tendency to manipulate and control the natural world, rather than harmonize with it. Such a domineering outlook suppresses natural psychic powers – and is usually disastrous for the environment, too.*

it remains unfathomable why a particular individual should telepathically 'tune in' to a particular crisis and not another. In the cases of Cassirer and Donne, both picked up some kind of signal from people with whom they had very strong emotional bonds, and at very critical times. But it seems hardly likely that the following instances of telepathically transmitted pain were the greatest emotional or physical crises suffered by the two couples involved.

Joan R. Severn, wife of the distinguished English landscape painter Arthur Severn, recounted to the art critic John Ruskin how, at about 7 am one summer morning in 1880, she woke up with a start, 'feeling I had had a hard blow on my mouth, and with a distinct sense that I had been cut and was bleeding under my upper lip, [I] seized my pocket handkerchief and held it...to the part...after a few seconds, when I removed it, I was astonished not to see any blood, and only then realized it was impossible anything could have struck me there, as I lay fast asleep in bed, and so I thought it was only a dream!'

Joan Severn noted the time, noticed too that her husband was not there and assumed he had gone out sailing – the Severns lived near Coniston Water, in the Lake District of Westmorland – and went back to sleep. About two and a half hours later, Severn came back from the lake for breakfast, and kept dabbing at his lip. Eventually he admitted that he had run into a squall while on the water: trying to get out of the way of the boat's suddenly swinging boom, he had had a sound crack across the mouth from the tiller. He had not been wearing a watch, but when his wife told him of her own sudden and painful awakening, calculated that the accident would have happened at about the same time as she started awake.

In 1947, Leslie Boughey was stationed with the RAF at El-Firdan in Egypt. He and his wife wrote to each other every day – she was in England, working in a factory near Stoke-on-Trent. He wrote to her one day telling how he had woken up in the night with 'the most excruciating pain' in one hand, and particularly in one finger. 'There was no mark on my finger, no swelling, inflammation, or anything, yet I just wanted to hold it and scream,' Boughey told researchers for the TV series *Arthur C. Clarke's World of Mysterious Powers*. Eventually, after a few hours of sweating and suffering, the agony subsided.

Boughey's letter telling his wife about this mysterious attack crossed in the mail with a letter from her. At work, she said, a fragment of metal had penetrated her finger, and the wound had turned septic. She had gone to the doctor, who had lanced the infected part. 'The extraordinary thing was,' said Boughey, 'the time of her operation coincided exactly with my painful experience: the same hand, even the same finger.'

TELEPATHIC TRAP

Telepathy, for some reason, is fickle: communicating quite trivial crises with excruciating force, and major ones with no more than a sudden pang of anxiety. And it is fickle too in its choice of subjects. It is not always people who have a close relationship or strong emotional ties who find themselves in touch by 'mental radio'.

Early one morning in 1980, 81-year-old Isabella Casas made her way slowly into her local police station in Barcelona, and stammered out a bizarre story to the officers there. She had just awoken from an appalling dream in which she had seen the face of her neighbour, Rafael Perez, 'twisted in terror', as she heard his voice saying, 'They are going to kill us.'

What stopped the police dismissing the nightmarish vision as merely a bad dream was Sra Casas's further concern. Perez, a 56-year-old chef, would normally visit her every day – but he had not called for ten

days. Even odder, she had had a note from him – delivered by hand – three days *after* she had last seen him, which said he would be away for several weeks. Why had he not called to tell her in person? The police decided to start a search for Perez.

They found him tied up in a utility room on the roof of his and Sra Casas's own apartment house. He had been hidden there by two men who had broken into his flat, forced him to sign 28 bank cheques so that they could withdraw his $30,000-worth of savings without being noticed, and made him write the note to Sra Casas to allay her suspicions before tying him up. When they had all the money, they said, they would return and kill him and the old lady. The

---

THE POLICE HAD TO DECIDE WHETHER THEY WERE DEALING WITH AN OLD LADY'S MENTAL WANDERINGS – OR AN UGLY MURDER.

Below: *A successful experiment in parapsychology. The typewritten 'target' phrase was hidden in a sealed box but was nevertheless accurately read by 15-year-old Monica Nieto Tejada in 1989.*

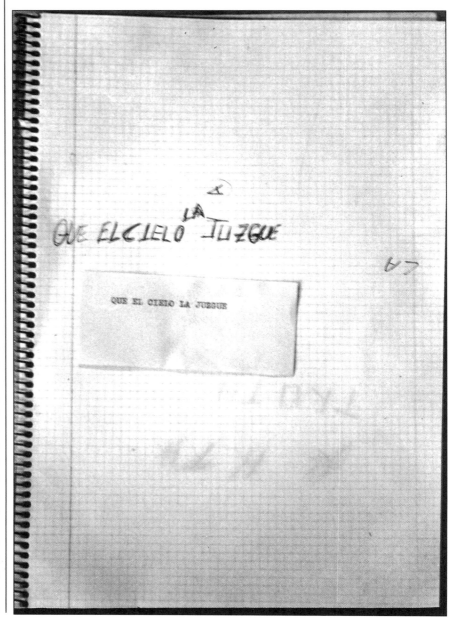

police simply waited for the two criminals to return, trapped them and arrested them.

THE BATTLE AGAINST NATURE

But why are these cases so rare, and why is telepathy so incomplete in the West, yet precise and part of the ordinary fabric of life for, say, an African Bushman?

To put it at its simplest, the great division between the modern Western outlook and that of traditional societies is this. The Western mind seeks to dominate the environment: it sees a plot of land, for instance, as something to exploit – to settle, to build hotels on, to bend to its will. It doesn't matter if this involves damming rivers, dredging harbours, razing forests and destroying wildlife. Success is measured by the extent to which things have been changed to suit the whim of human beings. At its worst, the Western mind treats the environment as an enemy.

The traditional way of looking at things is, on the other hand, passive: it seeks to absorb knowledge of the place, so that life – that is, the means of survival – can *fit in* with what already exists. Bridges may still be built, animals killed, the land tilled: but the traditional mind sees the natural world as something to listen to and co-operate with in order to make survival easier, not something to defeat.

The difference between the modern Western cast of mind and that of traditional societies is in essence the difference between confrontation with the environment and persuasion and compromise with it.

This tendency of the Western mind to see things in terms of black or white only, to see life as a series of oppositions and challenges and potential duels, may explain why laboratory experiments in telepathy and other forms of extra-sensory perception so often fail in the West, and fail in particular in the presence of sceptics. This phenomenon, known as the 'sheep/goat effect', has been noted many times by parapsychologists. A sheep, or believer in ESP, will get better results in ESP experiments than a goat, or sceptic – whether the sheep or goat is being tested *or is actually the person conducting the tests.*

In any case the notion of coldly testing for ESP in a laboratory is, in effect, a challenge, an implicit contest, in which one side or the other will 'win'. It is not an invitation to demonstrate a certain ability, but an obstacle to be overcome.

But in societies that keep the seemingly inevitable, perhaps inherent human propensity for competitiveness within carefully defined bounds – instead of making it a principle of 'good' conduct – and that have a relaxed, accepting outlook upon the natural world, psychic powers seem to flourish, along with other arts. And this is not wishful thinking. There is a wealth of historical and anthropological evidence that the most adept psychics within a tribe or community would certainly be regarded as unusual, but they would not be ostracized or even mocked. They would certainly not be ignored: it is more likely they would be revered. Such individuals might become a *shaman* or a medicine man – a '*witch doctor*' in crude colonialist terms, but actually the role is nearer that of priest, wise man, and tribal counsellor, rolled into one.

In the same way, the most talented poets or musicians would be recognized and elevated to a privileged position. Even in the West such 'acceptable' kinds of visionary still are so rewarded, if often grudgingly, since even the Western mind cannot bring itself wholly to deny the life of the spirit.

Western science, the epitome of logic and calculated thinking, cannot accommodate the life of the spirit, because it cannot measure it – or master it. Therefore it excludes it. While scientific thinking has come insidiously to dominate our lives, so that most people unconsciously assume that what cannot be proven by science cannot be taken entirely seriously, there are still eruptions of art, music and paranormal events to remind us that science's view of life may be powerful, but it is neither wholly true nor truly whole.

Below: *Medium Marvello Creti and members of his Societa Ergoniana. Creti was hailed as one of Italy's greatest inventors in the 1930s, but turned from material to spiritual interests. Today the society's base, a 16th-century former monastery near Sutri, contains machinery built by Creti to 'influence energy' in the human body.*

SLIPS IN TIME

Lost in foul weather and piloting a poorly equipped plane, Victor Goddard knew that his life depended on him finding the right direction. What he didn't expect to do was to fly into the future...

In 1934, Victor Goddard (later Air Marshal Sir Victor Goddard) of the Royal New Zealand Air Force had to fly a Hawker Hart biplane bomber from Scotland to England. On the way, he ran into bad weather and then had the nasty experience of going into a tailspin. After getting out of that scrape, he realized he was no longer sure where he was. The aircraft lacked sophisticated instruments and he was navigating by sight – and in that weather there was not much to be seen.

Goddard knew he ought to be within a few miles of Drem, an airfield that had been in use in World War 1 but had since been abandoned. Not long before, he had actually visited the place by car, just to find out if it was still possible to land there. He had found instead that the airstrip had been turned over to farmland, and that the former hangars were now being used as barns. But from the air he would certainly recognize Drem, and if he could find it, he could get himself back on course. Goddard lost height, flew under the cloud, and went to look for the disused airfield.

He found it. The first odd thing about the place was that it was bathed in sunlight, despite the inclement weather he had just encountered. Still more surprising – despite what he had seen just a few days previously – the airfield was now fully operational. The hangars had been repaired, and on the freshly laid tarmac apron sat four aircraft – one of them a monoplane fighter of a type he had never seen before. The final touch of strangeness was that these aircraft were painted yellow, and the ground crew around them were wearing blue uniforms.

It was weird enough to find an abandoned airfield suddenly in tip-top working order, but there were no aircraft in the RAF painted yellow, and in any case all RAF fighters in service at that time were biplanes: the first monoplane, the Hurricane, did not even fly until 1935. And RAF technicians wore khaki denim uniforms. What had suddenly happened at Drem? The place was real enough: Goddard took new bearings and completed his flight safely.

Reporting what he had seen to his wing commander, he was told unhelpfully but unambiguously to 'lay off the Scotch'. In 1938, Drem was reopened as a flight training station. By then, the first Hurricanes were entering RAF service, and training aircraft were routinely painted yellow to distinguish them from operational aircraft. Ground crew, too, were issued new working uniforms – denims in a dark shade of RAF blue. When

The RAF's first monoplane fighter was the formidable Hawker Hurricane (opposite), which entered service in 1935. Yet on a flight in 1934, Victor Goddard flew over an airfield where he saw not only a Hurricane, but one mysteriously painted yellow. He and his aircraft seemed somehow to have slipped forward in time.

Below: *RAF station officers – practical men like Victor Goddard, who had a timeslip in 1934.*

he eventually discovered and put together all these bits of the jigsaw, Goddard realized that he had seen Drem not as it actually was on that intemperate day in 1934, but as it was to be in the not too distant future. He had even managed to slip in time to a day when the weather was fine – helping him find his way home.

Goddard seems to have been a man with a charmed life when it came to narrow shaves in aircraft – later in his career he escaped a crash landing that should have devastated the aircraft he was in, and that he had been forewarned would result in his death. But there is a key difference between the premonitory vision that warned Goddard of that crash and what he experienced directly in 1934. For the premonitory vision was just that: a mental image of the future. In this case, Goddard – and his aircraft! – actually seem to have shifted, both together, from a foul-weather day in 1934 to a fair-weather day sometime after 1938. Goddard had experienced what psychical researchers call a timeslip.

TIME TRAVELLER

Goddard's experience was relatively unusual – but by no means unique – in being a slip *forward* in time. It is, for some reason, more common for those who have been subjected to timeslips to find themselves walking into the past. Joan Forman, who has researched and described a formidable range of these experiences (and on whose work any discussion of the phenomenon must rely very heavily), reported in her book *The Mask of Time* the intriguing case of an elderly man she called Mr Squirrel – who, like Goddard, slipped across time in pursuit of a particular personal need.

Squirrel was an enthusiastic amateur numismatist, a coin-collector, from Norfolk, England. Sometime in 1973 he found he needed some envelopes in which to store his coins, and he went to nearby Great Yarmouth, a resort on the coast, to find some. He had heard that there was a stationer's shop there that stocked exactly the thing he needed. Squirrel had never been to the shop before, but he did know how to reach it.

When he got there, he noticed that the street was still laid in old-fashioned cobbles, but that the shop itself looked bright, new, and freshly painted. When he went into the shop he found it empty, and glanced around at the place: the till was an old-fashioned box type; there was a frame full of walking-sticks for sale; decorated frames for photographs were on display. Then a young assistant approached him, wearing a long black skirt and a blouse with 'mutton-chop' sleeves; her hair was piled on top of her head.

Squirrel told her what he wanted, and she produced a brown box full of small, transparent envelopes. He commented that they had a surprising amount in stock. The girl explained that fishermen bought them all the time, to keep hooks in. She told him the price of his purchases was a shilling: he gave her a new 5p piece, which was then the same size, colour, weight and – most important – the same value as the old shilling coin. Then he left the shop. All the time he had been in it, there was no sound from outside and inside there had been absolute quiet apart from his conversation with the girl.

Squirrel thought little of these details at the time: many girls were wearing clothes with a Victorian or Edwardian flavour in 1973, and doing their hair to match; decimal coinage had been introduced only two years before, and he (like many people, especially the elderly) still thought of prices in the old money. The shop assistant apparently looked at the coin he gave her with some surprise, although she said nothing about it. However, the details of that visit did come to mind with some force when Squirrel went back to the shop a week later for more envelopes for his coin collection.

This time, there were no cobbles in the street, but ordinary modern paving stones.

Below: *In 1973, a Norfolk coin collector got a genuinely old-fashioned look from a shop assistant when he handed her a 5p piece – one of the decimal coins issued in 1971 and shown here – for he had, it seems, stepped back into the Edwardian era, when there were 20 shillings and 240 pence to the £1 sterling.*

The shop façade now looked weathered, not bright. Inside, too, the details had changed. The mature lady who served him denied any knowledge of a young girl assistant, and then said the shop not only had none of the envelopes Squirrel wanted – but had never stocked them!

This experience would have been uncanny enough; what makes it especially so was the fact that Squirrel still had the envelopes that he had bought in his brief visit to another age – and could not have bought them in 1973. Joan Forman tracked down their makers, who confirmed that they were sold in the 1920s, although they were first made before 1914.

Without the envelopes, it is reasonable to suggest that the elderly Mr Squirrel's experience, on its own, had been some kind of hallucination, or at any rate a purely mental journey across time. However, it is not possible to describe the set of new transparent envelopes that followed Squirrel back into 1973 as some kind of portable phantasm. This disconcerting detail raises even more questions about the nature of timeslips than does the apparent ability of Victor Goddard's very solid aircraft to travel with him into the future.

GHOSTLY MONKS

Two other intriguing instances reported by Joan Forman show a quite different facet of this mysterious phenomenon – and give yet another twist to the problem of what actually happens in a timeslip. Both timeslips happened to the same person, a Mrs Turrell-Clarke, who experienced them when she was living in the quaintly named village of Wisley-cum-Pyrford in Surrey. And both suggest that her timeslips, at least, were indeed a journey of the mind, or possibly even of the soul.

In the first of these strange events, Mrs Turrell-Clarke was cycling from her home to the village church, where she was going to the evensong service. Suddenly, the modern road under her turned into a path across a field; her bicycle vanished; and she found herself on foot. Approaching her was a man dressed like a 13th-century peasant. She herself, she felt, was wearing a nun's habit. The man stood aside to let her go by. Within seconds the scene shifted again, and the mystified Mrs Turrell-Clarke found

herself back on her bicycle in the middle of the 20th century.

Her second experience came a month later. This time she was actually in the church at Pyrford at a service. She was joining in the singing of a plainsong chant when the church – which dates back to the 13th century – apparently regressed in front of her eyes to its original state. The floor was of plain earth, the altar of stone; and in the centre of the church a group of monks in brown habits were in procession, singing the same plainsong chant that Mrs Turrell-Clarke had joined in singing just a few minutes before – or, to put it another way, some 700 years later!

The most curious part of the experience, however, was that Mrs Turrell-Clarke felt that, during the few moments it lasted, she was viewing this scene as 'one of a small group of people at the back of the church, taking little part in the proceedings'.

Pyrford church was originally a chapel belonging to nearby Newark Abbey. The monks there wore black habits, but Mrs Turrell-Clarke discovered that in 1293 the monks of Westminster Abbey had used the chapel – and they wore brown habits. Presumably it was members of this order that she had seen; at least the information gave some credibility to her odd experience.

Above: An Edwardian shop with the kind of fittings and decor that greeted the Norfolk numismatist in his timeslip in 1973.

SHE WAS A MIGRANT FROM THE FUTURE, SUMMONED TO THE PAST BY THE CHANTS OF THE BROWN-ROBED MONKS.

But what kind of experience was it, really? Both these timeslips could be regarded as in some sense imaginary, however authentic the details. Yet if in both these cases Mrs Turrell-Clarke did slip through time for a few minutes, who was she, and where was she, while she visited the Surrey of the 13th century? Were these simply very elaborate forms of ghosts that she saw – phantoms of the Surrey landscape and the Pyrford church, complete with inhabitants?

This seems unlikely, for she saw these things through someone else's eyes. In her first timeslip, she felt she was wearing nun's robes. But who was the nun? Mrs Turrell-Clarke in a previous incarnation? An innocent religious whose consciousness was briefly taken over by this migrant from the future? Or was some kind of long-distance, time-travelling telepathy involved, so that she saw the past through someone else's mind, but without taking it over? And was she still seeing through the eyes of the nun in her second timeslip, or through another person's? And for what purpose did they occur? No special information was passed on to the witness; no problem was solved – far from it: every aspect of these cases bristles with problems.

However, an especially interesting question is raised by the possibility that these visions were telepathic in nature. Did the person, or people, through whom she had these experiences in turn see into the future, while she looked into the past? The question 'Where was Mrs Turrell-Clarke during her timeslip?' becomes more and more intriguing – and more and more difficult to answer – if they did use her mind as a window onto times to come.

PHANTOM OMNIBUS

One interpretation of timeslips, as mentioned above, is that they are forms of haunting. If there is anything to this speculation, the 'ghosts' involved are not purely spirits, or spiritual representations, of dead people in the way we usually take ghosts to be. That spectres of inanimate objects do apparently exist is nothing new in the annals of psychical research: a famous example is the phantom No 7 omnibus belonging to London Transport that on various occasions in the 1930s was seen powering down Cambridge Gardens

*Below: **The parish church at Wisley-cum-Pyrford, Surrey, where one involuntary time-traveller saw monks from an order based at Westminster Abbey** (right), **who used the church only during the 13th century.***

in Notting Hill, causing at least one motorist to plough into parked cars in an attempt to avoid it.

Even if one accepts that a phantom path can haunt its descendant, a modern road, or that the past life of a church can cloak its modern interior, the timeslips experienced by Mr Squirrel and Mrs Turrell-Clarke were singular in that both the witnesses *interacted* with the so-called ghosts: a peasant stood to one side to let Mrs Turrell-Clarke go by; Mr Squirrel not only had a whole conversation with a phantom shop-girl in a phantom shop, he bought a set of phantom envelopes that nevertheless remained strikingly physical and material even when Squirrel himself had 'come out' of his timeslip.

The experience of Victor Goddard (and, as we shall see, others who have found themselves briefly inhabiting the future) also, rather comprehensively, disposes of the 'haunting' interpretation of timeslips. A complete collection of all the reports of hauntings from the future would make a very thin book indeed. The text would be something of an anticlimax, too. It would consist of three words: 'None so far.'

'GHOULE OF TOMORROW'

This does not mean that on his strange flight into the future Goddard and his aircraft might not have seemed spectral to anyone on the ground, had they bothered to look up. And perhaps a 13th-century Surrey peasant went home one night to tell the story of the nun he had seen unexpectedly appear on the path, and stood aside for, and seen vanish before his eyes…

Something like this may be reported in the distant future by a family living in what is now Germany. In the early 1980s a British family was travelling on one of the former West Germany's autobahns. The road wasn't busy, and their attention was taken by a lone vehicle approaching very

Below: A London omnibus of the 1930s – like the one that occasionally haunted Cambridge Gardens in London's Notting Hill district.

Are all ghosts spirits of the dead, or are some the spectres of living people caught in a timeslip? The driver of a ghostly Roman chariot (right) *may be as astonished to see us as we are to see him. A cross-haunting, or double timeslip, like this occurred between an 18th-century gentleman and healer Matthew Manning* (below) *when the latter was a teenager in the early 1970s.*

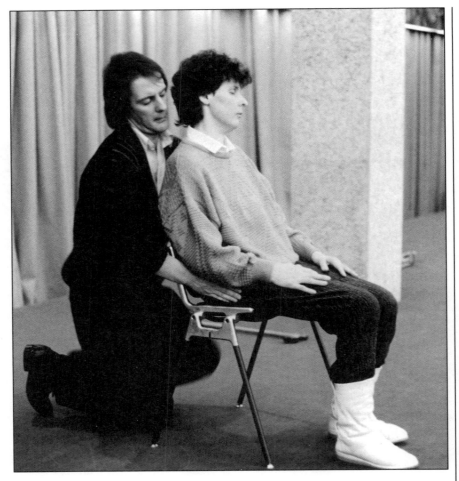

THE CAR WHICH HURTLED PAST THEM WAS A PHANTOM OF THE FUTURE, BUT ITS OCCUPANTS WERE FOUR VERY FRIGHTENED PEOPLE.

---

fast on the other side of the divided highway. It looked like no car they had ever seen – in fact it looked more like a UFO. It had no wheels visible, and was cylindrical in shape. There were four round porthole-like windows. As it flashed by, they saw four 'very frightened faces' staring at them out of the windows. If the British family saw a phantom from the future, it was clear the phantoms were equally astonished and alarmed to be seeing a ghostly automobile from what to them was the distant past – no doubt a sight as disconcerting as that of a spectral Roman chariot rattling down a modern *autostrada* would be today.

The British healer and psychic Matthew Manning experienced a bizarre series of episodes in his adolescence that bears out the notion that if there is an interaction with figures from the past or future during a timeslip, the other party involved will see the present-day witness as some kind of 'ghost'.

In 1971 Manning met an apparition of a man, walking with the help of two sticks, on the stairs of his parents' house – which dated back to the 17th and 18th centuries. The ghost was no translucent spectre, however: it was apparently solid, and Manning at first took it to be a living man – not least because he spoke to him. Rather matter-of-factly the man apologized for alarming Manning, and explained that he was taking exercise for the sake of his legs, which were bothering him. The entity claimed to be one Robert Webbe, who had in fact owned the house and had parts of it built. It was then that Manning realized he had encountered a ghost.

Webbe appeared many times after that. The apparition became almost part of the family, even playing pranks on them. At other times Manning communicated with Webbe through automatic writing. At one point in such a dialogue he asked Webbe if there were a ghost in the house. Webbe indignantly denied it: if there were, he would 'chase it away'. He added that he thought Manning was merely trying to frighten him.

Manning then asked Webbe whom he thought he was talking to. Webbe gave the following fascinating reply: 'I think sometimes I am going mad. I hear a voyce in myne head which I hear talking to me. But tell no one else they locke me away.'

Manning then explained why he was asking these questions. As far as he was concerned, he himself was in the here and now and solid flesh; Webbe, to him, was a ghost. At this, Webbe reportedly became distressed, and unable to believe what he was being told. He ended by insisting that Manning must be a 'ghoule of tomorrow'.

What seems to have happened in this case – especially given the notable solidity of Webbe's form, and his ability to have otherwise ordinary two-way conversations when he was actually visible – is a kind of *cross*-haunting – or a two-way timeslip. Both parties involved thought they were being haunted. It is as if two segments of time were interlocking – rather as if the circles of light from two spotlights were overlapping. But how this happens remains as mysterious as any other aspect of any other kind of timeslip.

STRANGE BLACKOUT

Timeslips may involve more than people and places. In at least two instances, they have featured radio transmissions from the distant past.

Alan Holmes, First Radio Officer of the Cunard liner *Queen Elizabeth 2*, was on watch in the radio shack aboard the ship during a transatlantic voyage some time in 1978, listening for messages on the frequency reserved for radio-telephone (RT) communications, when he received a message in Morse code: 'GKS GBTT QSX AREA 1A'.

There were several things wrong with this message. First, what was a Morse message doing on the RT voice frequency? Next, the message, once translated from Morse, was still using a code for ship-to-shore messages that had gone out of use years before. Third, the message appeared at first glance to be coming from the *QE2* herself, whose call sign is GBTT, or 'Golf Bravo Tango Tango'.

Holmes said: 'It was uncanny...The radio procedure used was dropped years ago...it came from another age. I can't believe it was sent by a ghost.'

If it was not a ghost, then the next most reasonable explanation seems to be that a timeslip had occurred. For the call sign

THE TIMID OLD GENTLEMAN WAS TERRIFIED OF BEING LOCKED UP IN A LUNATIC ASYLUM AND SO TOLD NO ONE ABOUT THE VOICES HE WAS HEARING.

Below: *The* **Queen Elizabeth 2,** *which in 1978 received a radio message out of the past from its long-since retired fellow-Cunarder* **Queen Mary.**

Above: *The liner* Queen Mary, *the apparent sender of a radio message that was not picked up until at least 11 years after its transmission.*

GBTT was also used by the old Cunarder *Queen Mary* – and she had been taken out of service in 1967, and sold to the City of Long Beach, California, where she was turned into a floating hotel and conference centre. And the form of the transmission was exactly the one that was in use when the *Queen Mary* was at sea. Holmes deciphered the anachronistic message as a routine position check from the old liner *Queen Mary* to the international shipping radio station Portishead, which is at Burnham in Somerset.

It's coincidence enough that the *QE2* had inherited the call sign from the *Queen Mary* before the code was discontinued; it is quite bizarre that the new ship, with that same call sign, should have picked up a message sent out at least 11 years previously.

Holmes suggested an explanation: 'Sometimes radio signals bounce off the moon and "turn up" in Australia. This message could have bounced out into space more than ten years ago and just zipped around until it found its way back to Earth and we picked it up.' He suggested that the signal might have bounced off something at least five light years away in space and, by an extraordinary freak, come back to Earth in such a way that the *QE2* had been in the way of the returning signal. The odds against that happening are, however, literally astronomical or 'inconceivable', as a spokesman for Portishead put it.

When Donald Mulholland, the station manager for Portishead, was interviewed about the affair in the Autumn 1978 edition of *Hello World*, the magazine of the Post Office External Telecommunications Executive, he suggested that the whole thing was a hoax. Holmes retorted by saying he was fed up with justifying the event: 'If I'd been alone on watch, I'd never have mentioned it. I was not alone in the radio shack at the time, and the message really did come in.' If it was a hoax, he went on, it would be difficult to lay on and hardly worth the bother. 'The hoaxer would have had to know exactly what frequency we were listening out on and when.'

BBC TV's report on 11 August 1978 about the bizarre message revealed a further curious detail: shortly after the *QE2* received the message, 'a mysterious blackout silenced all messages to and from Atlantic shipping for a time'.

Another strange case of a timeslipping radio message was also reported in 1978. After Mrs Helen Griffith wrote to the London *Daily Express* describing how she had heard the sounds of a World War 2 battle as she crossed the English Channel in 1977, a Mr A.J. Peterson wrote to the newspaper in response (the letter was printed in the 22 August editions), with another story of an inexplicable radio message that had somehow slipped in time. While his son was serving with the Green Howards in Borneo in 1968, his patrol picked up a radio message they couldn't decipher. 'Back at base they handed the message to intelligence who found that it was in a long-discarded code...[It turned out to be] a message sent during an action in the last war.'

ECHOES OF THE PAST

The sounds of battle are sometimes heard again years after the event. The most famous such case is that of two women who, while on holiday in Puys, near Dieppe, on 4 August 1951, claimed to have heard a blow-by-blow re-run of the assault on Dieppe by an Allied amphibious force on 19 August 1942. That battle left 3623 killed or wounded. The ladies' account seemed to tally with the military records, and investigators for the Society for Psychical Research stated their belief that it was 'a genuine psychic experience'. But whether this was a timeslip, a mass phantom, or a simple delusion, is open to question. It has also come to light that the ladies' oft-cited claim to have known nothing about the military details of the Dieppe raid may well be false.

The most recent such account maintains that sounds from World War 2 sea battles can still be heard echoing around the North Atlantic. The US Navy has a network of super-sensitive hydrophones called SOSUS (Sound Surveillance System) buried on the ocean floor to detect enemy submarine traffic. Armies of listeners compare the incoming sounds with vast computerized libraries of natural sounds and the known engine noises ('sound signatures') of vessels in the world's submarine navies. According to the magazine *US News and World Report*, sounds like distant explosions and cannon fire have been picked up ever since SOSUS was installed in 1952.

It has been suggested that the sounds were perpetuated by freak conditions that made the sea act like a superconductor. One expert in underwater surveillance thought the cause might be deep undersea channels, which do indeed exist, that 'act like huge natural telephone cables. Sound seems to be able to travel along them without deterioration in the signal. The sound goes back and forth, losing hardly any of its strength.' But, he said, 'not all sounds are "stored" in this way for years. The sounds apparently have to have occurred at the right place...but how [they] get into this system remains a mystery.'

Some apparent timeslips may, then, have a natural explanation, but most, it is absolutely clear, do not. The answer to the mysteries they present is buried somewhere in the extraordinary, and barely understood, capacities of the human mind.

THE RECEIVER PICKED UP
THE MESSAGE ACCURATELY
– BUT IT WAS A MESSAGE
FROM ANOTHER TIME.

Below: *British troops returning from the disastrous raid on enemy-occupied Dieppe in 1942. Nine years later, two English ladies on holiday nearby claimed they heard a replay of the battle.*

MIND OVER MATTER

Uri Geller seemed to prove the power of the mind over matter. Many set out to expose him as a fraud, and as the tests became more and more difficult, it seemed that Geller was bound to fail...

Probably the world's best-known exponent of the mind's power over matter is the Israeli psychic Uri Geller. As a result of the international attention that the media gave Geller in the early 1970s, hundreds of thousands, possibly millions, of people around the world became aware of the phenomenon of psychokinesis – the ability of the mind to affect material objects in unexpected ways.

Geller bent spoons under the glare of TV camera lights merely by stroking them; at his word, clocks and watches that had been put away as useless began ticking again; scientists watched him make Geiger counters go haywire and sail through standard ESP tests without a hitch. On one especially celebrated occasion he took a spoon from the Marquess of Bath's priceless gold cutlery service and made it fall in two pieces with hardly any visible physical effort – again, in full view of TV cameras.

Whatever the merits of Geller's claims to fame – and there has been a horde of noisy sceptics vociferously claiming that he is a fraud, and that they know how he does his tricks, pursuing Geller ever since he came to international attention – perhaps the best way to put any claim to psychokinetic powers is in its proper context.

SCEPTICS

To begin with, Geller's claims are by no means new. Many others before him have said that they can influence material things by mental powers alone and, without pretending that they understand how they can do so, have convinced trained, observ-

ant, and by no means gullible witnesses that they were indeed capable of just that. Some justified their abilities by ascribing them to the intervention of spirits; others offered no explanation at all, but the effects occurred nonetheless.

An even more important point about psychokinesis is that it is no more than an *extension* of the known ability of the mind. While almost all of Geller's predecessors in the history of psychokinesis have been attacked as fraudulent, sceptics have conveniently overlooked the fact that every day of their lives they themselves employ a faculty for 'mind over matter' – as do the rest of us, even people who have never heard of psychokinesis and could not care less about it.

Consider what happens when we feel thirsty. We get up and walk toward the nearest tap or we make for the nearest bar, or we brew a cup of tea. Similarly, what happens when we see the cat heading with remorseless determination toward our dinner of cold chicken that we left on the table while we answered the phone? We

Above: *Uri Geller performs an experiment in psychokinesis live on TV in Luxembourg. Geller has never shrunk from scientific investigation of his powers.*

Opposite: *Geller bends a key merely by holding it in one hand and concentrating on it, in a demonstration on Danish TV in January 1974.*

Right: *Others besides Geller have shown many times that psychokinetic metal-bending is possible. These objects were distorted in various experiments held in Europe and supervised by Dr Elmar Gruber between 1976 and 1982.*

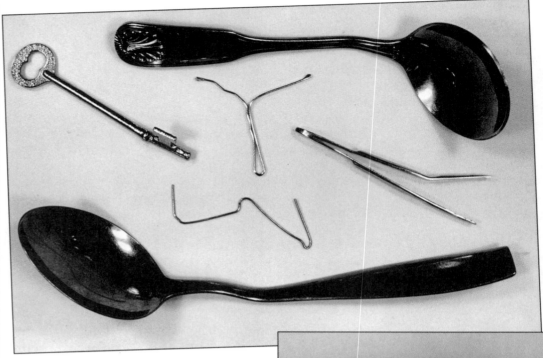

shoo it off, very quickly. What made the cat head inexorably for our chicken drumsticks in the first place?

The answer is simply that the cat is acting on the *idea* that those pieces of chicken would be very tasty indeed, thank you. Similarly the *idea* of wanting to slake our thirst drives us to a drink of some kind, and the *idea* that the cat not only does not deserve the dinner we have prepared for ourselves, but may well choke on splinters of bone, drives us to chase it away from the table. Mind influences matter every day, indeed every minute, of our lives. If it did not, sceptics of psychokinesis would not even be able to get out of bed of a morning, and certainly could not open their mouths to cry 'Fraud!' at the tops of their voices.

DOUBLE-TALK

The relentlessly materialist drift of modern science has gone so far as to deny this fundamental interaction between mind and matter. Some biologists would even deny the existence of human or animal consciousness on the grounds that it cannot be detected by instruments. The question of how they could reach such a ludicrous conclusion *without* a consciousness of some kind with which to think never seems to have crossed their minds – despite the obvious brevity of the journey demanded by the thought.

In his book *Knowing and Being*, philosopher and scientist Michael Polanyi quotes a number of neurologists on this point – among them Drs Hebb and Kubie. The former stated that 'The existence of something called consciousness is a venerable *hypothesis*: not a datum, not directly observable', while Kubie pronounced that 'Although we cannot get along without the concept of consciousness, actually there is no such thing.'

'Examples,' says Polanyi, 'of such double-talk and double-think could be multiplied from the whole range of biological sciences.' He brilliantly illustrates this obtuseness of the materialist view in his description of an episode that occurred at the annual meeting of the American Association for the Advancement of Science in December 1956. Polanyi had urged that gathering in New York to 'recognize the absurdity of regarding human beings as insentient automata'. Polanyi said he could not believe his ears at the response: 'The distinguished neurologist, R.W. Gerard, answered me passionately: "One thing we do know, ideas don't move muscles!"'

Polanyi's own view was encapsulated in his pithy aphorism: 'The mind is the body's meaning.' But when people live daily with the contradictions and constraints of a discipline that demands that they deny their own ability to move their own muscles in normal everyday life (if Gerard had been correct, he would have been unable to move his own lips, let alone follow his scientific vocation), it is hardly surprising that they reject the possibility that the mind may be able to move not only the body with which it is usually associated, but something outside its own flesh and bone. But that is what psychokinesis means.

PROOF OR FRAUD?

The problem with psychokinesis for physical scientists is at least a little more straightforward. Physicists don't have to pretend to themselves that people can't think, have no feelings, and don't know a joke when they hear it; but they cannot explain how a man in a television studio in central London can cause cutlery to bend in dozens of different homes around Britain. When Uri Geller succeeded in doing just that, physicists were among the first to voice their suspicions of trickery. To a physicist, the only proper way to bend a fork is to take it in one's hands and give it a hefty twist – or subject it to rather more heat than anyone would feel comfortable having in his or her hands.

Geller's first widely noted demonstration of his extraordinary powers occurred on 23 November 1973, when he appeared as a guest on the BBC TV show *The David Dimbleby Talk-In.* Geller gently rubbed two broken watches, and both began to work again. Then he made the hands of one of these watches bend upwards – *inside the glass*, that is, without touching them. While David Dimbleby held a fork in his hand, Geller gently stroked it, and it bent. Still more astonishing, a fork lying on the studio table between Geller and Dimbleby began to bend of its own accord. The most remarkable event of the show was the producer's announcement just before it closed: that dozens of viewers had phoned in to describe how forks and spoons in their own homes had bent and twisted by themselves while the programme was on the air.

THE TENSION MOUNTED AS GELLER GENTLY STROKED THE FORK, WILLING IT TO BEND.

Below: *Uri Geller at home today in Berkshire. His unusual talents are now employed largely in dowsing for mineral deposits, and bring in a handsome income from oil and mining companies.*

Astronaut Edgar Mitchell walks on the Moon (above) *during the Apollo 14 mission launched in March 1971* (right). *During this trip Mitchell attempted a number of experiments in ESP.*

Mitchell's secretary was wearing a gold ring. Geller asked her to take it off and cup it in her closed hand. Once she had done so, he then waved his hand back and forth over hers: there was no contact between them.

Feinberg reported what happened next: 'She opened her hand and the ring appeared with a crack in it, as if it had been cut through with some kind of extremely sharp instrument. Initially, there was a very small space...only a fraction of an inch. Over a few hours, the ring twisted and went gradually into the shape of an S.'

IMPOSSIBLE 'COINCIDENCES'

Geller became more ambitious as time went by. In Munich in 1972 he also appeared to have caused the Hochfelln cable car to grind to a halt in mid-air – on the fifth attempt – in answer to a journalist's challenge. The main power

Geller's mastery of metal is not his only psychic ability – he has performed extremely well in standard clairvoyance and telepathy experiments, and today enjoys a very high income from his skill at dowsing, which he uses to detect mineral deposits on behalf of international mining and oil companies. But his ability to affect a solid and intransigent material like metal is the most dramatic and demonstrable of his powers. Sceptics like the magician James Randi furiously showed how *some* of Geller's effects could be produced without calling on any paranormal abilities, but left much unexplained. And proof that fraud is possible is not, of course, proof that fraud has occurred.

A good instance of an entirely inexplicable Geller effect on metal occurred in August 1972, during his first visit to the USA. Geller was having lunch with the astronaut Edgar D. Mitchell – who, during the Apollo 14 moon mission, had carried out a number of ESP experiments from space – along with psychical researcher Dr Andrija Puharich, Gerald Feinberg (a physicist from Columbia University, New York), and Mitchell's secretary.

Far left: *Cable car in mid-journey, like the one halted by Geller in 1972.*

Left: *Big Ben, which Geller claims to have stopped dead at 12.35 pm on 17 December 1989. The clock is famous for its accuracy and is scrupulously maintained in perfect working order – so a 'coincidence' seems an unlikely explanation for the unusual event.*

switch at the control centre had apparently flipped off without warning. Given the short notice at which Geller managed this feat, it seems highly unlikely that he would have had time to organize a bribe in the right place. He was either extremely lucky, if a fraud, or he simply did what he said, and stopped the machinery by psychokinesis.

A few years later Geller was travelling between Spain and Italy on the liner *Renaissance*, when musicians from the ship's resident band dared him to stop the ship. Geller took up the challenge, and began to concentrate. Before long, the liner began to lose power, and finally her engines died. The ship's engineers found that the immediate cause was a crimped fuel line. Once again, the sceptical proposal that this was (for Geller) a 'lucky coincidence' is simply too feeble to contemplate. Ships' fuel lines are built to last – from metal. They don't suddenly get kinks in them of their own accord. Someone has to *put* a crimp in them, either by deliberately applied physical force – which means Geller had to have a very knowledgeable accomplice, and again in view of the short notice and spontaneous challenge, this seems a far-fetched explanation – or by some other means. Geller would appear to have used some 'other' means.

Geller's most spectacular large-scale feat took place in London in December 1989. He had been asked by an American games company to stop what is probably the world's most famous clock – *Big Ben*,

part of the British Houses of Parliament in Westminster – at midnight on New Year's Eve, 1989–90. (He has documentary proof of this request.) Geller, who was by then resident in England, went to Westminster around midday on 17 December – a day after he confirmed the deal with the company – to 'experiment'. At 12.35 pm, Big Ben stopped dead – an event almost unheard-of in the clock's history. If that was another mere 'coincidence' it was certainly a remarkable one indeed. The chances of a collaborator managing to penetrate the massive security around the Houses of Parliament are about nil. That leaves only one explanation – uncomfortable as it may be.

Below: *Psychokinetic effects were commonplace in Victorian spiritualist seances.*

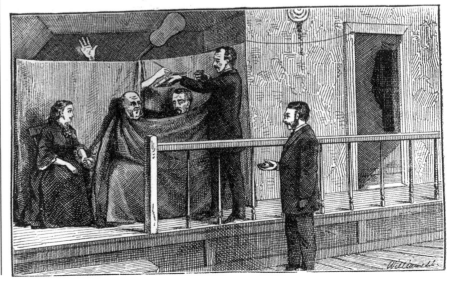

Above: *Daniel Dunglas Home's accordion – normal in every respect, except that Home was somehow able to make it play when no one was touching it.*

THE FAMILY WATCHED, MESMERIZED WITH FEAR AND AMAZEMENT, AS THE TINY HANDS MATERIALIZED OUT OF THIN AIR.

BEYOND REASONABLE DOUBT

Long before the world's television audiences were transfixed by Uri Geller, psychokinesis had been recorded and seriously researched by numerous eminent men of their day. Many psychokinetic effects were produced by spiritualist mediums in the seance rooms during the 19th century. Most of these mediums ascribed what happened while they were in trance to the activities of spirits beyond their control. A few, including one of the most remarkable of all psychics, Daniel Dunglas Home, were frankly baffled at their own abilities and did not pretend to know what was responsible for them. But as the 20th century wore on, fewer and fewer psychokinetic phenomena appeared at spiritualist seances. The present century has nevertheless been rich in people who have demonstrated these powers and have been extensively tested under controlled conditions that show beyond reasonable doubt that their powers are genuine. Few in recent years have attempted to explain the phenomena they produced as the work of spirits, but among those who did were the astonishing Schneider brothers.

Rudi and Willi Schneider were born in 1903 and 1908 respectively, in the town of Braunau, Austria (also, incidentally, the birthplace of Adolf Hitler). In 1919 the two boys began experimenting with a *planchette*. This device is said to have been

invented by a German milkmaid in the 1850s, and is a handy aid to producing automatic writing. It consists of a small, thin, heart-shaped platform. Two legs or castors project from underneath it, together with a pencil. The would-be medium places the planchette on a sheet of blank paper, puts his or her fingertips on the platform, and invites the spirits to communicate.

When the Schneider boys tried it, the planchette almost immediately showed they had made contact with a spirit who called herself Olga. She said that in return for having masses said for the repose of her soul, she would make the Schneider boys world famous. The Schneider family arranged for the masses and Olga kept her promise. Willi and Rudi were indeed to startle the world with the psychokinetic phenomena they produced over the next couple of decades.

TINY HANDS

The first of these took place soon after the masses were said. Olga told the family to cover a kitchen stool with a cloth, and to put various things – among them a handkerchief and a bowl full of water – nearby. When Willi sat next to the stool, water slopped out of the bowl, some of the objects began to move, the handkerchief rose up, disappeared under the cloth on the stool and then flew out with knots tied in all four corners. Weirder yet, two tiny hands materialized from nowhere and were heard to clap.

Several things suggest that these were genuinely paranormal events. First, they happened simultaneously – so that any ordinary degree of sleight of hand can be ruled out. Second, Willi, at 16 years of age, seems a trifle young to have developed such extraordinary powers of prestidigitation, even if the number and complexity of the phenomena did not make this too facile an explanation. And there is the testimony of one of the independent witnesses, a Captain Kogelnik, to consider:

'Not even the slightest attempt was made by [Willi] to support the supernormal phenomena through normal means. He never fell into trance; he himself watched the manifestations with as much interest as any other person present.'

Willi's abilities soon attracted the

attention of a number of scientists and other interested parties. By May 1922, 30 professors, 20 doctors, and 16 other 'savants' (one of them a general of the army, one the renowned novelist Thomas Mann) had witnessed or investigated Willi. After one seance in which a bell, which had been standing in Mann's full view on the floor, began to ring loudly of its own accord, he noted: 'Any thought of a swindle in the sense of a conjuring trick is absurd. There was simply nobody there who could have rung the bell.' Mann had arrived in sceptical mood.

Dr Eric Dingwall of the British Society for Psychical Research spent considerable effort in looking for hidden trapdoors, false walls and systems of pulleys in the Schneider household in Braunau's Stadtplatz, but found no sign that any conventional mechanism or trickery could account for the effects. Despite producing some remarkable phenomena, Willi's powers began to fade after 1922, but by then his brother Rudi had begun exhibiting his own paranormal talents.

Rudi Schneider's capacity for psychokinesis was thoroughly tested by the French psychical researcher Eugene Osty in Paris in 1931, and with fascinating results. Osty had realized that the key to proving the genuineness of any psychokinetic event lay in showing that nothing material had touched any of the objects that moved. Osty and his son Marcel, who was an engineer, devised a detection system that surrounded the 'target' objects with infra-red light. Anything – such as a human hand intent on a hoax – that broke the infra-red beams would automatically trigger a flash camera.

What actually happened was not what anyone expected. Rudi went into trance with various objects at a distance from where he was sitting. Olga 'came through' and announced she would pick up a handkerchief. The moment the handkerchief moved, however, the flashbulb exploded into life. Expecting to find evidence of trickery, Osty was mystified when the resulting photograph showed the handkerchief moving but no sign that anything material was interfering with it. He could only explain the result by inferring that his apparatus was faulty.

But the same thing happened several times more, even after Osty had made absolutely sure that his equipment was working perfectly. He eventually concluded that something paranormal was interfering with the infra-red beams. In due course, Olga – or whatever psycho-physical aspect of Rudi Schneider 'she' personified – interfered directly with the infra-red rays to trigger the camera on demand. Osty also found that the rays were affected

Top: *Thomas Mann, one of many distinguished witnesses to Willi Schneider's remarkable powers of psychokinesis. Initially sceptical, Mann was completely convinced of the genuineness of Schneider's abilities when he saw them demonstrated.*

Left: *Rudi Schneider is tested by psychical researcher Baron von Schrenck-Notzing in 1922.*

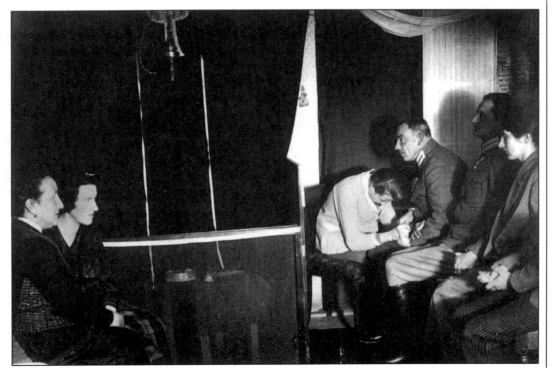

differently when Olga broke them than when they were broken by a material object. These experiments have been hailed by historians of psychical research as perhaps the most important of all investigations into psychokinesis.

EYELESS SIGHT

Just a few years before Uri Geller made headlines, Western parapsychologists had become intrigued by remarkable film featuring a former Red Army tank radio operator. The Russian ex-sergeant was a lady from Leningrad, born in 1928, called Nelya, or 'Nina', Kulagina.

Kulagina had first interested medical

THE RED ARMY TANK RADIO OPERATOR FOUND THAT SHE COULD SEE THINGS WITHOUT USING HER EYES.

Above: *Joe Mangini, a member of the SORRAT psychic research group based in Rolla, Missouri, bends a spoon – although it is sealed inside the bottle in his hand – on 3 January 1978.*

Right: *Monica Nieto Tejada with a strip of metal that she bent using psychokinesis.*

scientists at Leningrad's Institute of Brain Research in the 1960s, when she had discovered that she could detect the colours of sewing threads simply by touching them. In early experiments she also found that she could read newsprint by running her finger across the printed paper.

While these tests were being done, the researchers noticed that whenever Kulagina was practising her 'eyeless sight', any small object near her fingertips would move away from her. The discovery inspired a new, and quite different, series of tests. Film as well as published reports of

the results began to appear in the West, and it was these that aroused the interest of researchers there.

Kulagina's psychokinetic abilities never reached the grandiose heights of Uri Geller's later effect on Big Ben, but they were extremely varied in effect – and certainly no less intriguing.

GROTESQUE EXPERIMENTS

The Leningrad researchers reported that Kulagina psychokinetically moved small aluminium pipes and a box of matches over a distance of 3 in. In one of the films, she is seen to make a ping-pong ball levitate and hover in the air. In another, various small objects could be seen moving around under her influence inside a sealed transparent jar. For some strange reason, long or cylindrical objects – such as cigarettes or pencils – would stand on end before moving across the laboratory table.

In 1970, a team of American researchers went to Leningrad to watch Kulagina at work for themselves. They noted the variety of different materials that she could affect, from metals and plastics to paper and fabrics; and that objects moved quite inconsistently, sometimes in fits and starts and sometimes slowly and steadily, although never very far. In one test Kulagina made a solid gold wedding ring

turn in circles as she rotated her head above it. The possibility that she was using a magnet hidden in her mouth to create the effect is ruled out by the fact that gold does not respond to ordinary iron magnets and, the Americans observed, rigorous precautions were taken to ensure that Kulagina could not conceal such useful aids to fraud about her person.

Possibly the most extraordinary facet of Kulagina's power was her ability to affect living flesh. In one somewhat grotesque experiment a frog's heart was removed alive from its body. Normally, in these circumstances, the extracted organ will carry on beating at its usual rate for as long as four hours. Kulagina concentrated on this one, and slowed its pulse rate until it stopped beating altogether after only 12 minutes. In other experiments she simply laid her hand on another person's arm – with the result that they felt an extraordinary burning heat, which could be genuinely painful. Some subjects actually suffered burn marks on their skin.

BAFFLING SCIENCE

These are the most famous of those who have shown psychokinetic powers, but they are not alone. In the 1970s, too, the Muscovite Alla Vinogravada showed that she could make objects weighing up to 3 oz roll across a tabletop, and make those weighing a third of that slide across the surface they were resting on – all without touching them. New Yorker Felicia Parise demonstrated similar powers in tests at the Maimonides Medical Center in New York City, although it was only with great effort

and emotional tension that she succeeded, and then only with very small objects. In 1978, Joe Mangini of Columbia, Missouri, used psychokinesis to bend cutlery that had been sealed out of reach inside a bottle. In similar tests in 1989, the 15-year-old Spanish girl Monica Nieto Tejada bent metal strips sealed into glass tubes by holding them to her forehead and concentrating hard.

Earlier in the 1980s, several English schoolchildren convincingly demonstrated psychokinetic abilities in tests run by Professor John Hasted of the University of London. In a spin-off from this series of experiments, one schoolboy, Mark Briscoe, performed a truly remarkable feat in 1982, using wire made from the 'memory metal' nitinol. This alloy wire has the curious property of permanently holding its shape – that is, if it is bent out of its pre-formed shape, it will simply revert to its original configuration. The only way to reshape it permanently is – ostensibly – through heat-treatment under tension at temperatures of around $900°$ F. Mark Briscoe managed to produce a permanent alteration in *his* length of nitinol wire simply by stroking it.

As a change – some experimenters doubtless found it a welcome relief from watching cutlery bend – in 1984, the Polish teenager Joasia Gajewski managed to put a fork into free flight across a room in front of Japanese TV cameras. This was itself a change from her usual routine, which was to make lightbulbs explode at will.

No wonder the scientists are embarrassed as well as baffled.

Left: *Professor John B. Hasted of the University of London, who has conducted thousands of experiments that have satisfied him of the reality of psychokinesis. Hasted, in company with other distinguished physicists, suspects that quantum mechanics may hold clues to the mystery of how mind can affect matter so powerfully.*

KULAGINA CONCENTRATED ON THE PULSATING HEART, DETERMINED TO STOP IT BEATING FOR EVER.

Below: *These paperclips, held inside a glass sphere, safely away from physical interference by any means except the application of powerful magnets, were tangled together by the psychic power of a schoolchild.*

THE SORRAT STORY

Some considered Neihardt a charlatan and a fraud; others reserved judgement, but only the Oglala Sioux knew the truth about his astonishing powers. He founded the controversial society that set out to prove that pens write by themselves and metal rings could interlink without a single break.

In a basement in Rolla, Missouri, a pen sits up by itself and at lightning speed scribbles a message on a piece of paper. Two seamless leather rings shuffle toward each other. Without a break appearing in either of them, one ring connects with the other, and they interlink. Then they flip apart. Still, neither is broken. A letter,

addressed to a person in another country, is left in a sealed container without stamps on it. It disappears – and turns up a few days later at the correct address bearing a US postmark but Equadorian, not US Mail, stamps …

And so it goes on. The catalogue of major psychokinetic events that have taken place as a result of the work of the Society for Research into Rapport and Telekinesis (SORRAT), based in Rolla, is now

enormous. The group has been working together since 1961, and was established with the deliberate intention of bringing forth, once again, some of the more spectacular psychokinetic manifestations that amazed and graced the seance rooms of the Victorian era. Needless to say, SORRAT has met with its share and more of controversy in the years since 1961.

The arch-sceptic James Randi has said that he cannot believe anyone would take SORRAT's work seriously, and that it is 'not any more worth refuting than the Santa Claus myth'. Others have reserved judgement on the group's claims, but acknowledge that it has established a

Opposite: *Dr John G. Neihardt, poet, honorary member of the Sioux nation, and founder of SORRAT, at the age of 90 in 1972. With him is his secretary, Florence Boring.*

Above: *SORRAT researcher and experimental director W.E. Cox searches for the exact location of paranormal raps heard coming from the ground during a group session in September 1976.*

Left: *Skyrim Farm at Columbia, Missouri, where the SORRAT group first met under the guidance of Dr Neihardt in the hope of reproducing the kind of physical phenomena common in Victorian seance rooms.*

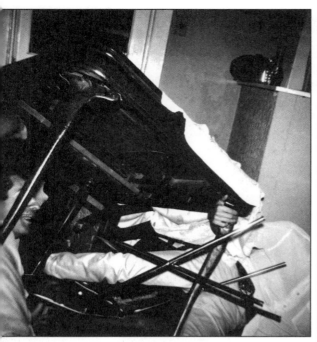

Left: *Two SORRAT members tangle with an 80 lb table as it crashes to the floor after levitating to ceiling height during a session in July 1966.*

Right: *A small table rises into the air at a SORRAT meeting with no physical assistance.*

method of investigating psychokinesis that should be a model for all researchers. Others acclaim the films and stills of the phenomena as a brilliant record, a more than reasonable proof, of the reality of psychokinesis. Meanwhile, SORRAT, unmoved, continue their work, and stand by their story.

What is that story?

PARANORMAL RAPPINGS

SORRAT was founded by Dr John G. Neihardt who, apart from being professor of English literature at the University of Missouri at Columbia, Mo., and poet

> **WHAT WAS MORE SIGNIFICANT WAS WHAT NEIHARDT CHOSE NOT TO REVEAL IN HIS BOOK.**

Below: *The apparition of 'Myra', which appeared to SORRAT members at Skyrim Farm on 27 June 1967. Myra had first communicated to the group using raps, telling them she had been a student at the University of Missouri and had died in about 1869.*

laureate of his native state of Nebraska, was the author of *Black Elk Speaks*. This extraordinary narrative, written in the 1930s, was the product of Neihardt's long and close friendship with the Oglala Sioux shaman Black Elk, and has been recognized as of enormous anthropological importance. The Oglala Sioux appreciated Neihardt enough to honour him with honorary membership of their tribe. Of more importance to psychical research, however, may be what Neihardt did not put in that book.

There is some evidence that Neihardt was himself initiated as a shaman, which implies that he had unusual mental, emotional and psychic strength – and physical stamina as well. Part of the shaman's task as a spiritual hub of the tribe is to make direct contact with the spirit world, which may be done through using hallucinogenic or psychotropic drugs; through drumming, dance and song, or ascetic, yoga-like exercises of self-deprivation; and often all of these together.

Whether the climactic shamanic 'flight' into the Otherworld to bring its wisdom back to the world of mortals is a real spiritual journey, an out-of-the-body experience, or an elaborate mystical illusion, no one who has not undertaken it can even begin to guess. But, whether or not Neihardt himself made this journey, his friend Black Elk certainly had; and the poet from Nebraska developed both a stern respect for the world of the spirit and a fascination for the paranormal. What particularly intrigued Neihardt was the fact that people with a powerful belief in a world of spirit could generate – or perhaps it was attract – psychokinetic effects. SORRAT was founded in part to explore that relationship.

In its early years SORRAT met every Friday evening at Neihardt's home at Skyrim Farm near Columbia. There was no solemn ritual involved; the group – the hard core numbered between 15 and 20 – simply sat about talking and joking and waiting for something to happen. Everyone recognized that months might pass before anything occurred; but the notion of 'rapport' among the members of the group, without which nothing would happen, was central to the SORRAT philosophy.

The first noticeable phenomenon was a peculiar coldness that surrounded objects left on a table during the sessions. Measurements showed them to be as much as 5° F colder than the surrounding room temperature. Within a few months, paranormal rappings began.

The raps were, it soon transpired, undoubtedly disembodied. They moved around the room on request, when everyone's hands and feet were visible, and even continued to sound outside the house, when they seemed to come from under the ground. Next, the group set up a code to communicate with the 'agency' – their carefully chosen neutral term for whatever was causing the sounds. Using the code they gradually encouraged the 'agency' to graduate to carry out simple 'tasks' – and to complete them would require some manifestation of psychokinesis.

By 1966 the SORRAT group had managed to levitate a massive oak table weighing 82 lb, and keep a light metal tray in the air – with no one touching it – for a full three minutes. Other effects were beginning to emerge, as well: mysterious lights appeared, objects appeared in the midst of the group as if from nowhere, others moved paranormally from place to place. Once, a life-like apparition materialized on the lawn outside Skyrim Farm, and was photographed. The 'agency' maintained that this was 'Myra', who had died over a century before.

FRAUD DETECTIVE

In 1969 there was a new development. Dr J.B. Rhine, professor of psychology and director of the Parapsychology Laboratory

at Duke University, Durham, North Carolina, had long been interested in Neihardt's work with SORRAT, and now suggested that the phenomena were so persistent and on such a scale that some professional help might be useful in gathering proof that they were indeed occurring. He offered the services of William E. Cox, his chief field investigator into psychokinesis. Cox had some 20 years' experience in researching psychokinesis, and was also a trained magician. Not only was he therefore well qualified to detect fraud, he also, as a result, knew how to prevent it.

One obvious solution to the problem of fraud – or even accusations of fraud – was

SLOWLY, UNBELIEVABLY, THE MASSIVE OAK TABLE ROSE IN THE AIR TOWARDS THE CEILING.

a locked container in which the 'agency' could be invited to do its work. Neihardt built a huge transparent chamber for the purpose, but the results were poor. Cox decided to take a leaf out of the original SORRAT book, and work gradually towards a fully sealed and equipped container. He decided to start with shallow wooden boxes, with transparent lids and simple seals, in which relatively minor psychokinetic effects could occur and be photographed.

These became known in the annals of SORRAT as 'coffee boxes', because more often than not the bottom of these sealed

Above: A 'coffee box', showing trails in the coffee grounds left by objects that were paranormally moved across the box's base.

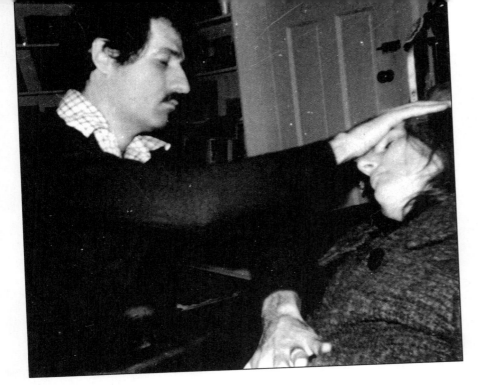

Above: *SORRAT member Joe Mangini performs psychic healing on Mrs Elaine Richards.*

psychology Laboratory at Duke in 1977, and settled in Rolla to monitor the psychokinesis that was occurring around Richards. Cox had made the extraordinary discovery that psychokinesis was possible even without the encouragement of the group when checking the state of the 'coffee boxes' at Skyrim, and – most astonishing of all – that psychokinesis would occur even when no one was even thinking about the boxes, SORRAT, or the group, let alone psychokinesis as such.

SEALED AND PADLOCKED

It was now time to put the achievements of SORRAT on record, and in a way that would, as far as possible, show that the psychokinetic effects they were able to produce were genuine.

(For those already convinced of the reality of psychic phenomena, SORRAT's greatest creation, out of infinite patience and dedication, was the circumstances in which spontaneous psychokinesis could occur at all. For psychical researchers, the invention of the mini-lab that followed as a direct consequence was an equally important accomplishment, if not more so. Here was a tool that could be deployed and adapted in a seemingly endless variety of ways not simply to test for psychokinesis, but to prove that it had occurred.)

The means Cox hit upon for this purpose was the 'mini-lab' – an elaboration on the original transparent chamber constructed by Neihardt. The first was a lidless Perspex™ box that was inverted to stand with its open side sealed against a heavy wooden base by steel strips and two heavy-duty padlocks. Inside it, Cox placed a number of objects, which the 'agency' was asked to manipulate in various ways. This spent some time at Skyrim before being moved to Dr Richards's home in Rolla, near Columbia.

Interesting things happened there. On one occasion Cox had set the mini-lab up in Dr Richards's sitting room. Inside the container were (among other things) a pencil and paper, dried peas that had been dyed white and blue, a small glass tumbler, some leather rings, pipecleaners, and six cotton spools strung on a wire that was twisted at the ends to hold them together. Dr Richards and a number of friends

trays was lightly and evenly covered in coffee grounds to track any movement of the objects inside. The coffee grounds also helped prevent the movement being effected by tilting the box, since they would reveal what had happened – by simply heaping up at one side or one end. A typical experiment was to put two dice in the box and ask the 'agency' to move only one – which it did successfully, and left tracks in the coffee grounds. Again, tilting the box would have made both dice move, and obscured any tracks.

Other boxes held nothing but carbon paper and a stylus. The 'agency' was invited to leave written messages by pressing the stylus on the carbon paper, so marking the pale wooden floor of the box. The results varied from meaningless scrawls to whole words. These early 'direct writing' experiments, though successful in their way, were to develop into something far more remarkable and elaborate in the years to come.

In 1973, SORRAT's founder, John G. Neihardt, died. As a result of that loss the group at Skyrim wavered somewhat in its purpose, but already a new and astonishing phenomenon was emerging with a few individuals. As a consequence, no doubt, of a dozen years' practice in letting psychokinetic events come forth, two of the founder members of SORRAT, Dr John Thomas Richards and Joseph Mangini were beginning to experience spontaneous psychokinesis in their everyday lives.

William Cox retired from the Para-

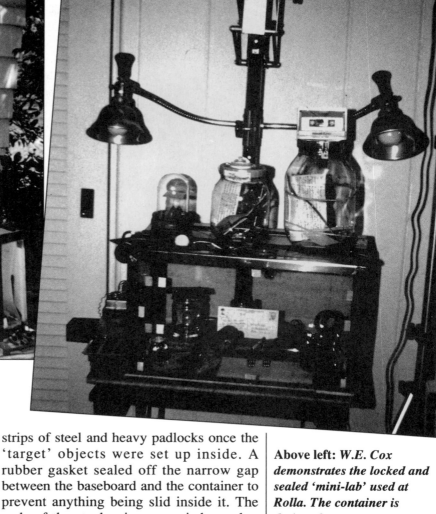

simply sat down in the room, turned out the light, and waited. In due course, noises came from the sealed mini-lab, and eventually stopped. When the light was turned on again, things inside the container were not quite as they had been – although the seals were unbroken and the locks still secure.

One of the six cotton spools had apparently vanished. The wire on which it had been strung had been retwisted. The glass tumbler now held 30 blue dried peas. The leather rings had moved. Two pipe-cleaners had been twisted into rings that were linked together.

The obvious difficulty about this event as evidence was that the only testimony to its truth was from those who had taken part in the session – and from Cox, who had arrived toward the end of the apparent movements inside the mini-lab. It was obvious that some kind of independent recording of what went on in the mini-lab, as it was happening, was necessary. Cox found a collaborator in a Mr S. Calvin, who helped to design and build a mini-lab that would provide the kind of evidence Cox wanted.

ASTOUNDING EVENTS

The new mini-labs were once again made of a transparent tank, upturned and capable of being sealed against a hefty base with strips of steel and heavy padlocks once the 'target' objects were set up inside. A rubber gasket sealed off the narrow gap between the baseboard and the container to prevent anything being slid inside it. The ends of the steel strips were tied together with plastic string, which was then melted; Cox impressed the warm plastic with the seal on a notary's ring, and then covered this with adhesive tape. Any 'break-in' to the mini-lab would thus be more than obvious.

A key difference between the old and new mini-labs lay in how the objects inside were set up. They were now placed on, or linked to, highly sensitive microswitches that would operate immediately if anything attached to them moved. These switches triggered lights and an 8 mm movie camera, which was linked to a timing device so that it would take 30 seconds of film every time a switch flipped on. A digital clock stood in front of the mini-lab to record when the events took place.

Two of these carefully prepared devices were put in the basement of Dr Richards's home in Rolla during the spring of 1979. It was here that the most remarkable of the SORRAT evidence for psychokinesis has been filmed, with reactions ranging from

Above left: *W.E. Cox demonstrates the locked and sealed 'mini-lab' used at Rolla. The container is designed to prevent any physical interference with the objects inside. If these move under psychokinetic influence, a movie camera is triggered to film the paranormal events as they happen.*

Above: *A similarly set up mini-lab in the laboratory of Dr Berthold Schwarz, in Vero Beach, Florida.*

THE SEALS WERE UNBROKEN AND THE PADLOCKS STILL SECURE – BUT INSIDE THE CONTAINER, IT WAS ANOTHER MATTER.

Above: *Paper rings link and catch fire during an experiment at Rolla in early 1992.*

Far right: *One of the most astonishing of the effects seen at Rolla. Inside the mini-lab, a pen writes a message without the assistance of a human hand.*

Right: *A message from the 'agencies' at work within the mini-lab, insisting that they are surviving spirits of the dead.*

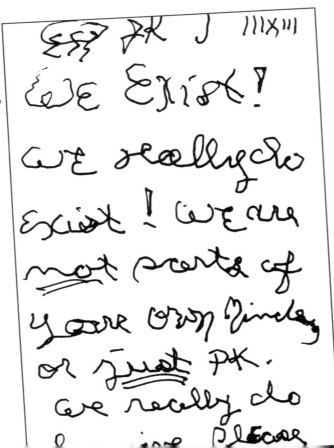

result the glass container cracked. Film also shows paper bursting into flames by itself – either effect would be difficult to achieve as a 'special effect', or in cruder terms, as a deliberate hoax.

• *Metal bending*
Spoons, forks and plain strips of metal left inside the mini-lab have been distorted by psychokinesis and the process has been recorded on film.

• *Spontaneous inflations*
Balloons have often inflated themselves inside the mini-lab. One such occasion was independently filmed by the production

crew of the Yorkshire Television series *Arthur C. Clarke's World of Mysterious Powers* on Labor Day 1983.

• *Direct writing*
There are many instances on record of pens taking it upon themselves to write messages without the intervention of any human agency, and at extraordinary speed. William E. Cox estimates that direct writing occurs at twice the average human writing speed at least. The quality of the messages received varies from the banal through the metaphysical to the unashamedly jokey in rhyming verse.

dismissiveness or rage on the part of sceptics, to undisguised and unadulterated delight on the part of believers.

The list of astounding events that have occurred since then in the mini-labs would fill many pages. But even a brief summary could not exclude the following:

• *Spontaneous combustions*
Film exists showing a candle igniting of its own accord inside the sealed mini-lab. As a

Left: *The block of marble (immediately to the left of the cylindrical container) placed by Dr Berthold Schwarz in the Rolla mini-lab with a request for the initials of a dead friend to be written on it. The picture was taken before the marble was placed in the mini-lab.*

HIS DEAD FRIEND'S INITIALS WERE CARVED DEEPLY INTO THE COLD MARBLE.

Below: *The marble after its sojourn in the mini-lab, clearly showing the letters CM – the initials of Dr Schwarz's dead friend – inscribed on it. No one was near the mini-lab when the inscription occurred, and none of those present knew what initials Dr Schwarz was hoping to see appear on the marble.*

On Easter Sunday 1991 an exceptional result was had from an experiment proposed by Dr Berthold Schwarz and set up in a plastic box with a cardboard liner at Skyrim Farm. In the container were a pencil stub and a block of marble, plus a note from Dr Schwarz requesting the 'agency' to give the initials of the person to whom the marble block was important. The box was left in the Skyrim study while a group of SORRAT members waited in the living room. Nothing happened for over an hour, and the group was ready to decide that nothing would, when the phone rang.

On the line was Maria Hanna, a SORRAT member living in Barstow, California; she had just had a series of paranormal raps in her home that, using the usual code, had said that a poem had appeared at Skyrim. Ms Hanna had had no idea that a SORRAT meeting was in session until she called. The group headed as one for the study to check the box. Inside, written in pencil on the cardboard liner, were the following lines:

I am you and you are I!
When the world is cherished most,
You shall hear my haunting cry,
See me rising like a ghost.
I am all that you have been,
Are not now, but soon shall be!
Thralled a while by dust and din –
Brother, Brother, follow me!

This, says Dr Richards, is a stanza from Dr Neihardt's poem 'The Ghostly Brother'. Yet more astonishing was what had happened to Berthold Schwarz's block of marble. Carved into it were the letters 'CM'. When told of this, Dr Schwarz confirmed that these were the initials he

had been hoping to have communicated (and that he had been keeping to himself). He then revealed that the marble came from the face of a building that had been named in memory of 'C.M.', who had been a close friend of Dr Schwarz and was now dead.

• *Linking rings*
It has long been a goal of para-psychological researchers to prove the successful working of psychokinesis by achieving the permanent interlinking of two separate rings of some seamless material – wood, leather, or metal, for instance. SORRAT films show momentary interlinking of leather rings (each cut from a single piece of hide). Messages from Cox and Richards to the 'agency' had persistently requested this achievement, but to no avail. One directly written response said testily: 'We've tried, but can't make the damn leather rings stay linked – sorry.' Another time, the 'agency' answered: 'When the psi energy is sufficient, we shall try to do this for you. However, do not expect to overcome the envious prejudice of your inferiors...'

However, in 1985, a metallurgist known only as Donald C. created two rings of a unique metal alloy whose formula only he knew. During an experiment at Skyrim Farm, the rings linked – and stayed that way. According to Dr Richards, 'Careful laboratory analysis shows that there is no cut or break in the metal of either ring.'

• *Levitations and extractions*
Film has shown the leather rings that are usually installed in the mini-lab, as well as numerous other objects, rising into the air of their own accord. Film has also shown letters being extracted from – and through – the envelopes that contain them, although the envelopes (and, of course, the mini-lab) have clearly remained sealed as the paper has come forth.

• *Psychokinetic sortings*
The original mini-lab event has been repeated more than once, with dyed dried

Above and right: *Rings placed inside the mini-lab before an experiment in December 1985 are clearly separate, but on retrieval after the experiment are no less clearly linked, without being broken or marked in any way.*

Above: *Another set of rings, put separately into the Rolla mini-lab, link spontaneously and without a break in the material.*

peas that have been left in the mini-lab in a mixed assortment of colours sorting themselves into single-colour groups.

• *Card calling*
Sealed sets of Zener cards, fresh from the makers and packed in random order, have been left in the mini-lab, and the 'agency' has been asked to call the order of the cards. Responses have been acquired through paranormal rapping, direct writing, and other means, and in about one attempt in three have been absolutely accurate for the whole run of the pack. In one unusual experiment conducted in 1991, Cox placed a blank audio tape next to a sealed pack of ordinary playing cards, which are always sold shuffled in random order. When the audio tape was taken from the mini-lab it was found to have on it a recording of a 'soft, feminine voice with an Arabic accent', correctly calling the order of the entire 52 cards in the deck – which remained sealed.

• *Apports*
Film exists of a piece of typewriting appearing from nowhere in front of the mini-lab. Other, mundane objects have also appeared inside the mini-lab.

• *Teleports*
Possibly the most controversial of all SORRAT's claims is that objects have been placed inside the sealed mini-lab and then appeared elsewhere with no human intervention. The first time this occurred was in May 1979, when Cox secured a green felt-tipped pen inside the container – and later found it on the floor of Dr Richards's basement, although the mini-lab remained untouched. Materials as varied as pipecleaners, water, matchbooks, peas, mica sheets, string, jewellery, film, and paper have transported themselves in or out of mini-labs. Films show such items appearing and disappearing and, yet more astonishing, actually passing through the glass of the sealed container.

These events led the experimenters to leave sealed, addressed, but unstamped letters inside the mini-lab to discover whether or not they would find their way to their intended destinations. They did. Often the letters have been adorned with unusual postage stamps – South American, Italian and even Australian ones have been attached to the envelopes – although they have all reached their destinations by way of the US Mail Office in Rolla and bear the Rolla postmark.

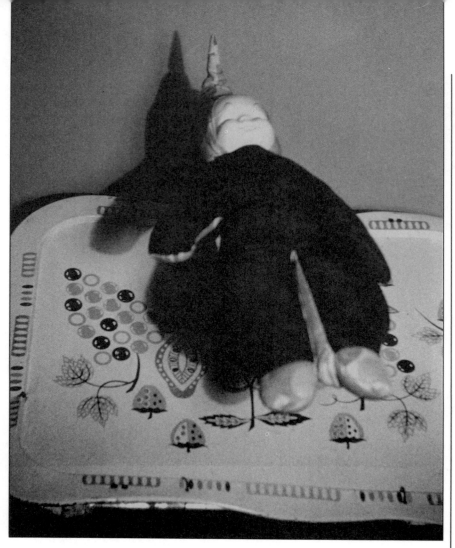

Above: *A doll levitates from a tray during a SORRAT session.*

THE LIGHTBULB WAS STILL UNBROKEN AND FIXED TO ITS BASE CONNECTOR, BUT THE COCKROACH WAS NOW TRAPPED INSIDE IT.

A number of psychical researchers around the world have received such letters, and during the Yorkshire TV filming mentioned previously, the production team left one – sealed but unstamped – in the mini-lab for paranormal posting to Arthur C. Clarke, along with several quarters (25-cent pieces), which were not in the envelope. Two weeks later, the letter and one of the quarters disappeared from the mini-lab. Both – with the missing quarter now in the envelope, which had somehow acquired stamps to the correct value for airmail – turned up at Clarke's residence in Sri Lanka shortly afterward.

One of the more startling teleports that the mini-lab achieved involved a living creature. In January 1992, psychiatrist and parapsychologist Dr Berthold E. Schwarz provided SORRAT with a large Florida cockroach from his home state and an ordinary clear lightbulb, with the request to the 'agency' behind the mini-lab to put the roach into the lightbulb. According to Dr Richards's testimony, 'the cockroach, some

white packing powder, and two slips of paper with notes paranormally written on them entered the sealed bulb'. One of the notes was written paranormally by the 'agency' to a SORRAT member, Eilly Fithian. The lightbulb remained unbroken and sealed to its base connector.

• *Paranormal sounds*
In another experiment using audio tape, Cox pre-recorded a cassette from beginning to end with the sound of a clock ticking. He left this tape in the mini-lab, again without a recorder. When it was retrieved and played, the tape also now held the sound of a series of paranormal raps – but the sound of the ticking clock had not been erased.

CONTROLLING SPIRIT

Who, or what, is responsible for the psychokinesis in the mini-labs and other SORRAT experiments? What is the 'agency'?

Opinions differ on this among SORRAT members themselves. Some believe the 'agency' is a product of members of the group's own subconscious. Some, including Dr Richards, prefer to think of the 'agency' as a group of spirits. The 'agency' itself has not always been consistent on this point. It has referred to itself by name, but at least once insisted that this particular personality resided in 'the fifth level of the subconscious' of one of the SORRAT members.

In the very first rapping experiments at Skyrim in the 1960s, the group asked whatever was behind the raps to identify itself. The answer was 'John King', the name of a spirit control (and long-dead pirate) that has allegedly acted as an intermediary between this world and the next for several mediums, including two of the most famous – and notorious – of the 19th century, Eusapia Palladino and Florence Cook. Since King announced 'himself' to SORRAT, a number of other names of alleged spirits or entities have cropped up in direct writing or through other communications. They have names like Explicator, Rector, Imperator, Mentor, IIIxIII, Eowald, and Expeditor – as well as, more mundanely, Sam, Mickey and Grady. Taken together these sound like the cast of some old-time spaceflight-and-sorcery

angle, panoramic view of the whole ensemble and its background would vastly reduce the set-up's vulnerability to fraud, as would either enclosing the cameras within the chamber or sealing the room in which the lab is placed with as much attention as has been devoted to the mini-lab itself. A 24-hour digital clock showing local time to the second as well as the date would both pinpoint events in time and verify the accuracy of timing of the camera runs. Using video cameras rather than movie film would improve the quality of the 'proof', as well – if only by reducing the opportunities sceptics have of crying 'Hoax!' and producing hilarious, but pointless, stop-action home movies of their own that purport to 'expose' the SORRAT work as fraudulent.

SORRAT has produced two major breakthroughs in psychical research: spontaneous, large-scale, and persistent psychokinetic phenomena; and the basis of a research tool that no serious para-psychologist interested in psychokinesis should be without. What will they do next?

radio serial. Whether they are genuinely disembodied entities (as they themselves claim) who happen to like slightly camp science fiction, or useful dramatizations from the collective unconscious of the SORRAT group, has to remain an open question.

Most psychical researchers would agree that the true answer to that question doesn't matter, for the time being at least. The value of the SORRAT work does not lie in any evidence it might contain for survival after physical death. The value of the independence of the alleged entities is that their manifestation removed any respons-ibility for producing paranormal effects from the members of the group. Apart from increasing the general relaxation of the meetings, so facilitating the 'rapport' that Neihardt believed to be crucial to producing psychokinesis, this lack of individual responsibility also meant that no particular member of the group would be deemed indispensable to the production of psychical phenomena. And it is the variety, depth and range of the psychokinetic effects that SORRAT has produced that is so impressive.

HOAX EXPOSED?

SORRAT's other great achievement is the invention of the mini-lab. It can, of course, be improved. Two cameras at right angles to each other, with a third giving a wide-

Left: *The message in this sealed bottle was written when an alleged psychic exerted conscious psychokinesis across a room during a SORRAT session. At the same time the safety-pin closed and the pipe-cleaners bent themselves into a stick figure.*

Below: *A Florida cockroach that was left inside the mini-lab with a plain lightbulb has been apported into the lightbulb – along with paper and white powder that, according to a message from the 'agencies' behind the event, was necessary 'to prevent breakage'.*

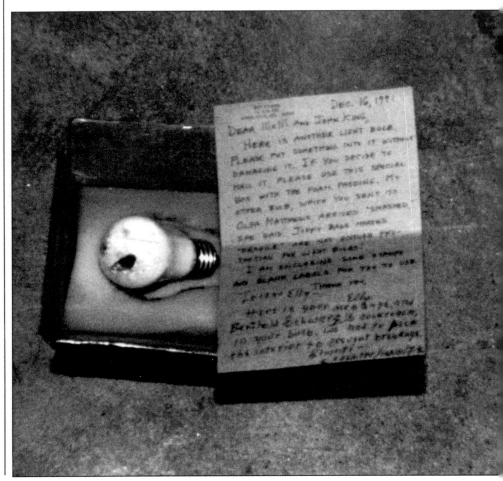

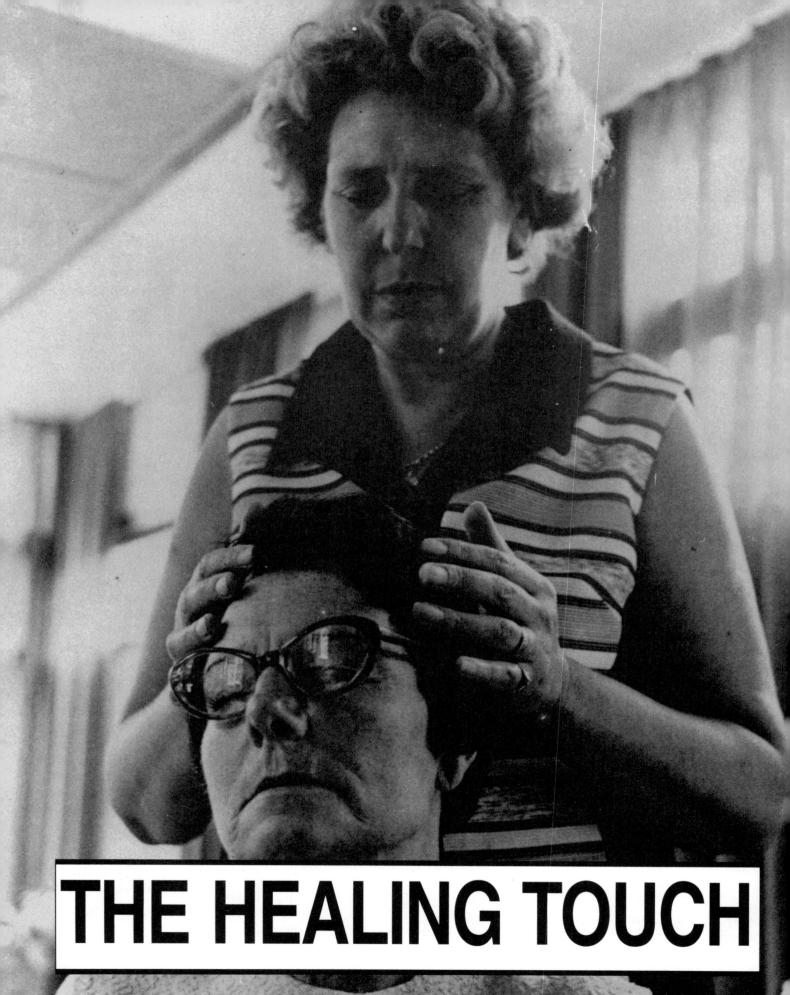

THE HEALING TOUCH

The sudden discovery that she was a healer brought Rose Gladden great joy. It was only later that she realized the gift could also be a burden that would drive her to the very edge of madness.

At the age of 19, in the 1940s, Rose Gladden discovered she was a healer.

'I had gone into a shop in London called Dyers and Chapman and found Mr Chapman, who had collapsed, lying under the counter. I asked him what was wrong and he said, "I'm in terrible pain. I have an ulcer."

'Now I didn't know where that ulcer was. All I thought was, "I wish I could help him," and I heard a voice say, "You can. Put your hand there."

'"But where?" I asked myself. "He hasn't told me where this ulcer is."

'With that I saw a little star, just as if it had fallen out of the night sky, floating over his left shoulder and, as I watched, the star floated down and stopped on the top half of the stomach.

'Mr Chapman confirmed that was where the ulcer was. As I put my hand there, I never saw but felt another hand come over mine and hold it steady. I felt my hand being filled with a tremendous heat. I couldn't move it away. It was as if it was glued to that part of the body. After a while, my hand was pulled like a magnet to his side and then away from his body.

'With that, he said, "That's gone, it's marvellous. Your fingers felt as if they were holding the pain and as you took your hand across, the pain went with it."

'I was absolutely overjoyed. I still didn't know you called it healing. I just knew I was beginning to realize why I was born and what I had to do was help people.'

THE PRICE TO BE PAID

Successful, unexpected and apparently simple as this discovery was, Rose Gladden did not find the process of

Opposite: *Healer Rose Gladden gives the healing touch.*

HER HAND WAS BURNING HOT AND, FRIGHTENED, SHE TRIED TO PULL IT AWAY.

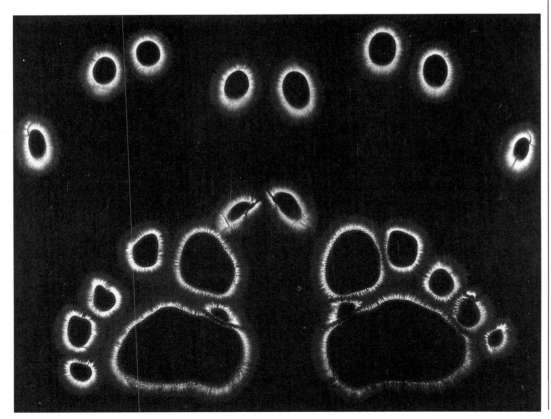

Left: *A Kirlian 'photograph' of fingertips and toes. The Kirlian technique detects static electricity on the surface of the skin – not, as some have claimed, the human aura that some psychics are apparently able to detect, or yet more fanciful attributes such as astrological or cheiromantic characteristics. Used by an experienced practitioner with proper medical training, the Kirlian technique can be an extremely useful diagnostic tool.*

becoming a full-time healer by any means easy. Since childhood she had seen 'forms and beings' that other people could not see; then, after her experience with Mr Chapman, during her twenties, she had a series of psychic experiences that were so intense and disturbing that she thought she might go mad. Today, she says she had to suffer in order to learn, and that without that distressing episode her work would be less effective. Although she is a psychic, not a 'spiritual' healer, and does not call on a spirit guide in her healing, she does believe that a spirit world exists and that it contains malignant as well as benign entities.

Rose Gladden has two ways of deciding how to go about treating a patient. She sometimes sees silver lines and spots mapped out on people's bodies, showing where the root of a particular complaint lies. She was at first mystified by the fact that these often showed in quite different places from where patients complained of suffering pain, although treating them (by laying her hands on the spot where the light showed) would effect a cure. It was years before she discovered that the lines and spots corresponded precisely with the lines and 'meridians' in the body identified by acupuncturists.

Rose Gladden is also one of those who claims to be able to see the human aura. This has been variously defined: as 'an envelope of vital energy, which apparently radiates from everything in nature' (from Harper's *Encyclopedia of Mystical and Paranormal Experience*); as 'a spiritual sphere surrounding everyone' (Swedenborg); as the physical body's 'etheric double' (Dr Walter J. Kilner, *The Human Aura*); some writers also identify the aura as the 'astral body' that is capable of leaving and returning to the physical body. A curiosity of the aura is that no two psychics see it in the same way, and often differ in their interpretations of the various bands of colour they are able to see in it, but there is general agreement that any physical sickness is reflected as disturbances in the aura, and may show there long before pain or other symptoms appear in the body.

Rose Gladden interprets this in an interesting way. She maintains that physical maladies are the *result* of imbalances and blockages of energy in the aura, not that an 'unhealthy' aura is a symptom of physical illness. Consequently she concentrates her treatment on the aura, not on the affected part, if that is the way the ailment presents itself.

MAGIC BULLETS

Rose Gladden is one of but a handful of healers who do not depend on a spiritualist interpretation of their gift. However, the evidence suggests that whether or not the healer considers the effect to be mediated

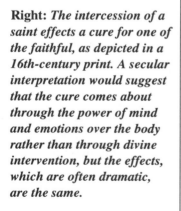

Right: *The intercession of a saint effects a cure for one of the faithful, as depicted in a 16th-century print. A secular interpretation would suggest that the cure comes about through the power of mind and emotions over the body rather than through divine intervention, but the effects, which are often dramatic, are the same.*

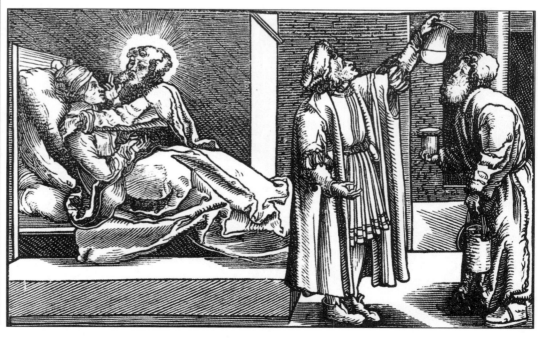

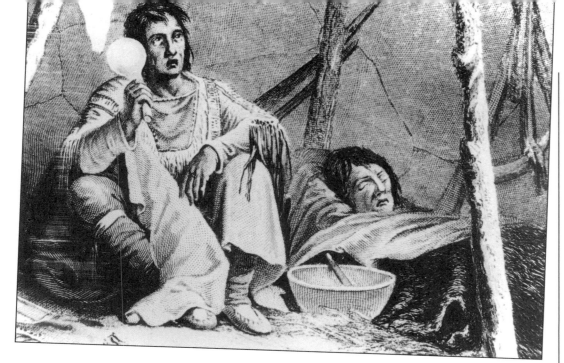

Left: *An Ojibway American Indian medicine man, or shaman, at work. Shamanistic healing centres on the patient's spirit – or on evil spirits within the sufferer's body – in order to cure physical ills. Sickness is seen as a symptom of the state of the soul, not merely a bodily condition demanding a purely physical cure.*

Below: *Conventional medicine is beginning to recognize that a patient kept confident and in good spirits will heal more quickly than one treated like an item on a production line.*

by the spirit world, or is directly from God (as with faith healers), or that he or she simply acts as a channel for a 'universal life force', the effects are the same: a very high proportion of the people who take their ailments to healers are cured.

Whatever the explanation or the source for the *healer's* powers, this would suggest that the state of the patient's mind, at least, has a massive degree of control over the state of the body. Part of the healing process, in other words, seems to depend on the confidence and reassurance that people gain by putting themselves entirely in the healer's hands. In effect, they heal themselves, as responsibility for the affliction is taken out of their hands and placed in someone else's.

Yet something more than this seems to be happening with psychic healing, and anyone might reasonably object to such a line of argument, not least an orthodox general practitioner. By taking an illness to a doctor you are also putting yourself in someone else's hands, even though conventional medicine addresses physical problems with physical methods such as surgery, or with physical tools, such as drugs, which are aimed like 'magic bullets' at the physical causes of specific ailments.

There is no doubt that in most cases, given an accurate diagnosis, conventional medicine works. The patient has entrusted a specifically physical malady to the doctor, and the doctor finds the physical cure. To that extent, mind and body are as one. But the exclusively physical approach does not always work. Given the mira-culous subtlety and complexity of the human body, and also the largely unfathomed intricacy of its relationship with the mind and with the emotions, this failure is not entirely surprising. Furthermore, conventional medicine traditionally regards *symptoms* as the clue to the underlying causes, and tackles those first.

If healers succeed where conventional

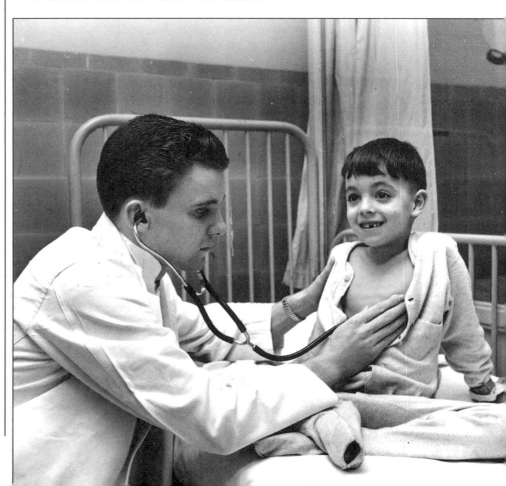

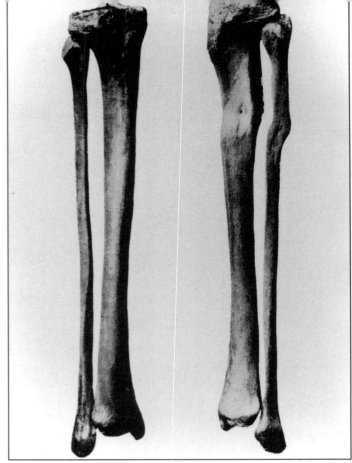

Belgian Pierre de Rudder (above, photographed in 1893) had one leg broken when a tree fell on him in 1867. He refused to have the damaged leg amputated and was in constant agony until April 1875, when he made a pilgrimage to the shrine of Our Lady of Lourdes at Oostaker, Belgium, where the pain miraculously vanished. Despite the distortion in his bones (above right, in a post-mortem photograph), De Rudder *thereafter walked normally and with perfect ease until his death in 1898.*

medicine fails, it may be partly because the patients entrust something different – something not merely physical, and something more than the physical symptoms of disease – to the healer. By accepting the reality and the importance of the interplay among mind, spirit and the emotions, and the part they may be playing in the illness, the patients implicitly put their whole being in the hands of the healer. And the healer, unlike the family GP or the specialist consultant, knows how to respond.

SERIOUSLY DISTURBED

This line of argument still supposes that suggestion plays a large part in the healer's art. However, as noted a few sentences earlier, something more seems to be happening when psychic healing takes place. When Rose Gladden laid her hands on the place where a bright light told her Mr Chapman's ulcer was, there was no 'suggestion' involved: neither Chapman nor Rose Gladden herself knew that she had the power to heal. And one of the wonders of psychic healing is that it can often deal with diseases that are intractable to modern medicine, such as cancer or multiple sclerosis.

Walter J. Kilner observed that the human aura reflected a person's state of health, and noted that 'weak depleted auras suck off the auric energy of healthy, vigorous auras around them'. Unhealthy parts of the aura, or the spirit, or one's general sense of well-being, will feed on the more vigorous parts in exactly the same way; but the overall effect is to disturb the system. The same is true of all energy systems: power moves from areas of high energy into areas of low energy, in an eternal and perfectly natural struggle to create and maintain a balance in nature.

You can see the same thing happening across the Earth's surface, nightly on the television weather forecast. Areas of low atmospheric pressure are fed by areas of high pressure in an attempt to even things out; the result in temperate climates is wind, cold fronts, rain...and the occasional spell of fine and balmy weather. An aura – or a person's psyche, or energy lines and meridians, or what you will – will constantly fluctuate in this way, but can, like the weather, become seriously disturbed. In meteorological terms, such a major disturbance in the balance of energies expresses itself as a storm or a drought; in terms of personal health, it means illness. And what, by all accounts,

Psychic healing may be practised at a distance, or directly. Russian healer Alexandr Ilyin of St Petersburg makes diagnoses from photographs of his patients (left), while John F. Thie's technique, known as 'Touch for Health' (below), uses direct manipulation as part of the therapy.

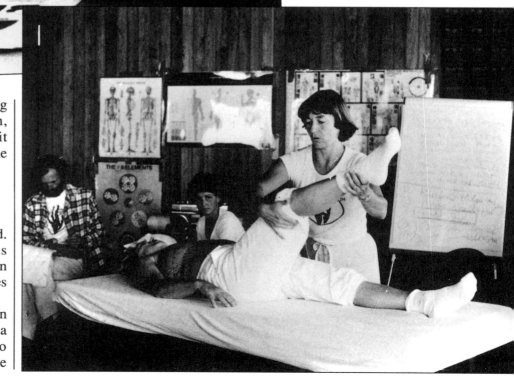

the healer does, is the equivalent of giving a troubled body an energy transfusion, which rights the balance – which, as it were, calms the storm or brings rain to the parched earth.

HIDDEN POWERS

The mystery in psychic healing is twofold. Exactly what that energy consists of is anyone's guess. And how it can work even when the healer may be thousands of miles from the sufferer is equally inexplicable.

The sensation that patients most often report feeling when they are touched by a healer is that of heat. Patients have also described tingling feelings, 'something like

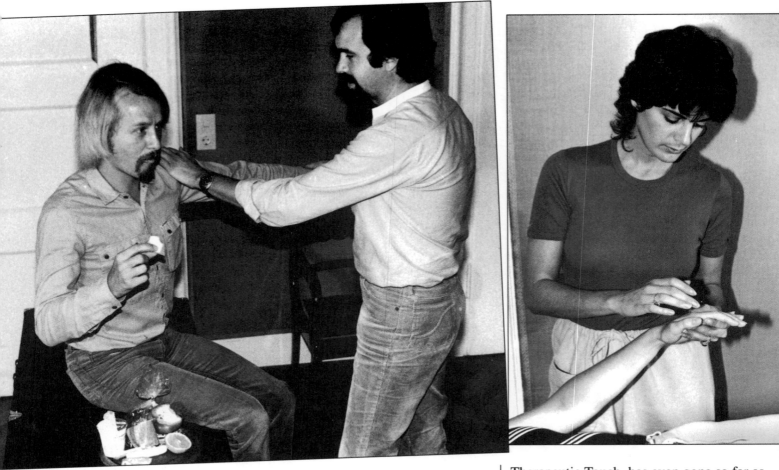

'Touch for Health' diagnoses involve testing for reactions to certain foods (above) and kinesiological testing (above right).

CAYCE REALIZED THAT THE STRANGE GIFT WAS OUT OF HIS CONTROL.

---

an electric shock', or even vivid impressions of colours before the eyes as the healer has touched them. At the same time, according to the Harper's *Encyclopedia* quoted earlier, healers have reported 'something of the consistency of heavy air' – whatever that may mean in practice – departing them, usually through the hands. The spiritualist healer Ambrose Worrall, in contrast, felt himself depleted of energy, indeed, but through the solar plexus.

These reports are both too various and too subjective to allow much of a guess as to what in fact has passed between the parties involved. And, intriguing and possibly helpful as they are, descriptions of what occurs in terms of the human aura really amount to explaining one mystery in terms of another. Only a relatively few people can see the aura, and they differ in their descriptions and analyses of it; it has stubbornly remained undetected by orthodox scientific means.

That something does pass between healer and healed seems to be beyond doubt, however. Dora van Gelder Kunz, a pioneer of a modern form of healing called

Therapeutic Touch, has even gone so far as to suggest that there is actually a two-way interaction between healer and patient, and that in the process both are made more whole and healthy.

THE FINAL HEALING

The mystery of psychic healing is only deepened by the ability of certain healers to treat their patients at a distance – even without meeting them.

The most famous exponent of distant healing was probably Edgar Cayce. Born in Hopkinsville, Kentucky, in 1877, Cayce followed the pattern of many other healers in being able to discern non-physical forms, and the human aura, from an early age. Until he was 21 he worked as a salesman, but had to abandon his job because of a chronic and apparently incurable sore throat, made worse by bouts of laryngitis. In 1898, Cayce lost his voice completely and, as a last resort, went to hypnotist Al Layne in the hope of getting some relief from his distressing condition.

Layne concluded that Cayce was immune to post-hypnotic suggestion (a command given during hypnosis to be carried out in the normal waking state), so he put Cayce into trance and asked him to identify the cause of his illness, and to suggest a cure himself. The ploy worked: Cayce was able to speak again at the end of the session. Layne suggested that Cayce should take up diagnosis and healing himself, in partnership with Layne.

Cayce refused, and promptly lost his voice again. Taking this as a sign that healing others was to be his destiny, he began to give readings – diagnoses and cures while in trance – in 1901. A key factor in Cayce's gift was that whenever he used it against his own principles – and he was a devout Christian – or even gave up readings, he would lose his voice. In this respect, and like many other psychics, Cayce was not entirely in control of his strange talent. He did not direct it; rather, it seemed to use him as a channel.

Thanks to a newspaper article about him in 1903, Cayce found a large following, and this increased still further in 1911 when a feature on his work – and his successes – in the *New York Times* brought him to national attention. By this time he was working in partnership with Dr Wesley Ketchum, a homoeopath who carried out the treatment that Cayce prescribed.

Cayce had begun his work by being hypnotized in the presence of the patient; now he needed no more than the name and address of the patient, and to put himself into trance. The reading would begin when someone (often Cayce's wife) would tell him: 'You now have the body of [here the name and address was read out]. You will go over this body carefully, noting its condition and any parts that are ailing. You will give the cause of such ailments and suggest treatments to bring about a cure.'

Cayce believed that every single cell in the body was individually conscious, and maintained not only that during a reading he could see every nerve, gland, blood vessel and organ inside his patient's body, but that the cells themselves communicated their condition to his entranced mind. The treatments he prescribed ranged from orthodox drugs or surgery (Cayce had no objection to conventional medicine where it was appropriate) through massage, manipulation, osteopathy and electro-therapy to herbal remedies (some of

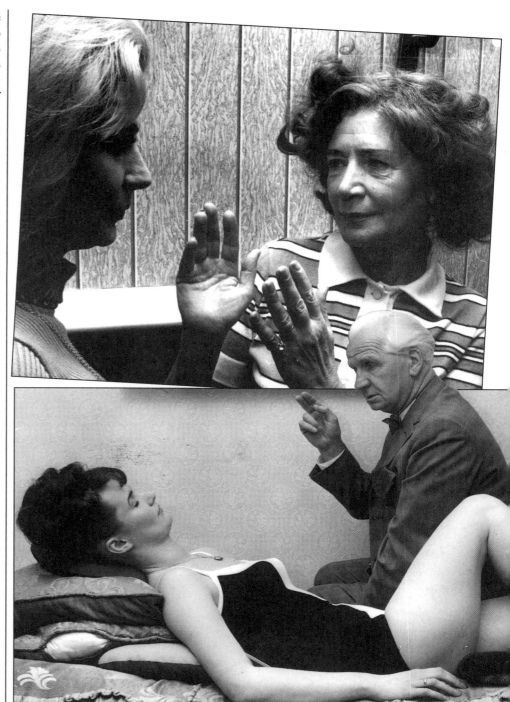

remarkable obscurity) and plain, simple exercise. The effectiveness of his prescriptions was vouched for by thousands of patients.

Many of Cayce's later ideas have been mocked – perhaps with some justice – for their outlandishness. For example, he came to believe that he himself was a reincarnation of one of the angels who inhabited the Earth even before Adam and Eve, and later was incarnated as an inhabitant of Atlantis. But as a healer he

One of the most widely used methods of putting the mind in control of the body is hypnotism. Doris Munday (top) specializes in treating nervous tension, while Harry Blythe (above) is seen here curing a would-be beauty queen of shyness.

Edgar Cayce's more extreme ideas – that he had been a citizen of the mythical lost continent of Atlantis (right) in a previous incarnation, and that still earlier he had been an angel existing 'before Adam and Eve' (below) – have been mocked as outlandish, but they did not affect his ability to give healing at a distance.

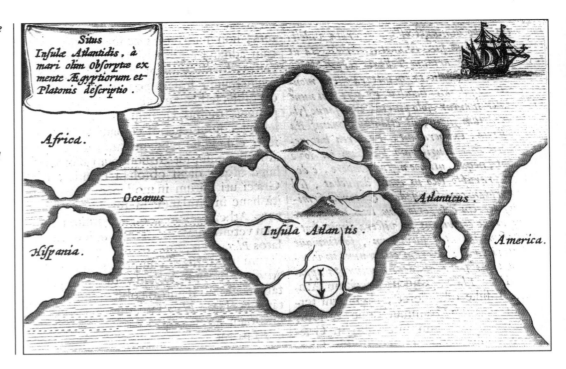

Situs
Insulæ Atlantidis, à mari olim obsorptæ ex mente Ægyptiorum et Platonis descriptio.

Africa.

Oceanus

Hispania.

Insula Atlantis.

Atlanticus.

America.

has had few equals.

The transfer of energy typical of healing took its toll on Cayce, who found the work exhausting. Warned that giving more than two readings a day would kill him, he nevertheless averaged four each day after 1942, in response to requests that flooded in as a result of the USA joining the war against Germany and Japan. In June 1943, he increased this to six a day; in August 1944 he collapsed from exhaustion, and was dead within five months. He had referred to his impending death as a 'healing'.

HE KNEW THAT TOO MANY HEALINGS WOULD KILL HIM, BUT HOW COULD HE IGNORE THE SUFFERINGS CAUSED BY THE WAR?

UNCANNY PRECISION

The most celebrated British clairvoyant healer was probably Harry Edwards, who died in 1976. During his prime in the 1950s he could fill London's giant Albert Hall with people anxious to receive his services. Edwards did not invoke spirit guides or use any ritual, whether healing at such a huge gathering or at home. He simply rolled up his sleeves and for a few moments put his hands on whatever part of the body was troubling the patient.

Astonishingly, Edwards took up healing virtually by chance. He seems to have had no inkling of any psychic capacities as a young man, and he was already in his forties when he made his first attempt at healing – and that was at a distance. This he did only after he had attended Spiritualist church services to please a friend. At these, he was told by a number of mediums that he had a latent ability as a healer, and that next time he knew someone who was ill, he should concentrate his thoughts on his or her recovery.

Edwards heard that a friend of a friend was terminally ill with tuberculosis, and decided to do what he could to help the man. He simply sat down and began to meditate. Then, images came into his mind of a hospital ward, and he found himself concentrating on the occupant of the last

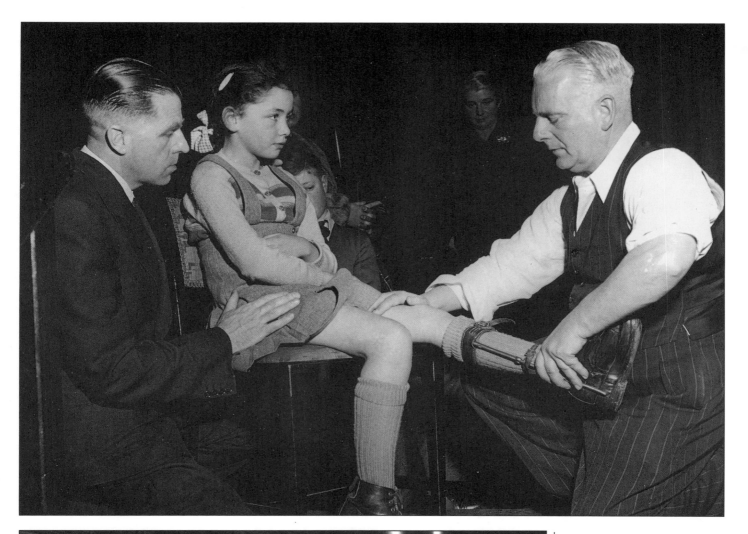

In the 1950s Harry Edwards (above) was Britain's foremost healer, and his fame was so widespread that he was able to fill the 8000-seat Royal Albert Hall (left) to capacity for his demonstrations.

Right: *Greek gendarme Costas Polychronakis is hypnotized and cured of a spinal disease by Harry Edwards during a brief stop that the healer made at Athens airport in April 1954.*

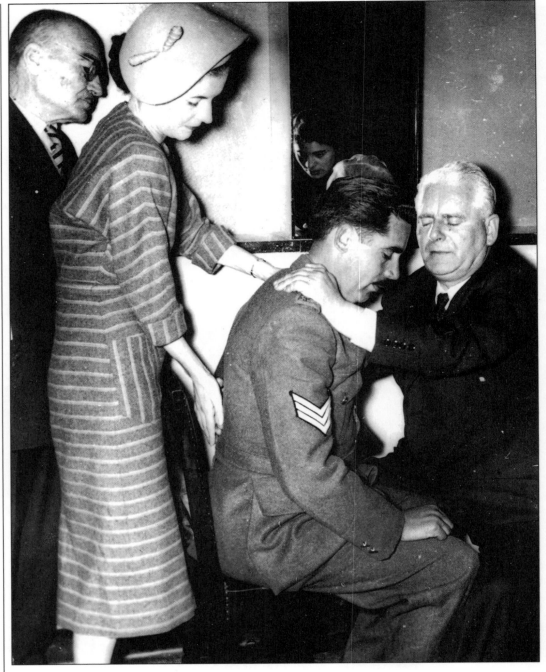

SHE WAS SCARED HE WOULD MOCK HER INTUITION AND NEVER CONFESSED HER SECRET.

bed but one in the ward, as seen from the point of view in his mind. Edwards sent out a 'get well' message as powerfully as he could, although without great confidence in its likely efficacy.

However, when Edwards described the scene he had had in his mind to his friend, he found that he had 'imagined' the ward in the hospital and the circumstances of the TB victim with uncanny precision. Better still, the patient had reported feeling better almost immediately after Edwards had made his attempt at healing. Within a few weeks the man was up and about, and soon

after that was back at work again – quite confounding his doctors, who had fully expected him to die.

The next encounter Edwards had with his paranormal gift – and it was one that lends some credence to the suspicion that the lives, let alone the talents, of healers are somehow beyond their control – came not long after this. Harry Edwards lived in Islington, London, and worked in a printing shop in the neighbourhood. One day a woman came into the shop, obviously distracted and, admitting she had no reason for bursting in, poured out her story to

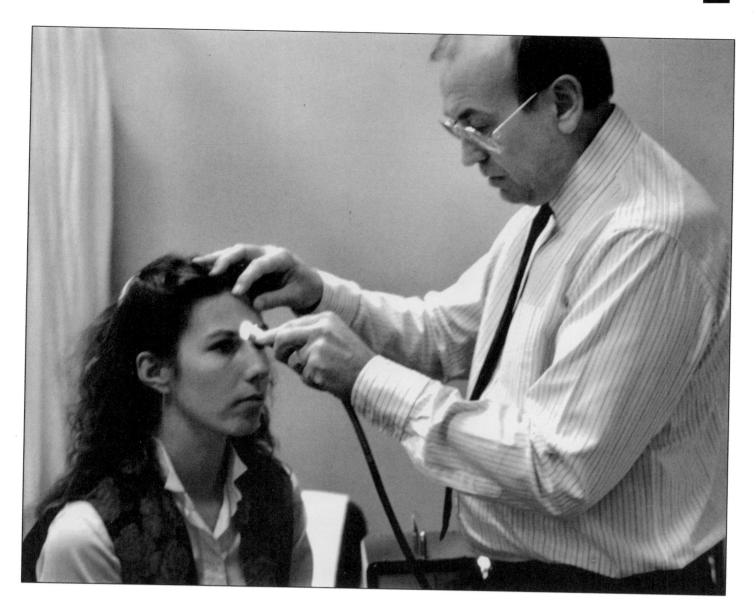

Harry. Her husband had lung cancer in an advanced degree: he was so far gone that he had been sent home from hospital – in short, to die.

Edwards personally believed there was little he could do to help (there was *nothing* he could do about the unfathomable way in which the distressed woman had found him), but made an effort nonetheless. Two days after her first visit, the woman dropped into the printing shop again. Her husband, she said, had already begun to recover. And recover he did: he lived for a score more years. The curious irony of this case was that he himself never learned of the part that Harry Edwards may have had in his sudden return to normal life. His wife never told him of her strange impulse to walk into a printing shop in Islington, for fear he would mock her intuition.

If this whole episode was no more than a crazy coincidence, it was fortunate as well as fortuitous. Edwards's third attempt at healing was also unusual, for it was the first time he actually had physical contact with his patient, a young girl suffering from TB of the lung. What marked the occasion for Edwards was what happened when he put his hands on the girl's head. He had experienced nothing of the kind before: his entire body seemed to come alive, filled with energy, which flooded down his arms and out of his hands into the patient. When this extraordinary sensation ceased, he heard himself telling the girl's mother that her daughter would be up in three days. Indeed she was, and at her next medical examination was pronounced completely cured.

These three events convinced Edwards

Above: *Naturopath Peter Mandel of Bruchsal, Germany, uses coloured light beams instead of needles to apply his own form of acupuncture to his patients.*

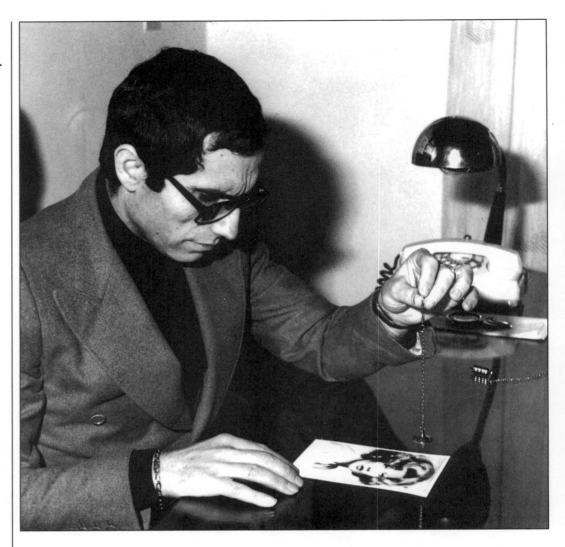

that he should devote himself to healing; in due course, he gave up his printing business and in 1946 established a sanctuary at Burrows Lea in Shere, Surrey, to carry on his work full-time. He was still working when he died in 1976. The sanctuary still thrives, run by a group of healers.

INEXPLICABLE PROOF

A number of healers have collaborated in tests to discover if there is any 'objective' element in what they do. The British healer Matthew Manning, for instance, has been involved in this research, attempting to influence the growth rate of seedling plants, to destroy cancer cells in the laboratory, and to increase the enzyme level in samples of blood. Testing on items like these removes the possibility that they may respond as a result of their own suggestibility – which may account for a

healer's success with human patients.

Much work along these lines was done by the biochemist Bernard Grad of McGill University in Montreal, Canada, during the 1950s. His research with the retired Hungarian army colonel Oskar Estebany was particularly revealing. Estebany had discovered his own healing ability by working not with people, but with horses of the Hungarian cavalry.

Grad tested the healer's ability to influence the growth of barley seeds successfully, but he performed one crucial experiment with Estebany. One involved 'wounding' a number of laboratory mice (actually just a tiny sliver of skin was painlessly removed from each one). Sixteen of the 48 animals were given healing treatment by being held in Estebany's hands twice a day for 20 days. Another 16 were put in incubators heated to body temperature for the same period twice a day, to simulate the warmth the first

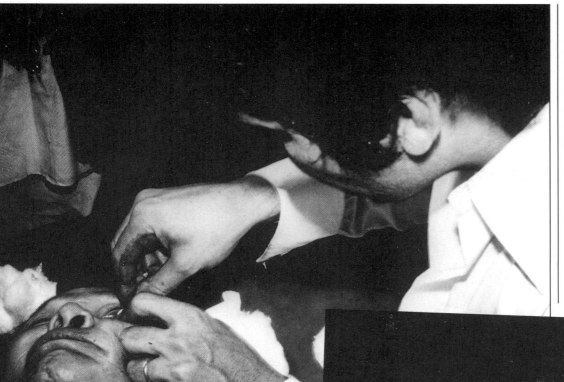

Left and below: *Ivan Trilha of Paraguay performs psychic surgery. Using neither anaesthetics nor conventional surgical instruments, psychic surgeons claim to be able to perform all the feats of modern medicine. Many of their patients have testified to the effectiveness of their work – but just as many of the 'surgeons' have been exposed as charlatans.*

group received from Estebany. A third group of 16 mice provided a final control: they were left to heal naturally.

By day 14 of the experiment, the size of the wounds of the control group had diminished as expected: about a third had reduced to less than half their original size, and the remainder were smaller yet. Of the 'heated' group, about half had reduced to about half their initial size; if anything, the group as a whole was healing more slowly than the control group – not surprisingly, since warmth encourages the multiplication of bacteria. Estebany's group had healed faster than either of the others: their three biggest wounds were smaller than *one-seventh* the size they had been initially; the rest were equal in size or (more often) smaller than those of the untreated control group.

Grad and Estebany were no nearer explaining the mechanism of the healer's art than anyone else, but they had shown that it had a real effect on live animals – who could not be accused of 'healing themselves' through auto-suggestion, faith, or any other psychosomatic means.

OUT OF THE BODY

The torture was agony but Ed Morrell refused to be broken. Even as his cruel jailers slowly squeezed him to the jaws of death, he found a way to escape.

Ed Morrell had the bad luck to be incarcerated in the Arizona State Penitentiary, rated one of the four most savage jails in the USA. One of the more refined methods of torture that Morrell suffered there was to be tied into not one but two strait-jackets; then water was poured over him, so that the jackets shrank. It was, he wrote in his book *The Twenty Fifth Man*, like being 'slowly squeezed to death'. But, time and again, Morrell escaped from this agony: his consciousness – some would say his soul, others would call it his 'astral body' – left his body to suffer, and floated away, free from pain.

In this 'out-of-the-body' state, Morrell was able to travel not only around the immediate vicinity of the prison, but to other countries. He seems even to have been able to travel in time. On one disembodied journey he saw a woman that he later was to meet in the flesh – and marry.

Out-of-the-body experiences (OBEs) are often associated with escape from extreme physical pain, as in Morrell's case; victims of road accidents, for instance, have often reported that their conscious self has floated free from their broken bodies, so that they survey themselves from a point above (and often slightly to one side of) their physical position.

The British secret agent Odette Hallowes positively looked forward to her OBEs when she was captured and tortured by the Gestapo during World War 2. When the pain reached a certain intensity, she would literally rise above it, leaving the sadists 'below' her to get on with their inhuman work while she, now free from any physical feelings, felt a profound sense of relief.

DRUG-INDUCED?

It is not necessary, however, to suffer extreme stress, shock or trauma in order to have an OBE. The experience can happen spontaneously and without warning to someone who is especially relaxed. One such episode was reported by a florist known only as Pat who, when she was 20, in April 1970, shared a flat in Canterbury, Kent, with her musician cousin.

'I [was] lying on the sofa for a few hours, listening to my cousin play the piano. I was completely relaxed and felt as if I were going to sleep,' she recalled. 'Suddenly I was aware that I had actually risen to ceiling height. I turned over and seemed to hover…I could see everything in the room quite clearly, even myself lying on the sofa…I suddenly found myself way up in the sky hovering over Canterbury. Only it wasn't April any more; it was a summery day.

'I didn't want to return, indeed I had a great sense of elation. But…what would happen if I travelled on into the unknown? As I was thinking about this I found myself staring down at my body again. I decided I

Opposite: Wartime secret agent Odette Hallowes with two dolls that she made while a prisoner of the Nazi Gestapo. Under torture, she would escape the harrowing pain by floating free of her body.

Below: An attempt to induce an out-of-the-body experience using coloured eyeglasses and aural stimulation through headphones, conducted at the Freiburg Institute in Germany in 1982.

THE BRAVE SECRET AGENT DID NOT SUCCUMB TO HER SADISTIC TORTURERS.

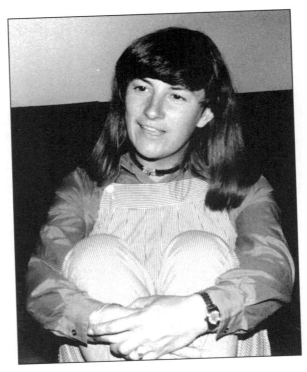

Psychologist Dr Susan Blackmore (right), who believes that OBEs are not actual journeys by the mind or spirit, but are created in the imagination.

Keith Harary (below) accurately reported details of distant locations – which he had never visited – during OBE experiments in the 1970s.

couldn't do it…as soon as I had made my decision I was back in my body before you could say "Jack Flash".'

Others have reported having an OBE as a result of sheer boredom – one lady office worker claimed she found her mind frequently drifting into a reverie during particularly tedious meetings, and she would find herself wondering, 'What's on the other side of that wall?' Then, she would 'float' out of her body, out of the meeting-room and 'have a good look round'. Relaxation and a relatively idle, non-concentrating conscious mind seem

essential to initiate this class of OBE. In 1971, psychologist Dr Charles Tart surveyed 150 regular smokers of marijuana and discovered that 44 per cent of them had had an OBE while using the drug. Other surveys have established that roughly one person in four has experienced an OBE at least once in their lives – suggesting that the state of fatuous euphoria typically associated with smoking dope increases the likelihood of you getting literally out of your head.

ASTRAL BODIES

These OBEs – brought on by intolerable physical stress or when the mind has, in effect, gone blank through relaxation or boredom – occur of their own accord; those who have them cannot control either their onset or, apparently, the way they end. But OBEs can be induced deliberately and enjoyed at will.

In their book *The Projection of the Astral Body* (1929), Sylvan Muldoon and Hereward Carrington describe several ways in which to achieve an OBE. All involve lying on your back in bed with the eyes closed. You might then concentrate on loosening the 'astral body' from the physical body, by rotating your point of view in the imagination around a central axis – so that you are looking at your own feet, for example, or at the length of your body. From these positions you should look at the ceiling, the wall on one side, the floor, and the wall on the other side.

Another suggestion is to hold the image and imaginary sensation of going up in a lift until you drift off to sleep, while telling yourself that you will wake up fully out of the body. A third method is to make sure you go to bed thirsty, and go to sleep while imagining going to the kitchen for a drink of water – and telling yourself to wake up, out of the body, at the sink. These methods do indeed work, although at first they take a great deal of concentration and willpower.

The fact that an OBE *can* be deliberately induced has meant that the true nature of the experience can be explored through tests and experiments. The first question to be answered, naturally enough, is: does the consciousness *really* leave the body during an OBE and wander about at will?

The anecdotal evidence that this does actually happen is conflicting. In Pat's OBE, cited earlier, it is curious that once out of her own basement flat and apparently high in the sky above Canterbury, the weather changed from that of a normal April day in England (which means it was raining) to that of a sunny summer day. Dr Susan Blackmore, a world authority on OBEs, became intrigued by the subject because she had them herself. In one, she floated to the ceiling, through it and above the housetops of her neighbourhood. Looking down, she could see the red roofs and chimneys of the buildings below as she flew over them...In her down-to-earth analysis of the event, Dr Blackmore noted wryly that in fact the roofs she supposedly floated over were actually made of grey slate, and that none of the buildings in the district had chimneys like the ones she saw.

Dr Blackmore has also had an interesting response from an experiment set up with a friend who lives 200 miles from her and who claimed that he had OBEs regularly and could 'travel' long distances at will. To find out if he did travel in reality or in imagination, Dr Blackmore left three items on the top of a cupboard in her kitchen, out of sight of any casual visitor. They were a small object such as a comb or a piece of candy, a three-digit number, and a short word. The arrangement was that when her friend paid a flying visit during an OBE, he would check the top of the cupboard, note what was there, and send her a postcard describing what he had seen. Each week Dr Blackmore changed the three objects. She did this for five years. No postcard ever arrived.

TRAVELLING CLAIRVOYANCE

Others have reported entirely different experiences. The American medium Eileen Garrett, for example, tells in her autobiography how she carried out an experimental OBE at the request of a doctor who lived in Newfoundland. Garrett lived in New York, and had never been to the doctor's home. She projected herself from New York to the house in Newfoundland, and there saw the doctor, who was himself somewhat psychic and was apparently able to detect her arrival. She noted a number of objects laid out on the

doctor's table, and also saw that he had a bandaged head. He told her, speaking out loud, that he had had an accident that morning. Next, he pulled a book from a shelf and opened it so that she could read the title page.

All this information and more about what Garrett had seen during her out-of-the-body visit to Newfoundland was written down and mailed to the doctor the same day. Next day, he telegraphed a reply confirming everything Garrett had reported.

Here we have two diametrically different accounts of OBEs, both from people renowned for their honesty. How can we account for the apparent contradiction?

First, let's suppose that Dr Blackmore is correct in thinking an OBE is essentially an imaginary experience – a 'dramatized reconstruction of a memory of the physical world', in Prof. Arthur Ellison's words.

Second, Eileen Garrett was one of the most accomplished mediums of all time. It seems likely, then, that what she saw on her OBE to Newfoundland was correct not because she was spiritually or astrally there in person, but because she was there psychically. The modern term for what she was doing is 'remote viewing', a form of extra-sensory perception that used to be called 'travelling clairvoyance'. Telepathy may have been involved too, for the doctor in the experiment was also psychic.

Third, it is well-known among psychical researchers that Dr Blackmore herself is

Above: *A sentimental Victorian depiction of the astral body – synonymous with the spirit form of the dead – watching invisibly over the grief-stricken living.*

OUT-OF-THE-BODY EXPERIENCES CAN BE INDUCED DELIBERATELY, AND ENJOYED AT WILL.

Above: *Psychical researcher Helmut Schmidt demonstrates a random-event generator of his own devising, for use in experiments in psychokinesis. Some experts have suggested that out-of-the-body experiences enhance psychic ability.*

TWO INVISIBLE HANDS FORCED HIM BACK INTO THE BEDROOM AND DOWN INTO HIS BODY.

---

distinctly un-psychic; she has remarked ruefully on the fact that she actually seems to inhibit extra-sensory perception many times. Her own lack of psychic gifts and her tendency apparently to block others' extra-sensory perception would not only explain the discrepancies between her view of her neighbourhood during her OBE and the actual facts about the place. It would also account for her friend's being unable to discover what she had put on the top of her kitchen cupboard – either she was blocking him from getting at the information telepathically, or he himself has no talent for extra-sensory perception (or both).

We've seen from accounts of many other psychic phenomena that extra-sensory perception (like an OBE) is often triggered by a crisis. It's also apparent that both extra-sensory perception and OBEs can occur as a result of profound relaxation that amounts to a trance state. An OBE may not make someone without any latent psychic ability into a sensitive, but it may make a chink in his or her psychic armour; and to someone moderately sensitive who has many OBEs it may help their extra-sensory perceptions develop. Thus Ed Morrell could see his future wife during one of his repeated OBEs. He was having a precognitive vision.

Even if OBEs are not literally journeys of the soul out of the body, but an extraordinary facet of the imagination, they are nonetheless replete with unsolved mysteries.

INTRIGUING EXPERIENCE

There are many reports of the curious effects experienced during OBEs – by both those undergoing them, and those researching them. One such series of oddities was recounted by Dr Arthur Ellison, professor of electronic engineering at the City University, London, until 1986 and at one time a president of the British Society for Psychical Research.

Ellison had himself induced his own OBEs as an experiment, but abandoned this line of research simply because he was exhausted by the lack of sleep it entailed. He did have one very curious experience during his second OBE, however. He had succeeded in floating out of his bedroom window and was aiming to drift down to the lawn below, where he intended to walk about. (It is, incidentally, a peculiar quality of OBEs that those who have them seem to travel about with a sense of having a body of some kind: hence the term 'astral body' used in many discussions of the phenomenon.) Ellison was starting his descent to the ground when: 'I had one of the most intriguing experiences to date. I felt two hands take my head, one hand over each ear, [and] move me...back into the bedroom and down into the body. I heard no sound, and saw nothing.'

Ellison felt, on balance, that it was more likely that an OBE was an imaginative reconstruction of reality and not an actual paranormal mode of travel. But there remained the problem of people who picked up undoubtedly genuine information during OBEs that they had no other apparent means of having acquired. Ellison decided to test for the possibility that information of this kind was acquired telepathically.

For his experiments he had an electronic machine built. This would generate a random number and show it on a standard digital panel at the back. No one would see this number at any time during the experiment, except for the subject – and then only if they could read it during their OBE. On the front of the machine, a second display would record the number that the subjects claimed to see and show whether the claim was correct or not. It could also tell whether individual digits in the three-figure number had been read correctly. It still did not show the original number.

Ellison chose as his subjects people who could be hypnotized and would then have an OBE. The advantage of this system was that they could report from their physical state what their ostensibly disembodied selves were seeing. The machine could thus display runs of 20 or more numbers, giving the answers statistical validity.

MACHINE MALFUNCTION

There were two intriguing results of Ellison's experiments with this device. He first tested the machine with a female subject and, to speed up this initial informal trial, checked the psychic's claims by looking at the numbers at the back of the machine himself. She achieved a correct score of almost 100 per cent. But when a completely secure run of numbers was made, she scored zero, and made some rather feeble excuses about not being able to read the numbers properly because they were 'too small' – which, strange to say, had not been a problem before.

The obvious conclusion was that when no one was actually aware of the target figures, she could not see them. Or, to put it another way, she could identify the numbers only through someone else's awareness – that is, by telepathy.

On two further notable occasions Ellison tested well-known psychics with his machine. The first, an American, achieved a score of eight correct numbers out of 20 without even going into an OBE – about eight times any score that one might expect by chance guessing. When Ellison tested the machine the following day, he himself – who makes no claim to psychic ability at all – achieved the same astonishingly high score. Checking the guts of the device revealed a fault in the circuitry.

The British psychic came up with exactly the same high score. Then, in a control run, so did Ellison. Once again, apparently, the machine had malfunctioned. Ellison concluded: 'An experienced psychical researcher…might observe that this kind of thing often happens. It is as though the unconscious mind of the psychic, knowing that a high score was required, achieved this by the easiest available method – by using [psycho-kinesis] on the microcircuit rather than clairvoyance. But it is impossible to prove this contention: it merely remains a possibility.'

CRISIS APPARITIONS

No less mysterious are those rare cases in which subjects having an OBE actually appear in front of someone they are visiting in their disembodied state.

On 26 January 1957, just such an encounter took place between 26-year-old Martha Johnson and her mother. During an OBE, Martha 'floated' to her mother's house 926 miles away, in another time zone. When she arrived, she found her mother in the kitchen. Martha took a couple of steps toward her, but then came abruptly back to her body. She looked at her bedside clock: it read 2.10 am.

For her part, Martha's mother wrote to her at once to tell her own side of the story – and, when she did so, she had no idea that Martha had been having an OBE. She had noticed nothing at first, then gradually became aware of Martha standing in the kitchen in a typical posture: with her arms folded and her head slightly tilted to one side. She started to say something to her daughter – but then Martha abruptly vanished. She noted in her letter how good Martha's new hairstyle looked. The time she had seen her, she added, was 'ten after two, your time'.

There was no sense of crisis or foreboding in this experience; Martha's mother seems to have taken the whole episode in her stride. Only when both parties were about to put the situation to the test by communicating did it break down: as if psychic reality and the mundane world were incapable of co-existing.

THE SCORE WAS UNEXPECTEDLY HIGH – BUT JUST HOW HAD IT BEEN ACHIEVED?

Below: Indian yoga adept Pushal Behen about to undergo an analysis of her brain-wave patterns with an electro-encephalograph. Out-of-the-body experiences are often deliberately induced by highly trained practitioners of yoga.

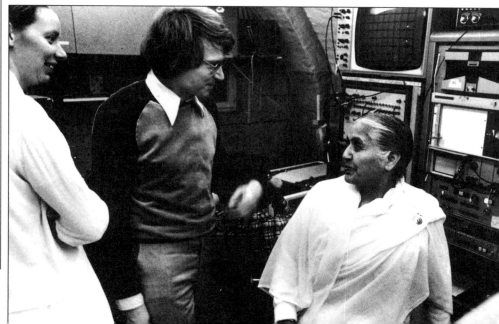

' Photograph of " vital radiations " issuing from the human body and impressing (directly) a photographic plate.

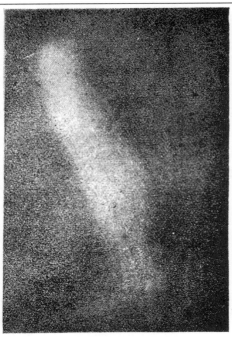

"Astral body" of Mme. Lambert obtained during the early experiments. (Note the imperfect outline of the body, and its swaying motion as though blown about by the wind.

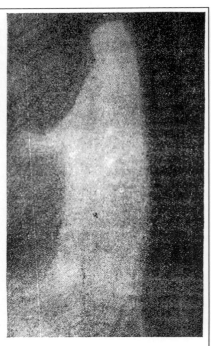

Later photograph of the "astral body." of Mme. Lambert, obtained after further experimentation. (Note the clearer outline and relative stability of the figure.)

Above: *These three photographs, published in the* Occult Review *of May 1916, purport to show the emergence of the astral body of one Madame Lambert from her physical form. Spiritualists and others remain convinced that it is the astral body which floats free of the body during an OBE.*

WHEN THEY RAN ROUND THE CORNER THE FIGURE OF THE SOLDIER HAD DISAPPEARED.

Circumstances were to say the least slightly different when Mr W. Lee of Bridgnorth, Shropshire, visited his mother in what seems to have been an OBE, in 1963. Lee was doing his stint of national service in the British Army at the time, and did not like it. He rebelled from time to time, and found himself at the mercy of an old Regular Army sergeant. He, on this occasion, landed Lee and three other conscripts with a punishment known by the innocuous name of 'pack drill'. At that time a standard infantryman's pack, fully loaded, weighed about 40 lb. Much of the kit inside was spare clothing. The sergeant ordered the four to fill their capacious packs not with issue kit but with housebricks, and then sent them out on the parade ground to drill with these back-breaking loads at a cracking pace.

It was a very hot day. One of the four kept collapsing. Lee, determined not to be beaten by the sadistic punishment, kept on marching. 'I just kept on going while the commands being shouted at us grew dimmer and dimmer,' he wrote years later. 'In the end I could not hear them. My heart did not seem to be beating and I could not see. Somehow I kept turning and marching but I was no longer there. Eventually the torture ended...'

That was all there was to that particular event, Lee thought, until the next time he returned home on leave. His mother then told him a curious tale.

On the same day that Lee had become an automaton on the drill square, his mother and his younger brother had been out shopping. 'They were about 100 yards from the nearest bus stop to our home,' he wrote, 'when a bus stopped and I got off in my Army uniform. [My mother] called to me as I walked up the road but I did not answer or turn round. It would be about 300 yards to the corner of our road, and my mother and brother...ran to try and catch me up, because I was walking very quickly. I rounded the corner four or five seconds ahead of them and when they too came round the corner I had disappeared. There was only a postman to be seen.

'My mother asked [him] where had the soldier gone and he told her nobody had come round the corner.'

In cases like these, the distinctions become blurred between what is an OBE, what is a *doppelganger* (the psychic double of a living person), and what is a 'crisis apparition' – the apparent ghost of someone who is, nonetheless, still alive. Even if most OBEs are the work of the imagination, incidents like these latter two show that we still only barely understand the phenomenon as a whole.